THE CONCEPT OF RIGHTS

Law and Philosophy Library

VOLUME 73

THE CONCEPT
OF RIGHTS

by

GEORGE W. RAINBOLT

*Georgia State University,
Atlanta, GA, U.S.A.*

 Springer

A C.I.P. Catalogue record for this book is available from the Library of Congress.

ISBN-10 1-4020-3976-X (HB)
ISBN-13 978-1-4020-3976-8 (HB)
ISBN-10 1-4020-3977-8 (e-book)
ISBN-13 978-1-4020-3977-5 (e-book)

Published by Springer,
P.O. Box 17,3300 AA Dordrecht, The Netherlands.

www.springer.com

Printed on acid-free paper

Printed in the Netherlands.

In Memory Of
John Corbin Rainbolt

Table of Contents

Acknowledgments

One of the pleasures of writing a book is that it gives one the opportunity to acknowledge those who have been instrumental in its production. My colleagues Kit Wellman and Andy Altman have provided not only stimulating conversation about rights but also their moral support through the ups and downs of working on a book. Bill Nelson read the entire manuscript and gave me many useful comments. In particular, he led me to see that I needed to distinguish between the simple and the complex justification of rights. Rex Martin read large parts of the manuscript and took time from his busy schedule to discuss it with me. I owe the existence of Chapter 1 entirely to him. He pointed out that I was not adopting Hohfeld but rather adapting Hohfeld. Three anonymous reviewers read the manuscript and their comments were uniformly detailed and useful. Reviewing manuscripts is a task which academia does not sufficiently acknowledge so I greatly appreciate the time these three scholars took to read my manuscript with such care.

Many years ago, I wrote a dissertation on rights and Carl Wellman commented on it even though he is at Washington University and I was studying at the University of Arizona. Little of that dissertation remains in this work. Central parts of it were flawed. What remains are the points Carl picked out. He also read the penultimate version of this book and provided many detailed comments of astonishing quality. I had been searching for a name for my view for more than 10 years but it is Carl who suggested "the justified-constraint theory." Intellectually, this work owes more to Carl than to anyone else.

My interest in rights began when I took a seminar offered by Joel Feinberg. Over the course of many years, we had many conversations about rights and he read many drafts of the early versions of this work. My greatest regret about this book is that it appears after Joel's death. Joel was a philosopher who wrote articles that revolutionized fields. He was also a profoundly good and decent person. I spent my time as a graduate student attempting to show Joel that he was wrong. I was forever in his office to tell him that he got this wrong here or that wrong there. My first article (written while I was one of his graduate students) was an attempt to show that the attack on paternalism found in his seminal four-volume work, *The Moral Limits of the Criminal Law*, was flawed. I consistently told him that his theory of rights was flawed. Only later did I realize how rare it is for a graduate student to have an advisor who does not seek disciples but rather encourages students to seek their own way. Joel was and is my central model of how to be a philosopher.

Amy Clashman provided crucial support as I went through a serious illness at the start of this project. My son Corbin helped me work on the book through a difficult personal time in my life. There is nothing like jumping up and down in the back of a pickup truck with a 4-year-old to help one clear one's mind and gain philosophical insight. My wife Madeline read the entire manuscript and corrected hundreds of small errors. She did more than her share of caring for a new baby so that I would have the time to make the final push on this work. She has made more personal sacrifices for me than any man deserves. Bises, Jolie.

Introduction

Discussions of rights are ubiquitous. One constantly hears things such as: "The Chinese are violating Tibetan rights," "Landlords have a right that their tenants pay their rent," "Students have a right to be graded fairly," "Animals have a right not to suffer merely to bring pleasure to humans," "Abortion violates a fetus' right to life," "We violate the rights of future generations when we pollute the water." These statements assert that Tibetans, landlords, students, animals, fetuses, and future generations all have rights. Tibetans, landlords, students, animals, fetuses, and future generations do not seem to have much in common. When one presses for clarity, it is very difficult to say precisely what a right is. What is it to have a right? That is the question this book seeks to answer.

To paint with an overly broad brush, previous answers to this question can be divided into two groups. Some hold interest/benefit theories of rights while others hold choice/will theories of rights. Perhaps the first person to propose an interest/benefit theory was Jeremy Bentham. Its most cited contemporary defender is Joseph Raz. The seminal statement of the choice theory was made by H.L.A. Hart. Carl Wellman is perhaps the most able defender of a will theory of rights. The debate between these two groups of theories has been a productive one. The theories have been developed and refined to avoid many of the objections to which the original versions were subject. Different versions of each of the basic views have been proposed with different strengths and weaknesses. This debate is now a mature one. It is now clear that all the theories in these two classic groups are fundamentally flawed. It is time to seek a third theory of rights. This work defends the view that a person has a right if and only if a feature of that person is a reason for others to have a particular sort of normative constraint. I call this the justified-constraint theory of rights.

Philosophical discussions of rights are usually carried on in a technical vocabulary proposed by Wesley Newcomb Hohfeld at the beginning of the last century. In order to take part in these discussions, the justified-constraint theory must be presented in Hohfeldian terms. Moreover, Hohfeld's work is of sufficient historical and intellectual importance that it is worth study for its own sake. Another reason to present the Hohfeldian terminology is that it makes this book more widely accessible. Many scholars of law, philosophy, and economics do not know of Hohfeld's work. For these reasons, Chapter 1 presents an Hohfeld*ian* vocabulary which follows Hohfeld's main lines while extending, revising, and clarifying certain features of his work.

Chapter 2 presents and defends an Hohfeldian version of the justified-constraint theory of rights. The analysis begins by noting that only claims and immunities imply a normative constraint on another. Because duties and disabilities are normative constraints on a person's acts and because the correlatives of duties and disabilities are claims and immunities, claims and immunities entail a normative constraint on another. The analysis continues by noting that rights constrain the acts of others. To modify a phrase of Hohfeld's, it is certain that even those who use the word "right" in the broadest possible way are accustomed to thinking of normative constraints as the invariable consequence of rights. That rights constrain the acts of others and that only claims and immunities constrain the acts of others gives us reason to think that one has a right if and only if one has a claim or an immunity.

On the other hand, it is very common to speak of rights corresponding to other Hohfeldian relations—e.g., liberty rights, power rights, etc. Chapter 2 goes on to argue that rights other than claim rights and immunity rights are packages of Hohfeldian relations which always include a claim or an immunity. In each of these packages, a claim and/or an immunity protects another relation. We label the right with the name of the protected relation. For example, a liberty right is a bilateral liberty protected by claims and/or immunities. Because the argument in Chapter 2 turns centrally on the notion of a normative constraint, this is the natural chapter in which to examine Rex Martin's theory of rights. Martin's views on the nature of this normative constraint differ from those of the justified-constraint theory, and juxtaposing both views brings each into relief.

One might be content to formulate an analysis of rights in purely Hohfeldian terms. There is much to be learned from Hohfeldian analysis. On the other hand, analyzing rights in purely Hohfeldian terms cannot answer all our questions about rights. Surely one's rights have some relationship to one's obligations and to what one is permitted to do. A purely Hohfeldian analysis cannot explicate those relationships. Suppose that everyone were to agree on an analysis of rights in Hohfeldian terms. We would still need to know the relationship between Hohfeldian relations and other normative concepts, concepts such as obligation and permission.

Chapter 3 argues that Hohfeldian relations can be analyzed in terms of the deontic modal triad (forbidden/permitted/obligatory) and the alethic modal triad (impossible/possible/necessary). While it is natural to speak of "having an obligation," there is no substantive corresponding to the adjectives "permitted," "forbidden," "impossible," "possible," and "necessary." So it is useful to stipulate the meaning of "to have an impossibility," "to have a forbidden," etc., and thus create the substantives corresponding to the adjectives. It then becomes clear that you have a claim if and only if someone has an obligation to you and that you have an immunity if and only if someone has an impossibility to you. From this and from the conclusion of Chapter 2, it follows that you have a right if and only if someone has an obligation or an impossibility to you. With both the Hohfeldian relations and the deontic and alethic triads on the table, we are in position to examine Joel Feinberg's influential view of rights as valid claims.

Although this is progress, the nature of obligations and impossibilities which are *to* someone requires clarification. People often recognize a difference between obligations that are *to* someone and obligations that are not. If I promise you that I will meet you for lunch, then it seems that not only do I have an obligation to meet you for lunch, but my obligation is *to* you. Assume that I have an obligation to give to charity. It does not seem that this obligation is *to* anyone. Obligations which are *to* someone are relational obligations. Obligations which are not *to* someone are non-relational obligations. The terms "relational impossibility" and "non-relational impossibility" are used in a parallel way. The task of Chapters 4 and 5 is to provide an analysis of relational obligation and relational impossibility. Chapter 4 presents and rejects the theories of rights offered by Raz, Hart, and Wellman. Each contains crucial insights that Chapter 5 assembles to reveal the justified-constraint theory of relational obligations and relational impossibilities. On the justified-constraint view, you have an obligation *to* someone if and only if a feature of that person is a reason for your obligation. You have an impossibility *to* someone if and only if a feature of that person is a reason for your impossibility. Thus, over the course of five chapters, the book works from an Hohfeldian analysis (rights as claims and immunities) to an analysis of rights as obligations and impossibilities justified in a particular way. We reach the view that a person has a right if and only if a feature of that person is a *reason* for others to have an obligation or impossibility. A person has a right if and only if a feature of that person is the justification of the obligations or impossibilities of others.

The title of this book bears a significant resemblance to Hart's *The Concept of Law* (1994). That is no accident. In part the title of this book is a homage to Hart's philosophical abilities and influence. Another reason for the similarity in title is that this book adopts much of Hart's philosophical method. In *The Concept of Law*, Hart sought an answer to the question "What is law?" He argued that "a central set of elements" were the best answer to this question (1994, 16). Hart was not seeking a definition. He was seeking a theory, an analysis. Oversimplifying Hart's complex theory, he held that the union of primary and secondary rules was key to understanding the law.[1]

[W]e shall make the general claim that in the combination of these two types of rules there lies what Austin wrongly claimed to have found in the notion of coercive orders, namely, "the key to the science of jurisprudence". We shall not indeed claim that wherever the word "law" is "properly" used this combination of primary and secondary rules is to be found; for it is clear that the diverse range of cases of which the word "law" is used are not linked by any such simple uniformity, but by less direct relations—often of analogy of either form or content—to a central case. What we shall attempt to show . . . is that most of the features of law which have proved most perplexing and have both provoked and eluded the search for definition can best be rendered clear, if these two types of rule and the interplay between them are understood. We accord this union of

---

[1] Very roughly, primary rules require people to do or not do certain actions. Secondary rules tell people how to create, change, or extinguish rules. See Hart 1994, chapter. 3.

elements a central place because of their explanatory power in elucidating the concepts that constitute the framework of legal thought (1994, 81).

I seek to understand the nature of rights. I will argue that the key to understanding rights is to see them as normative constraints on others that have a particular sort of justification. To modify Hart's words, I will attempt to show that most of the features of rights which proved most perplexing can best be rendered clear if rights are understood in this way. Rawls followed Hart but used a different terminology. Rawls distinguished between the concept of justice and conceptions of justice.

> [I]t seems natural to think of the concept of justice as distinct from the various conceptions of justice ... Those who hold different conceptions of justice can ... still agree that institutions are just when no arbitrary distinctions are made between persons in the assigning of basic rights and duties and when the rules determine a proper balance between competing claims to the advantages of social life. Men can agree to this description of just institutions since the notions of an arbitrary distinction and of a proper balance, which are included in the concept of justice, are left open for each to interpret ... (1971, 5).

In Rawlsian terms, this work defends a conception of rights. Like Hart, Rawls notes that definitions have no privileged status.

> A theory of justice is subject to the same method as other theories. Definitions and analyses of meaning do not have a special place: Definition is but one device used in setting up the general structure of a theory. Once the whole framework is worked out, definitions have no distinct status and stand or fall with the theory itself (1971, 51).

Another reason for the title *The Concept of Rights* is that an important feature of the justified-constraint conception of rights is that it sharply distinguishes substantive questions about rights from the conceptual question of what it is to have a right and holds that the line between conceptual and substantive questions should be drawn in a place different from where it is drawn in other theories of rights. It draws a sharp line between substantive questions such as "What is the scope of moral property rights?" from the conceptual question "What is a right?" On the justified-constraint conception of rights, any sort of individual feature is the correct sort of feature to ground rights. Interest and choice theorists have drawn the line between conceptual and substantive matters in the wrong place. Interest theorists think that a reference to the interests of the right-holder is a necessary part of an adequate conception of rights. Choice theorists think that the protection of choice is a necessary part of an adequate conception of rights. The justified-constraint theory of rights shows that both interest and choice theories are incorrect. The conceptual/substantive line should be drawn "further back" than they do.

A final reason for the title is that this work will not take up substantive questions of rights. Questions such as whether there is a moral right to private property or how the contours of the legal right to a divorce should be drawn will not be considered here. However, conceptions of rights are not merely of theoretical interest. We seek a theory of rights partially in hopes of making progress toward solving moral problems. The moral problems raised by rights are vast and diverse. One cannot hope to discuss all of them in one book. This book focuses on two that are particularly useful in comparing different theories of rights: the problem of conflicts of rights, and the issue of what sorts of beings can have rights. Chapter 6 is devoted to rights conflict. A new and plausible theory of rights conflicts follows from the justified-constraint theory of rights. Chapter 6 also contains a discussion of Ronald Dworkin's theory of rights as trumps. This is a natural place to consider his view because, on his view, conflict with non-rights-based moral considerations is a necessary feature of rights.

Chapter 7 considers the rights of presently existing things. The justified-constraint view reveals that the concept of rights places no limits on what sorts of beings can have rights. For example, the concept of rights does not imply that rocks cannot have rights. The limits on what sorts of beings can have rights are placed by other concepts and/or by substantive moral views. Many people (including myself) hold substantive moral views that imply that rocks do not have any rights.

Chapter 8 considers the rights of past and future things. The justified-constraint theory of rights applies, without modification, to the rights of past, present, and future individuals and shows that past and future beings can have rights. Key features drawn from Wellman and Raz allow for an account that unifies the rights of all beings whenever they exist. This is an important advantage of the justified-constraint theory of rights.

The evaluation of philosophical theories is a comparative matter. Perhaps it is possible in principle to provide an argument or set of arguments that, without reference to other views, shows that one's preferred view on a complex philosophical issue is true. In practice, I do not believe that this ever happens. On any issue worth philosophical ink, there will be a number of competing plausible theories. One defends one's view by showing that it is superior to competing theories. So one must compare one's preferred theory to other plausible views. Throughout this work the justified-constraint theory of rights will be compared to its competitors. In Chapter 9, these comparisons are brought together so that we may view all of them at one time.

1. Rights and Hohfeldian Analysis

Theorizing about rights has a long history. Discussions of rights have been occurring for at least the past 500 years.[1] But this work has a contemporary focus. As Steiner notes, when it comes to contemporary discussions of rights, "[t]he beginning of wisdom . . . is widely agreed to be the classification of juridical positions developed by Wesley Newcomb Hohfeld" (1994, 59). Hohfeld (2001) was a legal scholar who sought to clarify the law in general and the concept of rights in particular. He introduced the terminology that has been adopted in virtually all contemporary discussions of the concept of rights. The reason for its virtually universal use is that Hohfeld's relations uncover and remove serious ambiguities in the term "rights." They provide an essential pre-condition for thinking clearly about the subject. There is much to agree with in Hohfeld, but some of his views are incorrect and several points require amplification and/or clarification. In addition, other authors have failed to see the full power of Hohfeldian analysis. Therefore, this chapter does not present Hohfeld's terminology. Instead, it presents a new Hohfeld*ian* analysis. Let us call the analysis developed here "the neo-Hohfeldian analysis."

1. A NEO-HOHFELDIAN ANALYSIS

It is best to begin with a simplified presentation of the Hohfeldian relations and then proceed to a more complete discussion. There are eight Hohfeldian relations: claims, duties, liberties, no-claims, powers, liabilities, immunities, and disabilities. In typical legal systems, the owner of a car has a *claim* against others that they not drive the car and others have a *duty* to the owner not to drive the car. Claims and duties, like all Hohfeldian relations, have three parts: two agents and a content. Consider the statement that Evelyn has a claim against Joshua that Joshua not drive Evelyn's car. The two agents are Evelyn and Joshua. Evelyn is the *subject of the claim* and Joshua is the *object of the claim*. The *content* of this relation is "that Joshua not drive Evelyn's car." The content of an Hohfeldian relation is the act with respect to which one has a claim, duty, liberty, etc. The agent who is the subject of the dependent clause that is the content of the relation is the *subject of the content of the relation*. Joshua is the subject of the content of Evelyn's claim. The subject of the relation and the subject of the content of the relation are not necessarily the same agent.

The term "duty" used in the Hohfeldian sense is importantly different from the term "duty" as normally used. Hohfeldian duties always have an object. This is not

---

[1] For excellent reviews of this history, see Edmundson (2004) and Tuck (1979).

true of the term "duty" as it is used by normal English speakers. A normal English speaker can say that one has a duty to give to charity without implying that this is a duty *to* those who receive the charity. In what follows, "duty" will refer to Hohfeldian duties unless otherwise specified.

Claims and duties are correlatives. Correlativity is defined with a conditional. One relation is correlative to another if and only if it is true that *if* (1) both relations have the same content, (2) the object of the first relation is the subject of the second relation and (3) the object of the second relation is the subject of the first relation, *then* the relations are logically equivalent. Consider the following two statements:

(1) Evelyn has a claim against Joshua that Joshua not drive Evelyn's car.
(2) Joshua has a duty to Evelyn that Joshua not drive Evelyn's car.

The subject of the claim, Evelyn, is the object of the duty. The object of the claim, Joshua, is the subject of the duty. The content, "that Joshua not drive Evelyn's car," is the same in both relations. These statements are logically equivalent. Claims and duties are, to use a well-worn phrase, two sides of the same coin.

Suppose that Joshua wants to drive Evelyn's car next Tuesday and Evelyn agrees to sell Joshua a pass letting Joshua do so. There are two different sorts of passes Evelyn could sell Joshua. Evelyn might sell Joshua a pass that (1) states that Joshua has no duty to Evelyn not to drive the car next Tuesday and (2) puts Evelyn under a duty to Joshua to refrain from interfering with Joshua's driving the car (e.g., by hiding it) next Tuesday. Joshua has a claim that Evelyn refrain from interfering with Joshua's driving the car. Let us call this first sort of pass a claim pass.

On the other hand, Evelyn might sell Joshua a pass, which stated *only* that Joshua has no duty to Evelyn not to drive the car next Tuesday. The second pass would *not* put Evelyn under a duty to refrain from hiding the car. It would *not* put her under any duty to refrain from doing anything at all. It would not, for example, put her under a duty not to savagely beat Joshua to prevent Joshua from taking her car. This second sort of pass grants Joshua a *liberty* in the Hohfeldian sense. Let us call this second sort of pass a liberty pass. To say that one has liberty to do A is to say nothing more and nothing less than that one has no duty not to do A. If Joshua bought the liberty pass, then Evelyn would have a *no-claim* on Joshua that Joshua drive the car. Liberties and no-claims are correlatives. X has a liberty against Y that X do A if and only if Y has a no-claim on X that X do A.

A *power* occurs when a rule system allows one to change some Hohfeldian relation. In typical legal systems, Evelyn has the power to change Joshua's duty to refrain from driving Evelyn's car into a liberty to drive the car. Normally, Joshua has a duty to refrain from driving Evelyn's car. But if Evelyn says to Joshua: "You may drive my car," then Joshua no longer has a duty to refrain from driving the car. Correlative to Evelyn's power is Joshua's *liability*. Joshua has a liability with respect to Evelyn to have his duty to refrain from driving Evelyn's car changed into a liberty to drive the car. As with duties and liberties, it is important not to mistake Hohfeldian liabilities for normal liabilities. First, Hohfeldian liabilities are things one might want to have. Second, Hohfeldian liabilities always have an object. In this book, "liabilities" refers to Hohfeldian liabilities unless otherwise noted.

An *immunity* occurs when a system does *not* allow one to change some Hohfeldian relation. In typical legal systems, Evelyn has an immunity to Joshua's giving himself a liberty to drive her car. Suppose that Joshua said: "I hereby give myself the liberty to drive Evelyn's car." His act has no legal effect. It is a legal nullity. The legal system implies that Joshua's statement, unlike the one made by Evelyn considered above, has no legal effect. The correlative of an immunity is a *disability*. Another way to say that Evelyn has an immunity to Joshua's giving himself a liberty to drive her car is to say that Joshua has a disability to give himself a liberty to drive her car. Powers, liabilities, immunities, and disabilities necessarily concern the ability or inability to make changes in other Hohfeldian relations. Claims, duties, liberties, and no-claims do not necessarily concern changes in other Hohfeldian relations. In this sense, claims, duties, liberties, and no-claims are first-order relations while powers, liabilities, immunities, and disabilities are second-order relations.[2]

While this quick overview is a good place to begin a discussion of Hohfeldian relations, more needs to be said if we are to fully understand them. Moreover, when it comes to Hohfeldian relations and rights, the devil is often in the details. As we will see in this and subsequent chapters, getting the details right allows one to avoid many conceptual and practical muddles.

It will be useful to stipulate the meaning of some technical terms. It is a mistake to see the Hohfeldian system as an attempt to report the actual usage of either the public at large or of the legal community. It is better to see the system as a series of stipulations, which will, if all goes well, be useful in the analysis of rights.

"Hohfeldian statements" are statements about Hohfeldian relations. Here are some examples.

(1) George has a claim against Andy that Andy not hit George.
(2) Evelyn has the power against Joshua to change Joshua's duty to refrain from driving Evelyn's car into a liberty to drive her car.
(3) If Roy has a car insurance contract with Shirley and Roy is in a car accident, then Roy has a claim against Shirley that she pay for the damage to his car as specified in the insurance contract.

These Hohfeldian statements are simple ones. Anyone who has had even superficial contact with the law knows that Hohfeldian statements can be very complex. An "Hohfeldian rule system" is the set of all true Hohfeldian statements of a particular institution (e.g., a city, a county, a country, a university, a club, etc.). There are many examples of Hohfeldian rule systems. Probably the most obvious is the legal

---

[2]   I borrow the term "second-order" from Matthew Kramer. See Kramer et al. (1998, 20).

rule system. The legal Hohfeldian rule system of a country is the set of all true statements about people's legal claims, legal duties, legal liberties, etc. There are many other Hohfeldian rule systems. Organized sports, companies, clubs, and other social organizations often create Hohfeldian rule systems. Following Sumner, the term "rule" is used in a broad sense to cover such things as "by-laws, statutes, decrees, directives, edicts, ordinances, standing orders, regulations, injunctions, mandates, norms, precepts, guidelines, canons, principles or whatever" (1987, 21). Some prefer the term "norms" to the term "rules." If one would prefer, one can substitute "norm" for "rule" throughout the rest of this book. Again following Sumner (1987, 24), the broad use of "rule" implies that Hohfeldian relations are similarly broad. For example, "duty" covers what a particular rule system may label as "obligation," "responsibility," "expectation," etc.

The content of an Hohfeldian relation always contains a reference to an act. The term "act" is to be understood to include refraining from doing something as well as doing something. Both driving a car and refraining from driving a car are acts. In addition, changes in Hohfeldian relations are also included under the term "act." Suppose that Fielding has an immunity to Bill's extinguishing Fielding's liberty to burn the U.S. flag. Fielding is immune to the *act* of Bill extinguishing Fielding's liberty.

In English, the subject and the object of an Hohfeldian relation are linked by a preposition. The preposition used to indicate the object of an Hohfeldian relation is different for different relations. Above we have spoken of duties *to* others and claims *against* others. One naturally speaks of liberties *against* others, no-claims *on* others, etc. With some Hohfeldian relations, there is no natural English preposition to indicate the object. Therefore, one finds authors speaking of disabilities *vis-a-vis* or *with respect to* others. Different authors use different prepositions with the same relation. This can be confusing. Therefore, let us consistently use the following prepositions to refer to the object of a relation:

claim	against
duty	to
liberty	against
no-claim	on
power	against
liability	with respect to
immunity	against
disability	with respect to

Because we are analyzing rights, we need a preposition to indicate the object of a right. Let us use "against" to refer to the object of a right. We will occasionally need to discuss the object of relations generally. In that case, let us use "with respect to."

In addition to Hohfeldian correlatives, there are Hohfeldian opposites. Correlatives are logical equivalents. Opposites are logical contradictories. The following are Hohfeldian opposites: duty/liberty, claim/no-claim, power/disability, liability/immunity. To form the opposite of a relation, one keeps the same subject and object of the relation, but negates the content. Luc's duty not to hit Sienna is the opposite of his liberty to hit her. Although of interest to those who seek to formalize the Hohfeldian system, a theory of rights rarely needs to refer to Hohfeldian opposites. We will not often mention them in this work.

With these terminological matters behind us, let us turn to some provisional assumptions that need to be examined later in the work but which simplify presentation for the time being. Let us assume that there is a moral Hohfeldian rule system. The moral Hohfeldian rule system is the set of all true statements that someone has a moral claim, moral duty, moral liberty, etc.[3] For example, many think that the following statement is part of the moral Hohfeldian rule system: "Under normal circumstances, if a person, X, promises another person, Y, that he will do act A, then Y has a moral claim that X do A." This assumption will be defended in Chapter 3. All the examples of legal relations in this section are cases in which it is plausible to hold that the moral rule system and typical legal rule systems overlap. So all the examples of legal claims, legal duties, etc., given above are also examples of moral claims, moral duties, etc. For example, many think that the owner of a car has a moral, as well as a legal, claim against others that they not drive the car and the moral power to extinguish this moral claim. There might be cases in which moral and legal Hohfeldian relations do not overlap.

There is a great deal of controversy over what sorts of things can be subjects and/or objects of Hohfeldian relations. For example, some believe that groups cannot be the subject of Hohfeldian relations while others disagree. Some believe that a fetus can be the subject of relations but others disagree. Pending the results of Chapters 7 and 8, we will not make any assumptions regarding this issue. Until Chapter 7 and only for ease of presentation, let us use typical adult humans as examples of the subject and the object of Hohfeldian relations.

There is a series of common confusions regarding Hohfeldian relations. It is useful to point these out at the outset. We can begin with three common confusions, which can be quickly clarified.

First, Hohfeldian powers have nothing to do with physical powers. Suppose that Hyoung is physically unable to sign his name as the result of an accident. If the legal rule system required a signature to give another the liberty to drive one's car, Hyoung would lack the physical power to give others the liberty to drive his car. He cannot perform the triggering act specified by the legal rule system. But he does not lack the Hohfeldian power to do so. (In most legal systems, a legal power can be useful even if one cannot perform the triggering act because most legal systems have rules which allow representatives of a power-holder to exercise the power in the power-holder's name.)

---

[3] Non-cognitivists are free to replace the term "true" in this sentence with "appropriate," "valid" or whatever term they think ought to be used in place of "true" when referring to moral statements. Nothing in this book will be affected by such a substitution.

Second, one must be mindful of the distinction between the objects of Hohfeldian relations and the people and things, which are parts of the content of the relations. Suppose that Kyoto promises Devan that she will talk to Leslie. In that case, Kyoto has a duty to Devan to talk to Leslie. Kyoto's duty is to Devan. It is not to Leslie. Kyoto's duty is regarding but not to Leslie. The same point can be made with the other seven relations. (The issue of third-party beneficiaries will be discussed in Chapter 5.)

Third, Hohfeldian relations may be created by a rule system even if they are not explicitly stated in the rule system. A legal rule system might state that destroying another person's last will and testament gives rise to a valid civil cause of action. One can destroy a will in many different ways (shredding, burning, etc.), and it is not practical for statutes to explicitly list all the ways a will can be destroyed. Suppose that Jon runs Ellen's will through the washing machine. This would give Ellen a right to compensation under the legal rule system even though the statutes contain no explicit mention of the washing of wills.

2. The Nature of Liberties

Having mentioned some common confusions which require only brief discussion, we are in position to consider two more complex issues: the nature of liberties and the structure of Hohfeldian relations. At this point, the lines between stipulative definition, pointing out confusions, and arguing for a particular understanding of Hohfeldian relations begin to blur.

It is hard to overemphasize the importance and difficulty of correctly understanding what an Hohfeldian liberty is. Both the notion of a liberty itself and the relationship between liberties and other relations are frequently misunderstood. Consider the phrase "You are at liberty to go to church." Outside of Hohfeldian contexts, this implies that (1) you have no duty to others to go to church, (2) you have no duty to others not to go to church, and (3) you have claims against others that they refrain from preventing you from going or not going to church. Now consider the (very similar) Hohfeldian phrase "You have a liberty to go to church." It implies nothing about (1) or (3) and, with respect to (2), it asserts that you have no duty to X not to go to church, no duty to Y not to go to church, no duty to Z not to go to church, etc. In Hohfeldian terminology, "You have a liberty to go to church" is missing the object of the liberty and should be analyzed as a large set of liberties, each with a different object. In Hohfeldian terminology, (1) is a large set of liberties distinct from (2) and (3) is a large set of claims. In this book, "liberty" will refer to Hohfeldian liberties unless otherwise noted.

It is easy to read more into a liberty than is there. If Joshua has *only* a liberty to drive Evelyn's car next Tuesday (and no other Hohfeldian relations), then Joshua has no duty not to drive Evelyn's car—*and nothing more than that*. He does not have a claim that Evelyn not cut off his hand so that he cannot drive the car. He has no claims at all. Evelyn does not have a duty to refrain from blowing up her car or Joshua's house to prevent Joshua from using the car. Evelyn has no duties at all. If Joshua has only an Hohfeldian liberty, his position is precarious indeed. Because of the importance of a liberty in what follows, it is worth examining an illuminating example provided by Carl Wellman (1982, 8–9).

The parking regulations at Washington University have the effect of giving Wellman a liberty to park in the university parking lots. In general, it is illegal to park in the Washington University lots. But Wellman has purchased a parking pass. Suppose that he arrives one morning and discovers that all the parking spaces are full. He is simply out of luck. Unfortunately for Wellman, although his pass relieves him of the duty not to park in the University lots, it does not give him a claim that Washington University insure him a parking space. If the lots are full, he has no valid legal cause of action. For this reason, parking passes are known around some campuses as "hunting permits." Let us suppose that the president of Washington University has been given a special pass which gives him a claim that Washington University insure that he has a parking space in the University lots. He would have a valid cause of action if all the spaces were full. The importance of a liberty can be seen by comparing the legal positions of myself, Wellman, and the President of Washington University. I have a duty not to park in the University lots. I do not have a Washington University parking pass and if I park in the lots I have violated the law. Wellman has a liberty to park in the University lots. If he parks in the lots, he has done nothing illegal, but Washington University has no duty to provide him with a space. The president has a claim that Washington University provides him with a parking space. Washington University has a duty to provide him with a space.

Wellman's example illustrates why the concept of a liberty is important. However, Wellman does not have *only* a liberty to park in the Washington University lots. He has many claims as well. He has a claim that Washington University employees not be assigned to take baseball bats to faculty cars parked in the lots. He has a claim that the University not remove his car from the lot in which it is parked. Wellman's case is a good example of someone with a liberty. It is not an example of someone who has *only* a liberty. One must be careful not to think that the claim that Washington University employees not be assigned to take baseball bats to faculty cars is part of the liberty. It is not. It is a distinct claim. That is why it is best to consider an imaginary case (such as Evelyn and Joshua's) in which a person has *only* a liberty even though there is no actual legal rule system in which a person has a liberty to do A and no other relations.

Rowan (1999, 23) has worried that if there are no actual legal rule systems in which a person has only a liberty, then liberties do not seem "to have much moral significance . . . ." This is incorrect for two reasons. First, Wellman's example clearly shows that we need the concept of an Hohfeldian liberty to explain the difference between myself, Wellman's, and the president's legal positions with regard to parking in the Washington University lots. Second, even in the imaginary case, the liberty has a point. Suppose Evelyn sells Joshua the liberty pass. Joshua has no duty not to use Evelyn's car, and Evelyn has no duty not to savagely beat

7

Joshua to prevent him from taking the car. But suppose that Joshua manages to evade Evelyn and makes off with the car. Evelyn calls the police and Joshua is arrested for stealing Evelyn's car. His liberty pass, while it does not imply any claims against Evelyn that Evelyn not interfere with Joshua using the car, is a valid defense against a charge of grand-theft auto. That Joshua has the liberty pass implies that Joshua has no duty not to use Evelyn's car and therefore that Joshua did not steal it.

Rowan has asserted that "[p]rivileges [i.e., liberties] also differ from claims in that they are not relational in nature" (1999, 23). This is incorrect. One can have a liberty to do an act against one person but not have a liberty to do that same act against another person. Suppose that Stacy promises Jim and Barbara that she will meet them for lunch at the City Grill at 1 o'clock on a particular day. Stacy has a duty to Jim to be at the City Grill at one and a duty to Barbara to be at the City Grill at one. A friend offers her free tickets to an afternoon baseball game that starts at one. She calls Jim and he releases her from her promise to go to lunch. She calls Barbara only to discover that Barbara has already left for the City Grill. In this case Stacy has a liberty against Jim not to go to the City Grill but she does not have a liberty against Barbara not to go to the City Grill.

Because inanimate objects can have no duties, they have liberties. A thing has a liberty when it has no duty not to do some act. Consider a stapler. It, like all inanimate objects, has no duties at all. Therefore, it has no duty not to staple papers. Therefore, it has a liberty to staple papers. Liberties are defined as the lack of a duty. One way to lack a duty is to be the kind of being that can have duties but, in a particular case, does not. Another way to lack a duty is to be the kind of being that cannot have duties at all. Furthermore, because there is no act anyone can do that would remove a stapler's liberty to staple papers, a stapler also has an immunity to having its liberty extinguished.

Wellman (1984, 443) has argued that inanimate objects cannot have liberties because liberties are liberties to act in some way and inanimate objects are incapable of acting. It is true that liberties are liberties to act in some way. But "act" must be taken to include refraining from acting as well as positive acts. Many of the liberties we have are liberties not to do something. You have a liberty not to go to church. Although inanimate objects are clearly incapable of positive action, it is possible for them to refrain from acting. Indeed, it seems necessary that they refrain from acting. So although it is true that liberties are liberties to act in some way and that inanimate objects are incapable of positive acts, it does not follow that inanimate objects cannot have liberties. They have liberties to refrain from acting.

There may be arguments from act theory, which show that inanimate objects cannot refrain from acting. For example, one might argue that action and inaction must both have some linkage to intention or some other mental state. That would be a reason to hold that inanimate objects cannot have liberties. This is not the place for a discussion of act theory. The linkage between acts and intention is obviously complex and controversial. Rather than to enter that debate, it is better to note that, at this stage of the argument, there is an important reason to hold that inanimate objects have liberties and immunities. It is a very short step from the view that inanimate objects cannot have liberties and immunities to the view that they cannot have rights. The step is so short that those who think that inanimate objects can have rights would likely hold that the assertion that inanimate objects cannot have liberties and immunities begs the question against their view. So, at least until Chapter 7, it is best to assume that inanimate objects have liberties and immunities.

One can have Hohfeldian liberties and immunities because one is not subject to a particular rule system. I have no duty to pay French income tax. So, I have a liberty not to pay French income tax. I am also immune to the French government's extinguishing my liberty not to pay French income tax and replacing it with a duty to pay French income tax. Nothing the French government could do would give me such a duty. The laws of France apply only to the individuals subject to those laws, and I am not such an individual. (Of course, I could earn income in France and then I would be subject to French law.) The reason for my liberties and immunities against the French government is that I lack certain duties and they lack certain powers. The reason I lack these duties and they lack these powers is that I am not subject to French law.

Wellman (1995, 17) asserts that it is "pointless and misleading" to assert that I have a legal liberty under the French legal rule system. He thinks that I have no Hohfeldian relations under the French legal rule system. Let us suppose that my grandfather, whose name also happens to be George Rainbolt, were to earn income in France and that the French government, mistaking me for my grandfather, were to begin French legal proceedings against me for failure to pay French income tax. I would then think that my liberties and immunities regarding the payment of French income tax were very much on point. Indeed, because I would like to keep open the possibility of travel to France without risk of arrest for tax evasion, I would think it important to assert the liberties and immunities that I have because I am not subject to French law. I might well hire a French attorney to assert these liberties and immunities in a French court. The assertion of these liberties and immunities would be neither pointless nor misleading.

Powers are distinct from liberties. One can have the power to do A without having the liberty to do A. As Sumner notes

> It is . . . possible for me to do what I lack the liberty to do; any such act will be a violation of the rules. But it is not possible for me to do what I lack the power to do; any such attempt will be, as the lawyers say, a nullity (1987, 29).

Suppose that the mayor of a town has the power to appoint the members of the zoning commission. There are no qualifications for being a member of the zoning commission, so the mayor has the power to appoint anyone, from his mother to a child born yesterday. The laws of the town are then changed to say that if the mayor appoints someone under the age of 21, then that person is a full member in good standing of the zoning commission but the mayor will be fined $1,000. This gives the mayor a duty not to appoint someone under 21 but still leaves the mayor with the power to appoint someone under 21. The mayor has the power but not the liberty to appoint someone under 21. If one wanted to extinguish the mayor's power to appoint someone under 21, one would have to change the law to say that the appointment of someone under 21 is a legal nullity, that the mayor's naming a person under 21 as a member of the zoning commission does not make that person a member of the commission. The odd law which says that someone under 21 who is appointed is a member in good standing but that the mayor will be fined if she chooses someone under 21 creates a situation in which the mayor has the power to appoint someone under 21 but no liberty to appoint someone under 21.

Steiner has argued that it is not possible for one to have a power to do A without having the liberty to do A.

> Suppose that a set of rules imposes a duty on you to forbear from assaulting me, and invests me with the paired powers to waive and demand your compliance with that duty. Suppose further however that ... [this] same set of rules also imposes a duty on *me* to waive your duty of non-assault: that is, it denies me the liberty to exercise my power to demand your compliance with your non-assault duty. One and the same set of rules thus appears to vest me with that power and *disable* me from exercising it. [...] So rejection of the suggestion that possession of powers implies possession of corresponding liberties entails a straightforward contradiction (Kramer et al., 1998, 242–243).[4]

It is worth setting out Steiner's example in more detail. The imagined set of rules includes:

(1) X has a duty to Y that X not assault Y.
(2) Y has a power against X to extinguish (1).
(3) Y has a power against X to demand compliance with (1).

So far, so good. The set of rules is perfectly ordinary. But the set also includes:

(4) Y has a duty to X to extinguish (1).

If Y fulfills the duty in (4), then relations (1), (2), and (3) will be extinguished. Steiner claims that (2), (3), and (4) vest Y with a set of powers "and *disable*" Y from exercising these powers. This is not correct. (2) and (3) vest Y with powers. (4) does not disable Y. (4) is the statement of a duty, not a disability. (4) gives Y a duty to disable herself. From a practical perspective, being disabled and having a duty to disable oneself have almost the same effect. But the "almost" in the previous sentence is important. As the zoning commission example shows, in some cases it can make a practical difference whether one has a power without the correspond-ing liberty as opposed to having neither the power nor the liberty. If the zoning

---

[4] See also Steiner (1994, 60; footnotes 6 and 7).

commissioner had neither the power nor the liberty, then a 21-year-old she appointed would not be on the commission. If the zoning commissioner had the power but not the liberty, then a 21-year-old she appointed would be on the commission.

3. THE STRUCTURE OF HOHFELDIAN RELATIONS

Hohfeldian relations have a particular structure. As we will see in coming chapters, failure to correctly note this structure can lead one down many a dead end street. The full description of all Hohfeldian relations has the following form:

X has a [relation] with respect to Y that Z do A.

X is the subject of the relation, Y is the object of the relation and Z is subject of the content of the relation.

There are conceptual restrictions on the subjects, objects, and contents of relations. If

X has a claim against Y that Z do A

then, because claims and duties are correlatives,

Y has a duty to X that Z do A.

In these cases, Y and Z must be the same person. If Y has a duty it must be a duty that Y do A. One cannot have a duty that another person do something. The subject of a duty must be identical to the subject of the content of the duty. The object of a claim must be identical to the subject of the content of the claim.

If

X has a liberty against Y that Z do A

then, because liberties and no-claims are correlatives,

Y has a no-claim on X that Z do A.

In these cases, X and Z must be the same person. If X has a liberty it must be a liberty for X to do A. One cannot have a liberty that another person do something. The subject of a liberty must be identical to the subject of the content of the liberty. The object of a no-claim must be identical to the subject of the content of the no-claim.

Failure to note these restrictions can cause conceptual muddles. Judith Jarvis Thomson has asserted that, while one can have a liberty against everyone in the world, it is not possible to have a claim against everyone in the world. This is incorrect. Thomson notes that she has a liberty against everyone in the world to pinch her nose. This is correct. But she goes on to assert that

there surely are no claims that a person has against everything in the universe. B is under a duty towards A to stay off A's land so ... we may conclude that A has a claim against B that B stay off A's land. But you are under no duty toward A that B stay off A's land and I am also not under any such duty … (1990, 46)

Let us assume that "you" is C. It is true that C is under no duty to A that B stay off A's land. C cannot have a duty that A, B, D, or any other person do something. That is conceptually impossible. C can only have a duty that C do something. In light of this, it is clear that there are claims that people have against everyone. At this moment, many people have a claim against everyone else that they refrain from shooting them.

The content of the second-order relations (i.e., powers, liabilities, immunities, and disabilities) always includes two other Hohfeldian relations. Second-order relations are relations of change. They indicate the ability or inability to change a relation. Powers are abilities to change one Hohfeldian relation into another, and immunities are inabilities to change one Hohfeldian relation into another. The accurate presentation of a second-order relation must refer to three Hohfeldian relations. Consider Evelyn's power to change Joshua's duty to refrain from driving Evelyn's car into a liberty to drive the car. We need to refer to Evelyn's power, Joshua's duty and Joshua's liberty. Evelyn has a power to change Joshua's duty that he not drive her car into Joshua's liberty that he drive her car. This power is distinct from Evelyn's power to change Joshua's duty to refrain from driving Evelyn's car into a duty to drive Evelyn's car. (Evelyn might have such a power if Joshua had promised to use her car to pick her up from work the next time she asked him to.) If one is not careful, one can easily confuse the subjects and objects of these three relations. It is also easy to overlook one of the three relations. It is useful to have some terminology to refer to these complex Hohfeldian situations. Let us refer to the relation that has two relations in its content (e.g., Evelyn's power) as the *primary* relation. Let us refer to the relation that can or cannot be changed (e.g., Joshua's duty) as the *original* relation. Let us refer to the relation that can or cannot result from the change (e.g., Joshua's liberty) as the *resulting* relation.

The complete presentation of the second-order relations must, in addition to referring to three Hohfeldian relations, refer to a triggering act. Evelyn has the power to change Joshua's duty to refrain from driving Evelyn's car into a liberty to drive the car. Normally, Joshua has a duty to refrain from driving Evelyn's car. But if Evelyn says to Joshua, "You may drive my car," then Joshua no longer has a duty to refrain from driving the car. In this case, the triggering act is Evelyn's saying "You may drive my car." In the case of a power, the triggering act is the act that has the effect of causing the original relation to cease to exist and the resulting relation to come into being. Hohfeld refers to triggering acts as "some superadded fact or group of facts which are under the volitional control or one or more human beings" (2001, 21). The phrase "triggering act" is simpler and clearer.

However, in the case of immunities, the term "triggering act" might mislead. When it comes to immunities, the triggering act refers to the act that does *not* have the effect of causing the original relation to cease to exist and the resulting relation to come into being. If Evelyn and Joshua are strangers, then Evelyn has an immunity to Joshua giving himself a liberty to drive Evelyn's car. Suppose that Joshua said, "I hereby give myself the liberty to drive Evelyn's car." His act has no legal effect. In fact, Evelyn has a large set of immunities, one for each triggering act that Joshua might do that would fail to give him a liberty to drive Evelyn's car.

To fully describe second-order relations, all of the following must be filled in:

X has a [primary relation] with respect to Y that Z
change
    P has an [original relation] with respect to Q that R do A
into
    P has a [resulting relation] with respect to Q that R do A
by doing T.

"X," "Y," "Z," "P," "Q," and "R" are persons, "A" is an act and "T" is the triggering act. The content of a relation, "that Z do A," is common to all eight relations. In the second-order relations the act that is done is the act of changing or not changing relations. If any part of this full description changes, then a new relation exists. This is one way in which Hohfeldian relations can be "nested." A nested relation is a relation that is part of the content of another relation. All original and resulting relations are nested relations.

There are conceptual restrictions on the content of second-order relations. If

X has a power against Y that Z
change
    P has an [original relation] with respect to Q that R do A
into
    P has a [resulting relation] with respect to Q that R do A
by doing T,

then, because powers and liabilities are correlatives,

Y has a liability with respect to X that Z
change
    P has an [original relation] with respect to Q that R do A
into
    P has a [resulting relation] with respect to Q that R do A
by doing T.

In these cases, X and Z must be the same person. If X has a power, it must be a power that X do something. One cannot have a power that another person do something. The subject of a power must be identical to the subject of the content of the power. The object of a liability must be identical to the subject of the content of the liability.

If

X has an immunity against Y that Z
change
    P has an [original relation] with respect to Q that R do A
into
    P has a [resulting relation] with respect to Q that R do A
by doing T,

then, because immunities and disabilities are correlatives,

Y has a disability with respect to X that Z
change
    P has an [original relation] with respect to Q that R do A
into
    P has a [resulting relation] with respect to Q that R do A
by doing T.

In these cases, Y and Z must be the same person. If Y has a disability, it must be a disability for Y to do something. The subject of a disability must be identical to the subject of the content of the disability. The object of an immunity must be identical to the subject of the content of the immunity.

One might be tempted to hold that, when it comes to the second-order relations, the object of primary relation must be the subject of both the original and resulting relations. In the pattern

X has a [primary relation] with respect to Y that Z
change
    P has an [original relation] with respect to Q that R do A
into
    P has a [resulting relation] with respect to Q that R do A
by doing T,

one might be tempted to hold that Y and P must be the same person. However, upon reflection it becomes clear that while Y and P are often the same person, this is not part of the conceptual requirements of these relations. Evelyn has a claim against Joshua that Joshua not drive Evelyn's car. In addition, she has an immunity against Joshua that he not extinguish his duty not to drive her car.

Evelyn has an immunity against Joshua that Joshua
not change
    Joshua has a duty to Evelyn that Joshua not drive Evelyn's car
into
    Joshua has a liberty against Evelyn that Joshua drive Evelyn's car
by say "Joshua, you may drive Evelyn's car."

In this case, Y and P are the same person.

14

Fortunately for Evelyn, she also has an immunity against Steve that Steve not change Joshua's duty not to drive Evelyn's car into a liberty to drive her car. This is an example of an immunity in which Y and P are different people. If Evelyn did not have this immunity against Steve, Joshua could pay Steve to give him a liberty to drive Evelyn's car. Here is the complete description of Evelyn's immunity against Steve.

Evelyn has an immunity against Steve that Steve
not change
   Joshua has a duty to Evelyn that Joshua not drive Evelyn's car
into
   Joshua has a liberty against Evelyn that Joshua drive Evelyn's car
by saying "Joshua, you may drive Evelyn's car."

In this case, Y and P are not the same person. In this case, Steve's disability is with respect to Evelyn and merely regarding Joshua. These points about the conceptual restrictions on the subjects and objects of Hohfeldian relation may seem pedantic. However, in Chapters 2 and 5, we will see that clarity about these matters is essential to resolving puzzles about rights. In particular, clarity in these matters is crucial to the discussion of a central objection to the justified-constraint theory of rights.

Another way that relations can be nested occurs when a first-order relation has another relation in its contents. For example, one could have a duty not to exercise a power. To fully present this situation, one would have to refer to four relations: the duty, the power, the original relation in the content of the power, and the resulting relation in the content of the power. Moreover, there is no logical barrier to the nesting of relations continuing indefinitely. One might have a duty not to exercise a power to change a liberty to exercise a power into a duty to exercise a power. The nesting of relations is typically limited by the human inability to understand very complex situations.

Suppose that the president of a company has a legal power to authorize the company's vice-president to hire someone to work in the company's accounting office. This authorization is granted by signing a certain legal document. Let us use "P" to refer to the president, "V" to refer to the vice-president and "H" to an individual that the vice-president wants to hire for the accounting job. The full description of the president's power must include at least the following:

P has a power against V to
change
   V has a disability with respect to H to
   change
      H has no-claim on V that V hire H
   into
      H has a claim against V that V hire H
   by giving him a legal offer of employment
into

15

> V has a power against H to
> change
> > H has no-claim on V that V hire H
> into
> > H has a claim against V that V hire H
> by giving him a legal offer of employment
> by signing a certain legal document.

Even this is a simplification of the legal situation because the power to hire someone involves more than a power to change a no-claim into a claim. Hiring someone creates a huge set of relations. Strictly speaking, any change in any part of the above description results in a new relation. The president has an enormous set of powers. There is one for each different triggering act in either his power or V's power. There is one for each relation created when V hires H.

Uniformly using the full description of Hohfeldian relations presented above would make this already technical book even more technical. It greatly simplifies presentation if one changes the amount of the full description one uses as necessary for a clear discussion of a particular issue. In some cases, very little of the full description is necessary. However, in all cases, one could use the full description and in several crucial cases to be discussed below use of the full description is necessary to correctly understand what is going on.

Hohfeldian terminology is difficult to understand. In light of this, why have so many authors used Hohfeld's work to analyze rights? What is the payoff for all the effort required to understand Hohfeld? In an important sense this entire book is an answer to these questions. The rest of the book attempts to show that the conceptual apparatus just presented has an intellectual payoff. But one can quickly point to one obvious benefit of using the Hohfeldian terminology. Consider the following examples of rights: my right that you not hit me, my right to pick up and keep an interesting rock that I see on the sidewalk, my right to say that roses are red, my right to give the rock to a friend. Without Hohfeld's analysis, the crucial differences between these four rights cannot be explicated. My right that you not hit me is a claim right. I have a claim that you not hit me, and you have a duty not to hit me. My right to pick up a rock is not a claim right. You have no duty to refrain from picking up the rock. Rather, my right to pick up the rock is a liberty right. I have a liberty to pick up the rock, and you have a correlative no-claim. A crucial part of my right to say that roses are red is an immunity. I have a claim that you not interfere (in some particular ways such as gagging me) with my saying that roses are red and I have an immunity to you extinguishing this claim. Many important rights (such as the right to free speech and the right to freedom of religion) cannot be correctly understood without the Hohfeldian concept of an immunity. Similarly, my right to give away a rock that I have picked up cannot be correctly understood without the Hohfeldian concept of a power. Once I pick up an unowned rock and so gain a claim that others not take it from me, I have the power to transfer this claim to others. I use this power when I give the rock to someone else. Rights to buy and sell cannot be correctly understood without the Hohfeldian concept of a power. Here is the reason that H.L.A. Hart, Wellman, Joel Feinberg, and many others have taken the trouble to provide an Hohfeldian analysis of legal and moral rights. Hohfeldian terminology allows scholars to make important distinctions that were hidden until Hohfeld revealed them.

4. Disagreements With Hohfeld

There are several differences between this neo-Hohfeldian analysis and Hohfeld's analysis. The neo-Hohfeldian analysis offered here also differs from that offered by other jurists and moral philosophers. In theory, it is not necessary to point out these differences to make the arguments found in the subsequent chapters. However, in practice it is natural to see the analysis above through the lens of Hohfeld's own work. Therefore, it is useful to indicate the differences between Hohfeld's analysis and the neo-Hohfeldian analysis. Let us begin with a quick list of some differences that will be obvious to anyone who knows Hohfeld.

First, Hohfeld prefers the term "privilege" whereas the neo-Hohfeldian analysis uses the term "liberty." The majority of contemporary writers on rights theory prefer the term "liberty." Hohfeld himself suggests "liberty" as a possible substitute for "privilege." Second, Hohfeld does not use the term "rule system" as it is used in the neo-Hohfeldian analysis. Third, Hohfeld does not use "with respect to" in the way it is used in the neo-Hohfeldian analysis. Fourth, Hohfeld does not explicitly define correlativity. He merely offers examples. Fifth, the neo-Hohfeldian analysis does not follow Hohfeld in presuming a legal realist analysis of legal duties. Sixth, the neo-Hohfeldian analysis draws the distinction between physical and Hohfeldian powers more sharply than it is drawn by Hohfeld. Seventh, Hohfeld does not explicate the concepts of the subject, object, and content of Hohfeldian relations. While other authors have discussed the notions of the subject, object, and content of Hohfeldian relations, the neo-Hohfeldian analysis' specific understanding of these concepts is unique. Eighth, Hohfeld believes that one has a right if and only if one has a claim. Chapter 2 will argue that this view is false.

There are four other less obvious differences between the neo-Hohfeldian analysis and Hohfeld's. First, Hohfeld asserts that his eight relations are "fundamental" and "*sui generis*" (2001, 12). He believes that they are fundamental and *sui generis* in the sense that one cannot provide an analysis of them. He thinks that "attempts at formal definition [of the eight relations] are always unsatisfactory, if not altogether useless" (2001, 12). But Hohfeld is not true to his own word. He thinks that each relation is logically equivalent to its correlative. Moreover, as noted above, he points out that each relation has an opposite. With these correlatives and opposites, one can easily reduce the first-order relations to any one of their number. The first-order relations are interdefinable. One can also easily reduce the second-order relations to any one of their number. The second-order

17

relations are also interdefinable. Therefore, by Hohfeld's own logic, at most one of the first-order relations and one of the second-order relations is fundamental. Wellman (1985, 53; 1995, 18) asserts that two of the relations, duty and power, are fundamental, undefinable primitives. This is incorrect in at least two respects. Any one of the first-order relations and any one of the second-order relations can serve as the fundamental relation. Duty and power have no privileged place. Moreover, as we will see in Chapter 3, one can and should analyze the Hohfeldian relations in terms of the deontic and alethic modal triads.

Second, Hohfeld fails to see that the second-order relations can be analyzed in terms of conditional first-order relations. Consider

> Evelyn's power to give Joshua a liberty to drive her car by saying, "Joshua, you may drive my car."

One can express this same legal position with the use of a conditional which refers to the triggering act in its antecedent.

> If Evelyn says, "Joshua, you may drive my car," then Joshua's duty not to drive Evelyn's car ceases to exist and is replaced by his liberty to drive her car.

An immunity can be expressed as a conditional with the triggering act in the antecedent and the denial of a change in relations in the consequent. Consider

> Evelyn has an immunity against Joshua to Joshua's giving Joshua a liberty to drive Evelyn's car by saying "I may drive Evelyn's car."

One can refer to this same legal position as follows:

> If Joshua says, "I may drive Evelyn's car," then Joshua's duty not to drive Evelyn's car does not cease to exist and is not replaced by his liberty to drive her car.

Once one sees that the second-order relations can be analyzed in terms of conditional first-order relations, then it becomes apparent that one could pick any one of the first-order relations and refer only to this relation throughout this book. However, to write in this way would require confusing negations. While the following two sentences are logically equivalent, the first is much easier to understand than the second.

(1) Fred has a claim against Jane that Jane give Fred $10.
(2) Jane has no liberty against Fred that Jane not give Fred $10.

It is clearer to continue to use all eight relations.

Third, the neo-Hohfeldian analysis does not assume that the subject and object of a relation must be two different people. One is often the subject and the object of one's own powers. As noted by Wellman (1985, 24), most people have the power against themselves of changing their claim that others not hit them into a no-claim that others not hit them. Those who decide to box exercise this power. There is also the controversial matter of whether one can have a duty to oneself. Some people think that one can have a duty to oneself while others disagree. This issue will be discussed in Chapter 5. To avoid begging the question, it is best not to assume that the subject and the object of a relation must be two different people.

Finally, the neo-Hohfeldian analysis does not assume, as Hohfeld does, that all claims, duties, liberties, no-claims, power, liabilities, immunities, and disabilities are with respect to someone. It distinguishes between Hohfeldian claims, duties, liberties, no-claims, power, liabilities, immunities, and disabilities, which necessarily have an object, and non-Hohfeldian claims, duties, liberties, no-claims, power, liabilities, immunities, and disabilities, which do not have an object. Indeed, Chapter 5 will argue that there are non-Hohfeldian duties. To minimize the repetition of the adjective "Hohfeldian" let us use the terms "claim," "duty," "liberty," "no-claim," "power," "liability," "immunity," and "disability" in the Hohfeldian sense unless explicitly stated otherwise.

5. Agreements With Hohfeld

This long list of disagreements between the neo-Hohfeldian analysis and Hohfeld might lead one to think that overlap between the two is minimal. This would be incorrect. The neo-Hohfeldian analysis agrees with much of Hohfeld, and it agrees with Hohfeld on fundamental matters.

First, the neo-Hohfeldian analysis preserves Hohfeld's most basic insight: that one must carefully distinguish among the eight relations he describes in order to remove serious ambiguities in the term "rights," ambiguities that are extremely detrimental to thinking clearly about the subject. Like Hohfeld's, the neo-Hohfeldian terminology is not intended to accurately reflect actual English usage of the terms "claim," "duty," "liberty," etc. (Hohfeld sometimes seems to hold that his usage reflects actual legal usage. But his own long list of jurists who do not use the terms as Hohfeld thinks they should be used belies that view.) Both Hohfeld and the neo-Hohfeldian analysis seek to improve on actual English usage by stipulating a technical and specific meaning for a set of terms. The concept of rights is best analyzed in neo-Hohfeldian terms (and those to be introduced in Chapter 3). As Matthew Kramer (Kramer et al., 1998, 22) puts it, Hohfeld's terminology was meant to be "purificatory." It seeks to clean up normal English usage so as to avoid confusions and bring out overlooked similarities. Thus attacks on Hohfeldian terminology on the grounds that it does not reflect common usage or legal usage are misplaced. Neo-Hohfeldian terminology is also stipulative. To attack the use of the terminology, one must argue that it is not useful. For example, one might assert that it obscures important distinctions or that it makes distinctions where none should be made.

Second, both the neo-Hohfeldian analysis and Hohfeld hold that one relation can, all by itself, be a right. Some, such as Wellman, have held that only a package of Hohfeldian relations can be a right. This issue will be considered in Chapter 2.

Third, both the neo-Hohfeldian analysis and Hohfeld hold that Hohfeldian relations relate no more than two agents. Wellman has argued that this is not so. His argument consists of three examples intended to show that there are cases in which Hohfeldian relations relate more than two people.

> Suppose that Judge Jones decides a medical malpractice suit in favor of the plaintiff and against the defendant ordering the doctor to pay $50,000 to the patient. [...] The judge brings into existence a legal claim of the patient to be paid $50,000 by the doctor and imposes upon the doctor a legal duty to pay the patient $50,000. Nor, by Hohfeld's own logic, can the judge's legal power be analyzed into two separate and independent legal powers, the legal power to create a claim of the plaintiff and the power to impose a duty upon the defendant, for the concepts of a legal claim and a correlative duty refer to one and the same legal relation seen from the different perspectives of the parties between whom it holds (1985, 24).

Wellman has overlooked the complexity of Hohfeldian analysis. The content of a power contains references to two other relations, the original and resulting relations. The subject and object of the original and resulting relations need not be the same as the subject and object of the primary relation. So a power can, and in this case does, require reference to three distinct individuals to be completely described. However, it is still accurate to say that the judge has two distinct powers; the power to give the patient a claim and the power to give the doctor a duty. The object of the first power is the patient while the object of the second power is the doctor. Describing the judge's two powers in more detail makes the difference between them clear. The first power is

> The judge's power against the patient to
> change
>> the patient's no-claim on the doctor that the doctor give the patient $50,000
> into
>> the patient's claim against the doctor that the doctor give the patient $50,000
> by issuing a court order.

The second power is

> The judge's power against the doctor to
> change
>> the doctor's liberty against the patient that the doctor not give the patient
>> $50,000
> into
>> the doctor's duty to the patient that the doctor give the patient $50,000
> by issuing a court order.

While the full Hohfeldian description of the situation requires reference to three individuals, each of the three relations referred to in the full description of these two powers relates only two individuals.

Here is Wellman's second example:

> Another illuminating example is that of contracts that confer a legal right upon some third party. Although not all contracts intended to benefit some third party create a legal claim of the beneficiary to the intended benefit, some do precisely that. Let us imagine that the party who will become legally bound to perform some action beneficial to the third party has made the relevant offer. The first party now has the legal power to create, by accepting the offer and tendering the specified consideration, both a legal duty binding upon the second party and a legal claim of the third party. Once more it is impossible to analyze this legal power into two separate legal powers because it is the power to make precisely the sort of contract that has both second and third parties (1985, 24).

This example is not as good as the first. The problem is that there are some, such as Hart (1979, 18), who deny that contracts can confer rights upon a third party. But even if we set that issue aside, this example has the exact same problem as the first. Wellman has confused the fact that the full description of the first party's powers refers to three individuals with the claim that the powers in question have two individuals as objects. Once again, if one describes the two powers in more detail, one sees that they are distinct because they have distinct objects. The object of the first party's power to create the second party's duty is the second party. The object of the first party's (distinct) power to create the third party's claim is the third party.

Wellman's third example is of a different structure:

> Consider a bank account in the name of John Doe *and* Jane Doe, rather than in the name of John Doe *or* Jane Doe. Although neither John Doe nor Jane Doe has any legal right to write checks against this joint account individually, John Doe and Jane Doe do have such a right together (1985, 97).

It is likely that Wellman would hold that this is an example of a claim with two subjects. Wellman underestimates the power of Hohfeldian analysis. Hohfeld would surely respond that in the case of this bank account, neither John nor Jane has a claim to the money in the bank. John has instead a power to give Jane a power to give herself a claim to the money in the bank and a power to give Jane the power to give John a power to create his claim to the money in the bank. Jane has a power to give John a power to give himself a claim to the money in the bank and a power to give John the power to give Jane a power to create her claim to the money in the bank. Imagine that money is drawn from this account by check only and that the check must be signed by both John and Jane. John's signing of a check has the effect of giving Jane the power (by signing the check herself and presenting it to the bank) to create a claim against the bank that they give her the money in the account. John's signing of a check also has the effect of giving Jane the power (by signing the check herself and giving it to John) to give John the power (by presenting the check signed by both of them to the bank) to create his claim to the money in

21

the account. Jane's signing of a check has the effect of giving John the power (by signing the check himself and presenting it to the bank) to create a claim against the bank that they give him the money in the account. Jane's signing of a check also has the effect of giving John the power (by signing the check himself and giving it to Jane) to give Jane the power (by presenting the check signed by both of them to the bank) to create her claim to the money in the account. So what Wellman sees as a claim with two subjects is actually a complex Hohfeldian collection of powers and claims, each of which relates only two individuals. I can think of many cases in which Hohfeldian relations relate one or two individuals and no cases in which, if fully described, the relations relate more than two individuals. Hohfeld's view that his relations relate no more than two individuals is correct.

Relatedly, Hohfeld was correct to hold that rights *in rem* can be analyzed as a large set of rights relating precisely two agents. A right *in rem* is a right that holds against everyone. The classic example is the right not to be assaulted. You have this right against everyone. Everyone has a duty to refrain from assaulting you. Rights *in rem* are to be distinguished from rights *in personam*. A right *in personam* is a right that holds only against a particular individual. The classic example is the right of a creditor to repayment from his debtor. If Jefferson lends Lyvona $20, then Jefferson has a right *in personam* that Lyvona give him $20. His loan does not generate a right that anyone else give him $20. (Some, such as Hart (1979), refer to rights *in personam* as "special" rights and rights *in rem* as "general" rights.) Joseph Raz holds that:

> Hohfeld's insistence that every right is a relation between no more than two persons is completely unfounded and makes the explanation of rights *in rem* impossible . . . (1980, 180).

Hohfeld can easily offer a plausible explanation of rights *in rem*. Hohfeld holds that what we refer to as a right *in rem* is a package of rights. One's right *in rem* not to be assaulted is a large set of claims not to be assaulted. For each person in the world, you have claim of which she or he is the object, you are the subject and the content is that she or he not assault you. Hohfeld and the neo-Hohfeldian analysis hold that rights *in rem* are packages of rights *in personam*. This is a natural and plausible explanation of rights *in rem*.

Sumner asserts the related view that a non-relational liberty is a liberty against everyone.

> Out of the relational notion of a liberty we can, of course, easily construct a non-relational notion: I have a liberty tout court to do something just in case I have a liberty with respect to everyone to do it . . . (1987, 26).

Hohfeld was right to hold that a liberty against everyone is a liberty *in rem*. A liberty *in rem* is a large set of liberties *in personam*. A non-relational liberty is not a liberty against everyone. It is a liberty that does not have any object at all. It is a liberty against no one.

Another issue on which the neo-Hohfeldian analysis and Hohfeld agree is best illustrated by focusing on powers. MacCormick (1981, 75) provides a useful example. A tramp, seeing the coming of winter, carefully chooses a town with a particularly comfortable jail and commits, in full view of a police officer, an offense with a mandatory sentence that lasts until the arrival of spring. Hohfeld and the neo-Hohfeldian analysis hold that the tramp has the power to create the police officer's duty to arrest him and the judge's duty to sentence him to the mandatory sentence. Or, to make matters sound even more odd, consider a variation on an example provided by Corbin (1918). Suppose that Katie wishes to be declared bankrupt but finds that she does not have enough debt. To solve what she perceives as a problem (her lack of debt) she assaults Craig with just enough force to avoid a jail sentence but create a duty to pay him damages in an amount sufficiently great to make her debt rise above the level necessary for a judge to declare her bankrupt. Hohfeld (and Corbin) were correct to hold that Katie has the power, by assaulting Craig, to give herself a duty to pay Craig a certain amount of money.

Wellman argues that the acts of the tramp and Katie should not be construed as the exercise of a power. He acknowledges that "one *can* view the [tramp's] act of committing a crime as an exercise of a legal power" but he thinks that "it is more illuminating to restrict the concept of a legal power to a narrower range of legal abilities" (1985, 45). According to Wellman, "what is required for the efficacy of a legal power is the imputation of some rough knowledge of the legal consequences attached to one's action and the intention of effecting something like those consequences" (1985, 46). (Raz (1984) agrees with Wellman.) The two restrictions in this quote do not imply that the tramp and Katie are not exercising a power. Both are committing their crimes with knowledge of the legal consequences attached to their act and the intention of bringing about consequences that they find desirable but which most people do not. It is true, as Wellman notes, that one needs terminology to express the distinction between the intentional and the unintentional use of a power. People do sometimes do things that they do not intend to do, and one needs to be able to indicate that this has occurred. Of course, Wellman could stipulatively restrict the definition of "power," but it is simpler and less misleading to use phrases such as "the intentional exercise of a power versus the unintentional exercise of a power" rather than to follow Wellman and use the term "ability" to intentional or unintentional exercises of an ability and restrict the term "power" to intentional exercises of an ability.

2. Normative Constraints

Commentators beginning with Hohfeld have noted a special relationship between claims and rights. Hohfeld held that rights are claims and that any other use of the term "right" is loose talk. But commentators since Hohfeld have rejected his strict identification of rights and claims. (See Lyons (1970) and Wellman (1985) among many.) They argued that there are rights corresponding to other Hohfeldian relations. Immunities, liberties, and powers are thought to be the most likely candidates. So it has become common to distinguish four sorts of rights: claim rights, immunity rights, liberty rights, and power rights. As noted above, this fourfold distinction allows us to distinguish importantly different sorts of rights. On the other hand, the distinction leaves a crucial question unanswered: Why are all of these different things rights?[1]

1. CLAIM AND IMMUNITY RIGHTS

Suppose that a landlord has a right to $250 from her tenant at the first of each month. This is a claim right. Suppose that a citizen has a right not to have the President change her liberty to burn the flag into a duty to refrain from burning the flag. This is an immunity right. These are paradigm cases of rights. The central Hohfeldian relation involved in these two cases is clear. The landlord has a *right* to $250 and the landlord has a *claim* to $250. The citizen has a *right* not to have the President extinguish his liberty to burn the flag and the citizen has an *immunity* to having the President extinguish his liberty to burn the flag. We have identified two different rights—rights that are claims and rights that are immunities. We have reason to think that if one has a claim or an immunity, then one has a right.

The only relations that imply a *normative constraint on another* are claims and immunities. This is a crucial and overlooked feature of Hohfeldian relations. (In what follows, the adjective "Hohfeldian" refers to the neo-Hohfeldian analysis defended in the previous chapter.) If a rule system implies that a person has a duty or a disability, then her acts are restricted or constrained. For example, according to typical legal rule systems, I have a duty to refrain from torturing people and a disability to give myself a liberty to drive your car. These duties and disabilities restrict or constrain my acts of torturing people and giving myself a liberty to drive your car. Duties and disabilities are different sorts of normative constraints. My duty to refrain from torturing people is a constraint on my action because there is

---

[1]   This chapter is a much revised version of Rainbolt (1993). For a useful collection of work on the questions discussed in this chapter and the next, see Wellman (2002), vol. 3.

some act that I *may not* do. My disability to give myself a liberty to drive your car is a constraint on my action because there is some act that I *cannot* do. To say that there is some act that I cannot do is to say that there is no way to do a certain act. According to typical legal rule systems, if Joshua says, "I hereby give myself the liberty to drive Evelyn's car," his act has no legal effect. This is a constraint on his ability to have the liberty to drive Evelyn's car.

Because duties and disabilities are normative constraints and the correlatives of duties and disabilities are claims and immunities, claims and immunities entail a normative constraint on another. If X has a claim against Y, then Y has a duty to X and so Y has a normative constraint on her actions. If X has an immunity against Y, then Y has a disability with respect to X and so Y has a normative constraint on her actions. No other Hohfeldian relations imply normative constraints on another. Duties and disabilities entail a constraint on the person who has the duty or the disability, not on another. To say that X has a liberty to do act A implies no normative constraint. It only implies that X has no duty to refrain from doing A. Similarly, to say that X has a power to do A implies no constraint. It only implies that X can change an Hohfeldian relation. Because liberties and powers imply no normative constraints, their correlatives (no-claims and liabilities) also imply no normative constraints.

What is a normative constraint? A constraint is something that restricts or limits a person's action.[2] There are different sorts of constraints. Physical constraints are restrictions on action created by the laws of physics. If one is locked into a room, one is under a physical constraint. Logical constraints are restrictions on action created by the rules of logic. It is logically impossible for one to be at one's desk and not be at one's desk at the same time. This is a restriction, a constraint, on one's action. Sumner's analysis of normative constraints is useful.

> Rules do not constrain in the way that ropes or bars constrain, and it is usually physically possible to break them. But the analogy between a physical and a normative constraint is instructive. Just as the former reduces the range of options physically possible for me (i.e., compatible with the laws of nature), the latter reduces the range of options deontically possible for me (i.e., compatible with the rules of conduct). The analogy between the two kinds of constraints serves to remind us that deontic categories (required/forbidden) are counterparts, or perhaps special cases, of alethic modal categories (necessary/impossible) (1987, 22).

---

[2] My use of the term "constraint" is importantly different from Nozick's (1974). His side constraint view is a substantive view on what rights people actually have. To oversimplify, he holds that all rights are rights that others refrain from doing certain acts. He holds that there are no rights that another do an act. Because my interest is the question, "What is a right?" and not "What rights do we have?" Nozick's view is not relevant to the issues in this book.

(In the next chapter we will see that Sumner's suggestion of a link between the Hohfeldian relations and the deontic and alethic concepts is a fruitful one. Although his analysis of this link is not developed, it does point toward a move crucial to the understanding of rights.)

Although normative constraints are clearly different from physical and logical constraints, it is notoriously difficult to determine exactly what sort of constraints normative constraints are. In other words, it is hard to determine exactly what is the case when one may not or cannot do something. For example, consider your legal claim that your physician not treat you without your consent. She may not treat you without your consent. In addition to this claim, you have the legal power to sue her in the event that she treats you without your consent. Some might hold that the mere legal claim by itself, the mere presence of a legal duty without your power to sue, would not constrain your physician's actions. On this view, constraints do not exist unless there is force or threat of force to back them up. This view might lead one to hold that there are no moral constraints. Others reject the view that normative constraints do not exist without force. Here we enter issues in meta-ethics. The justified-constraint theory of rights will inherit from one's meta-ethical views an analysis of normative constraint. An attempt to resolve these meta-ethical issues would take us outside a theory of rights. I assume without argument that there are normative constraints. I assume without argument that it makes sense in law, morals, and in other contexts to talk of what one may not do and of what one cannot do. The justified-constraint theory of rights does not include an analysis of "may not" and "cannot." In this sense, it is not a complete theory of rights. The justified-constraint analysis follows Sumner (1987, 29) in ending with the unexplicated notions of "may not" and "cannot." Every analysis must end somewhere. The rest of this book will show that significant philosophical insights can be gained if one ends here.

Rights constrain the acts of others. To modify a phrase of Hohfeld's, it is certain that even those who use the word "right" in the broadest possible way are accustomed to thinking of normative constraints as the invariable consequence of rights. As Steiner notes, "any right entails a prescribed restriction on the activities of persons other than that right's holder . . . " and this sort of "constraint is an uncontested feature of rights . . . " (1994, 55, 59). The landlord's right to $250 is a normative constraint on the actions of her tenant. The tenant is constrained to pay $250. The citizen's right that the President not extinguish her liberty to burn the flag is a normative constraint on the actions of the President. The President is constrained not to extinguish the liberty. I have a right to drive my pickup truck and others are constrained to refrain from certain acts which would interfere with my driving my truck. My students have a right that I grade their papers and I am constrained to grade their papers. My next door neighbor has a right that I not dispose of my trash by throwing it over the fence onto her yard and I am constrained from throwing my trash onto her yard.

Both claims and immunities and only claims and immunities place normative constraints on others. Rights necessarily constrain others. Therefore, there is reason to think that claims and immunities, and only claims and immunities, are rights. More precisely,

X has a right against Y that Y do A if and only if
(1) X has a claim against Y that Y do A, or
(2) X has an immunity against Y that Y do A.

To be brief, we can say that one has a right when one has a claim or an immunity.[3] It will be useful to have a name for this theory of rights. Let us call it "the justified-constraint theory of rights." This name is appropriate because it points to a key feature of rights, that they constrain the acts of others. In Chapter 5, I will argue that rights are constraints which have a particular sort of justification. This explains the "justified" in the name of the theory defended in this book. That only claims and immunities constrain others, that rights necessarily constrain others, and that claims and immunities are paradigm cases of rights combine to give the justified-constraint analysis initial plausibility.

A virtue of the justified-constraint analysis is that it explains *why* both claims and immunities are rights. Both claims and immunities are rights because they (and only they) entail normative constraints on the actions of another. As we look at other examples of rights, we will find that rights always entail a normative constraint on the actions of others. Therefore, we will always find a claim or an immunity in a right. Chapter 5 will argue that normative constraints do not entail rights.

The justified-constraint analysis of rights implies that the correlativity thesis is false. According to the correlativity thesis, all rights necessarily imply duties and all duties necessarily imply rights. Whether the second half of the thesis is true depends on whether one thinks that there are non-Hohfeldian duties. Chapter 5 will argue that there are. If all duties are Hohfeldian duties, then all duties imply rights. But if there are non-Hohfeldian duties (that is, duties which have no object), then some duties do not imply rights. The first half of the correlativity thesis—that all rights imply duties—is false. It is false because there are immunity rights and they imply disabilities, not duties. (The existence of immunity rights also shows that Rowan (1999, 26) was incorrect when he asserted that all rights imply claims.)

Kramer has correctly pointed out that, for Hohfeld, the correlativity thesis was true by definition (Kramer et al., 1998, 24–27). Hohfeld defined rights as claims and then defined duties as the correlatives of claims. If one makes these two stipulations, then the correlativity thesis is a logical necessity. One must not attempt the futile task of refuting Hohfeld's stipulations. On the other hand, it is appropriate to

---

[3] Kramer has noted that "immunities are the second-order counterparts of rights." (Kramer et al., 1998, 21).

consider whether the best theory of rights implies that all rights imply duties and all duties imply rights. On the best theory of rights, is the correlativity thesis true or false? An answer to this question is neither an objection to nor a consideration in support of a theory of rights. The correlativity thesis is far too technical an issue to matter in that way. However, because the thesis has been discussed by many commentators, it is worth noting that the justified-constraint theory of rights implies that there are some rights that do not imply duties and therefore the theory implies that the correlativity thesis is false.

Hobbes (1964, Chapter 14) holds that a mere liberty is a right. A Hobbesian could either (a) reject the view that rights necessarily constrain the acts of others or (b) hold that liberties entail normative constraints on others and therefore are rights. Evelyn sells Joshua a pass which states that he has a mere liberty to drive her car next Tuesday. The Hobbesian would agree that Evelyn has no duty to refrain from hiding the car, locking the car, destroying the car, taking the car to Alaska, removing the battery, etc. But, the Hobbesian might continue, even a mere liberty does constrain Evelyn in a certain way. If Joshua has a liberty, then Evelyn cannot prevent him from taking the car by citing his duty not to take the car. This, the Hobbesian might argue, is a normative constraint on Evelyn's action and therefore a mere liberty is a right. Alternatively, the Hobbesian could attempt to defend the view that a mere liberty is a right by granting that liberties do not constrain the acts of others but denying that rights necessarily constrain the actions of others.

There is an important reason to prefer the justified-constraint view over the Hobbesian view. It better matches the ordinary language of rights. Suppose that Hassan has a mere liberty to say that Richard Nixon was a crook. This liberty does not imply that others have a duty to refrain from gagging Hassan to keep him from speaking, threatening to arrest him if he says Richard Nixon was a crook, or doing any of the thousands of other things which would keep Hassan from speaking. If no one has any duties to refrain from these sorts of acts, then Hassan does not have a right to say that Richard Nixon was a crook. One who says, "You have a right to say that Richard Nixon was a crook but I may gag you if I wish," reveals an Orwellian confusion. As Hart put it:

> There would be something not only strange but misleading in describing naked liberties as rights: if we said, for example, that a class of helots whom free citizens were allowed to treat as they wished or interfere with at will, yet had rights to do those acts which they were not forbidden by the law to do (1982, 173).[4]

The Hobbesian view is "strange" and "misleading" because it is out of line with our normal usage of the term "rights." The puzzled reactions of students also indicate

---

[4] For similar views, see Sumner (1987, 34–35), Raz (1984, 20), Wellman (1985, 63), and Steiner (1994, 61, footnote 9).

that the Hobbesian usage is odd. For example, students have a great deal of trouble understanding how Hobbes can hold that one has a right to some bit of property if the state may take it for any reason. A teacher must explain that Hobbes *did not mean* by "rights" what we mean by the term.

Hart is correct and Hobbes is wrong. Mere liberties are normatively too weak to be rights. A mere liberty is not a right because it does not imply the kind of normative constraint on others that is essential to rights. Those who think liberties are rights have allowed the normative force of the normal English use of "liberty" to creep into their view concerning Hohfeldian liberties. In Chapter 1 we saw that there is a more natural and full-bodied sense of "liberty." Liberties in this more full-bodied sense are sets of Hohfeldian liberties and *claims* and do constitute a liberty right. But mere Hohfeldian liberties are not rights.

2. LIBERTY AND POWER RIGHTS

What of the other two sorts of rights mentioned by commentators, liberty and power rights? Liberty and power rights are packages of Hohfeldian relations, which are rights because they contain a claim and so entail a normative constraint on another. Perhaps the most famous example of a liberty right is Hart's.

> [A] man has a right to look over his garden fence at his neighbor; he is under no obligation not to look at him and under no obligation to look at him. [The neighbor] has certain legal obligations or duties . . . which preclude some, though not all forms of interference (1982, 166).[5]

This right contains three Hohfeldian relations—a liberty to look over the fence, a liberty not to look over the fence, and a claim against interference. One has a liberty right to do A if and only if one has (1) a liberty to do A, (2) a liberty not to do A, and (3) a claim that protects these liberties. A liberty right is a *right* because it contains a claim. It is the claim that entails the normative constraint on another. A liberty right is a *liberty* right because it contains two liberties.

In some cases, an immunity is added to a liberty right. For example, Hassan's legal liberty right to say that Richard Nixon was a crook contains, in addition to the liberties to say and not to say that Richard Nixon was a crook and claims against interference, an immunity to having these liberties extinguished. That is the effect of the First Amendment to the U.S. Constitution. The immunity adds further protection of the liberties by further constraining the actions of others. Hassan's right under the U.S. legal rule system to say that Richard Nixon was a crook is a liberty right (which contains a claim right) and an immunity right.

---

[5] Because Hart does not think that the criminal law creates Hohfeldian duties, he would disagree with my analysis of his example. Chapter Four defends the view that the criminal law creates Hohfeldian relations.

A word needs to be said about phrases such as "a claim that protects a liberty." The word "protects" in such phrases could be read in two ways. It could refer to

(i) a claim that protects the doing of the act which is the content of the liberty

or it could refer to

(ii) a claim that protects the liberty relation itself.

Suppose one says: "Laural has a claim against Gene that protects her liberty to go swimming." This could mean (i) that Gene has a duty not to do things that would interfere with Laural's swimming (e.g., draining her pool). On the other hand, it could mean (ii) that Gene has a duty not to extinguish Laural's liberty itself. For example, Gene might have the power to extinguish the liberty, but it might be illegal for him to exercise this power. As used in this work, "a claim that protects a liberty" refers to (i). If others are constrained to act in certain ways, this may aid one in doing what one has a liberty to do. In that case, the claims that constrain the acts of others protect the liberty. This way of using the phrase is not ideal because read literally the phrase seems to refer to (ii). However, it would be tedious to use the longer "a claim that protects the doing of an act which is the content of a liberty," so the rest of this book will use the shorter "a claim that protects a liberty" to refer to (i). "Protects" will be used in the same way to refer to claims protecting other relations and to refer to immunities protecting a relation. A liberty can be and usually is protected by many claims and immunities. Such a package of claims, immunities, and liberties is often referred to as *a* right.

There are two ways liberties can be protected. First, some claims or immunities protect liberties when they constrain people to refrain from interfering with others' liberties. This is the sort of protection that occurs in the example of the right to look over a fence. Second, claims or immunities protect liberties when they constrain people to take positive actions that aid people in doing what they have a liberty to do. In the U.S. legal rule system, part of Hassan's liberty right to say that Richard Nixon was a crook is a claim that the police take positive actions (e.g., assigning officers to demonstrations) to protect Hassan when he exercises this liberty.

Commentators have overlooked the fact that many rights not traditionally thought of as liberty rights have the liberty right structure of Hohfeldian relations. Consider the right to have a decent minimum income. If I have this right, then I have a liberty to have a certain sum of money, a liberty not to have this sum of money, and a claim that others give me this amount of money if I do not have it. This claim helps me to have what I have a liberty to have, in this case a certain amount of money. This is the same structure of Hohfeldian relations found in Hassan's liberty right to say that Richard Nixon was a crook with its claim to positive protective actions by the police. The term "liberty right" is a technical philosophical term, and so one might wish to define liberty rights by their content and thereby restrict them to the traditional list. But, because of the structural similarity, we ought to consider adding rights such as the right to a decent minimum income to the list of liberty rights. However we decide to use the term "liberty rights," it is important to note the structural similarity between the right in Hart's original example and rights such as the right to a decent minimum income.[6]

A classic example of a power right is the legal right to change another's duty to refrain from driving one's car into a liberty to drive the car. Like a mere liberty, a mere power is not a right. Suppose that Evelyn has the power to change Joshua's duty not to drive her car into a liberty to drive her car but no claims, immunities, liberties, etc. As Steiner (1994, 61, footnote 9) notes, the normative constraint essential to having a right is missing. Evelyn has no claims that others refrain from interfering with her changing Joshua's duty into a liberty. Others have the liberty to hit her on the head to keep her from saying that Joshua may drive her car, to destroy her car, to destroy official documents necessary for her to give Joshua the liberty to drive the car, etc. In typical legal rule systems, a power right includes, in addition to a power to change a duty to a liberty, a claim that others not interfere with this power.

In typical legal rule systems, a power right also includes the liberty to make the change that one has the power to make. But this is merely a contingent fact. Evelyn could have:

(1) the power to change Joshua's duty not to drive her car into a liberty to drive her car,
(2) claims that protected this power, but
(3) no liberty to make this change.

In this atypical situation, she would have the power to change Johsua's duty to a liberty but also a duty not to change his duty to a liberty. She would not have a power right. One cannot have a power right to do what one has a duty not to do. To have a power right one must have, in addition to the power to make a change, the liberty to make this change.

Evelyn's power right contains five relations: a power to give Joshua the liberty to drive the car, a power not to give him the liberty to drive the car, a liberty to give him the liberty to drive the car, a liberty not to give him the liberty to drive the car, and a claim that protects her liberties and powers. One has a power right to do A if and only if one has (1) a power to do A, (2) a power not to do A, (3) a liberty to do A, (4) a liberty not to do A, and (5) a claim that protects these liberties and powers. A power right is a package of Hohfeldian relations. It is a *right* because it contains a claim. It is a *power* right because it contains two powers. As with liberty rights, an immunity may be added to the power right.

Liberty and power rights are classic examples of active rights, rights to do something oneself. On the other hand, passive rights are rights that another person do or not do something. Both active and passive rights are subdivided into positive

---

[6] For example, this sort of similarity might have implications concerning libertarianism.

and negative rights. An active positive right is a right in which the right-holder has a right to perform an act. My right to drive my pickup is an active positive right. An active negative right is a right in which the right-holder has a right not to perform an act. My right not to drive my pickup is an active negative right. A passive positive right is a right that another person do something. A passive negative right is a right that another person not do something. I have a passive positive right that Georgia State University pay me. My right that you not hit me is a passive negative right. Claim and immunity rights are necessarily passive rights. They can be either positive rights or negative rights. All active rights are packages of Hohfeldian relations, and all of them contain passive claim and/or immunity rights.

Sumner offers a different analysis of power rights. He notes that power rights contain claims but thinks that the other parts of a power right are different from those I have noted.

> In the case of powers ... there are two further ingredients whose addition to the package is necessitated by the fact that powers are second-order normative positions. The first is an immunity against the like power of others. We would ... not think much of my 'right' to make a will if, while I have the power to do so or not as I choose, others have the same power (to make a will for me or not as they choose). We ordinarily assume that my right to make a will confers on me exclusive control over whether anything will come to count as *my* will. [...] We would also not think much of any 'right' to make a will if, while I have the power to do so or not as I choose, I also have the duty not to do so. Thus we must add to the power at least the higher-order liberty to exercise it. Must we also add the liberty not to exercise it? If I am to have full control over whether anything will come to count as my will, then my full power must be accompanied by a full liberty to exercise it or not as I choose. But just as we can make some sense of first-order mandatory rights ... so we can also make some sense of second-order mandatory rights .... Thus, for example, a university registrar may be empowered to issue academic transcripts but also be required to do so in the case of any applicant who satisfies some specified conditions. It would not be a gross abuse of the language of rights to say that the registrar has the right to issue transcripts, despite the fact that (when the conditions are satisfied) he lacks the liberty not to (1987, 36–37).

He holds that a power right is composed of (at a minimum) (1) a power to do A, (2) a liberty to do A, (3) an immunity to others doing A, and (4) a claim that protects these liberties and powers. The registrar has a right and this right is a Hohfeldian bundle that contains a power, but it does not seem to me useful to call his unusual right a power right. This right is not a classic power right. It is a variant. The classic power right contains the elements (1) through (5) noted above.

On the other hand, it would not be profitable to spend too much time arguing over the nature of power rights. Hohfeldian bundles that are rights can come with a wide variety of relations in them. Hassan's legal right to free speech as currently interpreted by the U.S. Supreme Court is a bundle of Hohfeldian relations containing at least the following relations:

(1) a liberty to say that Richard Nixon was a crook,
(2) a liberty not to say that Richard Nixon was a crook,
(3) a claim that the police provide protection when he says that Richard Nixon was a crook,
(4) a large set of claims that others not interfere with his saying that Richard Nixon was a crook, and
(5) a set of immunities to having the above relations extinguished.

So the right to free speech in the U.S. legal rule system is a claim right, an immunity right, and a liberty right. Because we often label complex Hohfeldian bundles as a single right, many rights we speak of as single rights will fall into more than one Hohfeldian category. Indeed, every sort of right is a claim right and/or an immunity right and all power rights are liberty rights.

Rule systems can combine Hohfeldian relations in thousands of ways. Below I will argue that in addition to power and liberty rights there are duty, disability, liability, or no-claim rights. However, this classification is not exhaustive. Some rights will not be power, liberty, duty, disability, liability, or no-claim rights. Sumner's registrar example is a case in which a person has a power to do A, a liberty to do A, and a claim that protects the power and the liberty. This is a claim right but, because the liberty and power not to do A are missing, not quite a power right (as I have defined it). One should not attempt to provide a label for all of the sorts of Hohfeldian bundles that would be a right of some sort. This section attempts to show that classic cases of the different sorts of rights have the relations noted above and to point out overlooked similarities between rights. How one classifies odd cases is a matter of convenience. The crucial point is that one has a right of some sort if and only if one has a claim or an immunity.

3. DUTY, DISABILITY, LIABILITY, AND NO-CLAIM RIGHTS

Lack of an adequate analysis of rights has caused commentators to overlook the fact that there are rights corresponding to all the rest of the Hohfeldian relations: duty rights, disability rights, liability rights, and no-claim rights. Each of these sorts of rights is a right in just the same sense that liberty rights and power rights are rights. Each is a package of Hohfeldian relations that contains a claim that protects the relation after which the right is named.

Let us begin with duty rights. The phrase "duty right" sounds odd. Yet there are clear examples of such rights. I have a duty to grade my students' papers and a claim that others refrain from interfering with my grading the papers. I have a duty right. One has a duty right to do A if and only if one has a duty to do A and a claim that protects this duty. Duty rights are common. According to typical legal rule systems, I have a duty right to pay my debts, to refrain from killing people, etc. Judges typically have a legal duty right to impose sentence. Duty rights frequently go unmentioned because people tend not to demand to do their duties. Therefore, they tend to keep quiet about their duty rights. It is only when people want to do their duty that they point out their duty rights. I would mention my duty right to grade my students' papers only if someone attempted to interfere with my grading and I wanted to grade the papers. (It is not often that I want to grade papers.) One of the most common mistakes made when discussing rights is to overlook the distinction between having a right and having a right that one wants to mention, assert, or demand. One can have a right without mentioning it. Rights that people have but do not want to mention will, of course, not be mentioned. But that does not mean that these rights do not exist. Many unmentioned things exist.

Some duty rights are mentioned. A police officer might well have a right to arrest someone and a duty to arrest as well. The officer, especially if she were a plainclothes officer, might well be asked, "What right have you to arrest me?" The officer might then produce an order from a judge which directed her to arrest the individual in question. The president of a university might well have the right to preside at meetings of the university faculty and, if no one else may preside, a duty to do so as well. One has a duty to care for one's children. One also has a right to care for one's children. If someone were to try to prevent me from fulfilling my duty to care for my son, I would cite my duty right to care for him in defense of my duty to care for him.

Other examples of duty rights that are mentioned from time to time include what Feinberg (1980, 157) calls "mandatory rights." According to some legal rule systems, such as those of the former Soviet Union and Australia, people have a duty to vote. The duty is protected by claims. For example, one has a claim that others refrain from interfering with one's voting. But it is not clear that people in the U.S.S.R. had an Hohfeldian duty to vote. Hohfeldian duties are always with respect to someone, and it is not clear who the object of the duty to vote is. If people in the U.S.S.R. had a non-Hohfeldian duty to vote, then they had a non-Hohfeldian duty right. They had a non-Hohfeldian duty protected by claims. If they had an Hohfeldian duty to vote, then they had an Hohfeldian duty right. (The question of whether there are non-Hohfeldian duties will be considered in Chapter 5.) If one wished, one could use the term "mandatory rights" instead of "duty rights." The phrase "duty right" is preferable because it calls attention to the Hohfeldian structure of these rights. Moreover, as we will see later in this chapter, the phrase "duty right" points to a structural parallel between duty rights and other rights that will lead us to classify duty rights as members of a larger group of "non-basic rights." (The other common example of a mandatory right, a child's right to go to school in those jurisdictions in which children are legally required to go to school, is also a duty right.)

Another example of a mentioned duty right can be found in *Albertsons v. Kirkingburg* (527 U.S. 555, 1999). Federal Motor Carrier Safety Regulations

(49 CFR §391.11) require Albertsons, a grocery store chain, to hire only truck drivers who meet certain federally-specified vision standards. Albertsons hired Kirkingburg on the basis of an examination that erroneously certified that his vision met the federal requirements. At a subsequent physical, Kirkingburg's true, monocular, vision was discovered and Albertsons fired Kirkingburg. The Department of Transportation was, at that time, undertaking a study of the Federal Motor Carrier Safety Regulations. Part of the study involved granting waivers of the vision standards to certain individuals. Kirkingburg applied for and was granted one of these waivers, but Albertsons refused to rehire him and he sued claiming that Albertsons' actions violated the Americans with Disabilities Act of 1990. The Supreme Court ruled that Albertsons did not violate this Act. In discussing the case, the Court first presented the situation as it would be if the Department of Transportation had not undertaken the experimental waiver program.

> If we looked no further [and ignore the waiver program], there would be no basis to question Albertsons' unconditional obligation to follow the regulation [which requires them to fire Kirkingburg] and its consequent right to do so (527 U.S. 555, 570, 1999).

Here the Court explicitly notes that Albertsons has a duty right to fire Kirkingburg. Given his vision, federal rules require Albertsons to fire Kirkingburg and therefore they have the right to do so. (The Court went on to conclude that the experimental waiver program did not modify the federal regulations and that Albertsons still had a liberty right to fire Kirkingburg.)

Duty rights reveal something important and surprising about rights in general. Rights are not necessarily things one wants or things one will insist upon. All of us have rights we would prefer not to have. Under the U.S. legal rule system, I have a duty right to pay my debts. I would prefer not to have this right. So when a duty is protected by a claim or immunity there is no implication that the protected duty is a duty one prefers to have. X can protect something of Y's that Y does not want. In a battle a captain might protect a position that her general does not want protected. A claim protects a duty that one does not want to do when the claim constrains others in ways that aid one in doing a duty that one does not want to do.

The existence of duty rights also reveals that those such as Benditt (1982, Chapter 4) who hold that

(1) X has a right to do A

entails

(2) X has no duty to do A

are mistaken. According to the U.S. legal rule system, I have a duty right to pay my debts. But my having this right does not entail that I have no duty to pay my debts. Those who think (1) entails (2) have focused too much of their attention on liberty rights. As we will see below, this is a common mistake among rights theorists. It is true that

(3) X has a liberty right to do A

entails

(4) X has no duty to do A

because if X has a liberty right to do A, then X has a liberty to do A and a liberty not to do A. And if X has a liberty not to do A, then X has no duty to do A.

The excessive focus on liberty rights has also led authors to the false view that

(1) X has a right to do A

implies

(2) X has a liberty to do A.

Obviously, one cannot have a liberty right to do A unless one has a liberty to do A. It is equally obvious that rights that *another do A* do not necessarily contain a liberty. My claim that you not blow up my car is a right even if I do not have any liberties. Claim and immunity rights are passive rights, rights that *others* do or not do something.

Waldron (1981) has pointed out that there are counterexamples to the view that one cannot have a right to do A unless one has a liberty to do A. Suppose that a member of the Ku Klux Klan runs for political office in my state. She fills out the appropriate forms and gets the appropriate number of signatures to be on the ballot. According to the moral rule system, I would have a moral right to vote for the Klan member. It is equally obvious that I have a moral duty not to vote for her.[7] One can have a moral right to do A and still have a moral duty not to do A. In such cases, one will not have a moral liberty right because one does not have a moral liberty. One will have moral claims and/or moral immunities that protect one's ability to do something that one has a moral duty to refrain from doing. One could construct a legal rule system that contains the same structure of claims and duties. One could write laws that give a person legal claims and/or legal immunities which protect one's ability to do something that one has a legal duty to refrain from doing. There would seem to be no good reason for putting such a structure of claims and duties into a legal rule system. In the legal case, if the legislature passes a law creating a duty not to do some act, it would be odd for them to give a person legal claims and/or legal immunities that protect one's ability to perform the act in question.

The justified-constraint analysis of rights has no trouble explaining how one can have a moral right to do what one has a moral duty to refrain from doing. That I have a moral right to vote for the Klan member implies I have moral claims that others

---

[7] The duty not to vote for the Klan member may or may not be a Hohfeldian duty. But that is irrelevant to the point being made here.

not interfere with my voting. This rights statement, like all claim and immunity right statements, is a statement of the duties and disabilities *of others*. It has no implications concerning *my* duties. In particular, it does not imply that I have a moral liberty to vote for the Klan member.

Disability rights are similar to duty rights in that one does not usually demand one's disability rights. Disabilities are usually not things one wishes to have. But one can easily imagine disability rights that someone might demand. Suppose that you are a first-year faculty member and that, according to the rule system of the university, first-year faculty cannot hold the office of tenure-giver. The tenure-giver decides who, among those eligible, receives tenure. In Hohfeldian terms, you have a disability to give someone tenure. You might well be glad that first-year faculty have this disability. So if someone tried to make you the tenure-giver, you might assert that you have a disability to be the tenure-giver and claims that protect this disability. You might have a claim that others not change your disability to give tenure into a power to give tenure. You have a disability right. One has a disability right if and only if one has a disability to do A and a claim that protects the liberty and the disability. Disability rights often include an immunity in addition to the claim. In the tenure-giver case, you might have an immunity to having your disability to give tenure changed into a power to give tenure. There are many disability rights. Under the U.S. legal rule system, I have a set of disability rights not to perform thousands of people's marriages and a disability right not to be on thousands of committees. I am glad that I have these disability rights.

As Wellman (1985, 86–91) has noted, one example of a liability right is the right to marry. In typical legal rule systems, the legal act of marriage is more complex than most people realize. Despite what many think, two people cannot, by themselves, become married. If Fred and Wilma attempt to go off *by themselves* and get married, they lack the legal power to do so. In typical legal rule systems, a marriage requires two individuals to be married by an appropriate official. At least three people are required to create a legally valid marriage. Only certain designated officials have the power to create the complex set of claims, liberties, etc. that is a legal marriage. Correlative to the officials' power is the liability of two unmarried individuals over a certain age to be married. The liability is protected by claims (e.g., others have a duty to refrain from kidnapping people on their way to be married). In such a rule system one has a liability right. In typical legal rule systems, thousands of people have the liability right to be married. One has a liability right to do A if and only if one has a liability to do A and a claim that protects the liability.

No-claim rights, like disability and duty rights, are common but unmentioned. Recall again the liberty pass situation. Evelyn owns a car and she sells Joshua a pass granting him nothing more than a liberty to drive her car next Tuesday. Since Joshua has a mere liberty to drive the car, he does not have a claim that Evelyn not hide the car to prevent him from driving it. Correlative to Joshua's liberty is Evelyn's no-claim. Suppose that, when Tuesday rolls around, Evelyn decides that she does not want Joshua to drive the car. She goes out to hide it. Now the legal rule system might well imply that others have duties to refrain from interfering with her hiding the car. In that case Evelyn has a no-claim right. She has a no-claim that Joshua drive her car and a claim that protects the no-claim. One has a no-claim right to do A when one has a no-claim that another do A and a claim that protects the no-claim.

Claim rights and immunity rights are *basic rights* in the sense that only claims and immunities are rights even if no other primary relation is present. All the other sorts of rights are packages of various relations in which a claim protects another relation. We label the right with the name of the protected relation. These *non-basic rights* (liberty rights, power rights, duty rights, disability rights, liability rights, and no-claim rights) are no different in kind from the constitutional right to free speech in that all are packages of Hohfeldian relations. The word "primary" in the first sentence of this paragraph is necessary because, as Sumner (1987, 37–38) has noted, there is a sense in which an immunity cannot exist if no other relations are present. Because an immunity is a primary relation, its content always includes both an original relation and a resulting relation. On the other hand, the original and resulting relations are *part* of the immunity. The relations in the packages which are liberty, power, duty, disability, liability, or no-claim rights are not part of each other in the way that the original and resulting relations are part of an immunity.

Because non-basic rights are packages of Hohfeldian relations that contain a claim and because mere liberties, mere powers, etc. are not rights, it is tempting to recommend the elimination of the terms "liberty right," "power right," etc. in favor of phrases such as "claim right that protects two liberties," "claim right that protects two powers," etc. These phrases would be more accurate descriptions of the normative situation. On the other hand, the terms "liberty right," "power right," etc. are standard and useful terms. We will continue to use them. However, one must keep in mind that non-basic rights are crucially different from basic rights. That "liberty right," "power right," etc. have the same grammatical form as "claim right" must not lead us to think that mere liberties, powers, etc. are rights. We must also remind ourselves that "liberty right," "power right," etc. refer to packages of Hohfeldian relations while "claim right" and "immunity right" do not.

4. SOME OBJECTIONS

With the Hohfeldian version of the justified-constraint theory on the table we can turn to five possible objections.

One possible objection to the justified-constraint view begins by correctly noting that, on this view, a statement that someone has a right is logically equivalent to a statement about claims and immunities. Montague (1980, 373) would object to any theory that holds that rights are logically equivalent to the duties or disabilities of others on the grounds that rights are frequently cited to justify duties and disabilities. One often hears people citing rights in arguments intended to show that people have certain duties. A fetus' right to life might be cited to justify a duty to refrain from abortions. Montague thinks that any theory that holds that rights are logically equivalent to duties or disabilities cannot explain this use of rights. According to Montague, rights cannot justify duties if they are logically equivalent to them.

Logical equivalences can justify. Consider my belief that the sum of the squares of the two sides of a right triangle equals the square of the hypotenuse. That belief is justified by reflection on the definition of a right triangle. The justification of my belief in Pythagoras' theorem is not undermined because it follows from the definition of a right triangle. Similarly, it is odd to claim that the justification of a duty is undermined because it follows from the definition of a right.

Montague's view might be based on the belief that normative reasoning has a foundational structure. On this foundational structure, statements of rights justify statements of duties, but statements of duties never justify statements of rights. Here I can do no more than assert that normative reasoning does not have this sort of foundational structure. Some sort of coherence theory is the correct theory of normative reasoning. One might begin with statements of rights and justify statements of duty or begin with statements of duty and justify statements of rights. If normative reasoning has a coherence structure, then the logical equivalence of statements of rights and statements of duty or disability is no barrier to the former justifying the latter or the latter justifying the former. (For an example of a coherence theory of normative reasoning see Rawls (1971, 46–53). For a useful discussion of this issue see Kramer et al. (1998, 37–40).)

There is another interpretation of Montague's objection. He might be pointing out that definitional justification runs the risk of begging the question. If statements of rights and statements of duties or disabilities are logically equivalent, there is a danger that one will beg the question in an argument for certain duties or disabilities by asserting without argument a right that necessarily implies those duties or disabilities. The other party to the debate might then simply assert the existence of a right which necessarily implies the duties or disabilities that he favors.

The phenomenon just described occurs all too frequently. Among politicians and special interest groups, the abortion debate often takes this form. One also sees it in non-philosophical discussions of libertarianism. That such a pattern of abuse of rights can occur is no objection to the justified-constraint analysis of rights. In fact, the justified-constraint analysis explains why this abuse is common. Because rights necessarily imply duties or disabilities, it is tempting to justify duties or disabilities with unsupported assertions of rights. But the justified-constraint view does not force one to follow this path in seeking to justify statements about rights. As noted above, one can use some sort of coherence theory of justification (e.g., some form of reflective equilibrium method) to justify one's view on rights. One might justify an assertion of some particular right by claiming that it is logically equivalent to some duty and then provide independent grounds for thinking that such a duty exists.

Steiner (1994, 75) has raised a second sort of objection to the justified-constraint analysis of rights. One might argue that claims that protect a liberty cannot be a part of a liberty right because, in typical legal rule systems, these claims would exist even if one did not have the liberty. According to this objection, I do not have a liberty right to look over my garden fence because my claim that others refrain from interfering with my looking over the fence would, in typical legal rule systems, exist even if I did not have the liberty. My neighbor's duty to refrain from preventing me from looking over the fence by hitting me would exist even if I had a duty not to look over the fence (perhaps because, in return for some payment, I agreed not to look over the fence). The same sort of objection might be made against the analysis of the other non-basic rights.

A rule system need not explicitly conjoin the liberty, the power, the duty, etc. and the claims that protect it. In typical legal rule systems, there is no explicit statement of the liberty right to look over one's fence, but we clearly have this right. A rule system may simply imply certain claims that create a liberty right when they protect a liberty, create a power right when they protect a power, etc.

The third objection to the justified-constraint theory of rights argues that manifesto rights are counterexamples to the view that all rights imply duties or disabilities. For example, one might assert that (1) people in very poor countries have a right to a certain amount of food and that (2) no one has a duty to provide them with food because it is physically impossible to do so. These people have manifesto rights. One must be careful here. People in positions of wealth have an incentive to underestimate what it is possible for them to do. For the sake of argument, assume that there are some cases in which (1) and (2) are true. In that case, should we say that the people in poor countries have a right to some food? It is better to hold that such people do not currently have a right to the food, but, given their need, they would have a right if it were possible to feed them. Many will think this option is better because it limits rights proliferation. If one adds manifesto rights to the list of rights that actually exist, then there will be more rights. Many will see this as a reason to reject manifesto rights. Whatever one thinks of this reason for rejecting manifesto rights, there is an independent theoretical reason for rejecting them. Feinberg (1973, 67) was correct in thinking that people in these circumstances have "possibilities of rights," although they do not actually have rights now. This is a better description of the situation because it preserves the direct connection between rights and normative constraints on others. If we wanted to incorporate the manifesto sense of rights into the justified-constraint analysis, we would have to hold that rights actually *or counter-factually* constrain others. Spelling out the appropriate counter-factual conditions would be a difficult task that we can avoid if we hold that people in these circumstances do not now have a right but that they do have important needs that would justify a right if it were possible for someone to meet those needs. This analysis of the situation does not in any way imply that these needs are less morally important. It only acknowledges the possibility that in a world of limited resources there may be extremely important needs that we physically cannot meet.

The fourth possible objection to the justified-constraint view is a particularly interesting one. Wellman has argued that a single relation cannot be a right.[8] The justified-constraint theory, following Hohfeld, holds that one relation can be a right. A claim all by itself is a right. An immunity all by itself is a right. Neither of these relations needs to be joined with any others to be a right. On Wellman's view, only a package of Hohfeldian relations can be a right.

> A single legal claim, in and by itself, could not possibly constitute a legal right holding against any second party. Imagine that a creditor C has a legal claim to repayment against a debtor D, but that none of the other Hohfeldian elements normally associated with a legal claim-right is present. Could C's legal position be accurately said to constitute a legal right to repayment? D would lie under a legal duty to C to tender the amount owed on the due date and C would have the legal power to take legal action in the courts in the event that D failed to fulfill this duty. But if this single claim were the *only* element in C's legal position, then, according to Hohfeld's own logic, C would lack the legal liberty to accept repayment if and when it is tendered by D. It strikes me as linguistically and conceptually odd to say that under these circumstances C has "a right" to repayment. Surely some element of liberty enters into any genuine legal right. Again, C's legal claim to be repaid in and of itself implies absolutely no sort of legal immunity against D. Let us imagine, therefore, that D has the legal power to extinguish C's claim simply by snapping his or her fingers in the creditor's face and repeating the legally prescribed formula "I hereby cancel my debt to you." Under these circumstances, C's legal claim to repayment would not hold fast against the debtor as any self-respecting legal right surely should (1985, 59–60).

Wellman would surely re-enforce his objection by correctly pointing out that the justified-constraint view disagrees with his view that a claim implies a power to take action in the event that the duty implied by the claim is not fulfilled. The reason that Wellman says that "D would lie under a legal duty to C to tender the amount owed on the due date *and C would have the legal power to take legal action in the courts in the event that D failed to fulfill this duty*" (emphasis added) is that he holds that a claim implies a power to take this action. For reasons that will become more apparent when discussing Rex Martin's theory of rights, rights are not necessarily enforceable.

There is a great deal of truth in the quote above. In typical legal systems the legal right to repayment of a debt is more than a single claim. It includes the power, the liberty, and the immunity that Wellman mentions. But the issue at hand is not

---

[8] Feinberg would probably make a similar point. He holds that "[w]hen a person has a legal claim-right to X, it must be the case (i) that he is at liberty in respect to X ..., and also (ii) that his liberty is the ground of other people's duties to grant him X or not to interfere with him in respect to X" (1980, 148).

the proper analysis of the legal right to repayment, but whether it is possible for a single claim to be a right.

The first point to make in response to Wellman's objection is that it concerns the analysis of a legal position that does not exist in any actual rule system. No actual rule system gives people a single claim all by itself. So the issue here concerns the analysis of an imaginary legal position. *Ceteris paribus*, that a theory implies that normal English usage does not correctly classify a purely imaginary legal position is a less serious objection than one that points out that a theory implies that normal English usage does not correctly classify a common legal position.

The second and more important point to make in response to Wellman's objection is that there are counterexamples to his claim that no single relations are rights. Suppose that you are going to visit Squam Lake, New Hampshire and that I have fond memories of an old girlfriend who lived on Squam Lake. For sentimental reasons, I ask you to promise me that you will stick your feet in Squam Lake for me. You agree to do so. Assume that this is sufficient for me to have a legal claim that you stick your feet in Squam Lake. In this case, unlike Wellman's, no liberty of mine is relevant to whether you fulfill your duty or not. I need no liberties for you to stick your feet in Squam Lake. I have a claim that you do an act that requires nothing of me. To make the case parallel to Wellman's, let us assume that I explicitly waive the power I would normally have to sue you if you did not stick your feet in Squam Lake. Let us assume that I do not have a legal immunity to your extinguishing your duty to stick your feet in Squam Lake because you have the power to extinguish your duty by snapping your fingers in my face and repeating the legally prescribed formula "I hereby cancel my promise to you." In spite of my lack of this power and my lack of this immunity, I still have a right. My legal position would, of course, be stronger if I had the power and the immunity in addition to the claim. But the question before us is not whether the addition of a power and an immunity would strengthen my legal position. It is whether having a claim is sufficient to have a right. Why is my mere claim that you put your feet in Squam Lake a right? Because you have a duty to put your feet in Squam Lake and, as Hohfeld put it, "it is certain that even those who use the word and the conception 'right' in the broadest possible way are accustomed to thinking of 'duty' as the invariable correlative" (2001, 13). To put this in the terminology used in this book, your promise to me, even if I do not have the power and the immunity mentioned above, places a normative constraint on your actions. If you did not wish to put your feet in Squam Lake, you would need to take the time and trouble to snap your fingers in front of my face and repeat the legally prescribed formula.

It seems to many philosophers (particularly those inclined toward the choice or will theories) that "some element of liberty enters into any genuine . . . right." This view is false. As noted above, philosophers tend to place an excessive focus on liberty rights. There are passive rights, e.g., claims that another do or not do something. These rights contain no liberty held by the right-holder whose subject is the same as the subject of the right.

43

Many things we call *a* right are in fact packages of Hohfeldian relations. *The* right to free speech is a complex package of rights. Wellman is correct that one does not have the package we call *the* legal right to repayment unless one has a liberty to accept the repayment. However, that does not settle the issue of whether one has a right *tout court* if one has a claim that another gives one some money but lacks the liberty to accept the money. In this second case, one would have an odd right (but not the rights package we call the legal right to repayment). The person who owes you the money has a duty which constrains her actions. She must offer you some money (and you must refuse to take it). The normative constraint key to the existence of rights is present even in this odd case.

It is worth a small detour to note that the Squam Lake example also shows that there are rights that are not exercisable. Steiner holds that:

> The idea that rights are things which are exercisable deeply permeates both ordinary language and standard legal usage. Next to our minds and our muscles, rights are what we exercise most (1994, 57).

In addition to the assertion that ordinary language and legal usage favor the view that all rights are exercisable, Steiner (1994, 74) defends this view by noting that it follows as a consequence of the choice theory of rights. In Chapter 4, we will consider and reject this theory. Therefore, let us set aside this part of Steiner's argument for the time being. It is not true that ordinary language and standard legal usage indicates that all rights are exercisable. Steiner has fallen into the trap of an excessive focus on active rights. There are clearly a great many cases of exercisable rights. Active rights are, by definition, exercisable. But Steiner is not asserting that most rights are exercisable. He is asserting the stronger view that it is a necessary truth that all rights are exercisable. So, like Wellman, he is committed to the view that a single claim or a single immunity cannot be a right. But the Squam Lake example shows that there are pure passive rights (i.e., a claim or an immunity that is not part of a rights package). Cases such as the Squam Lake case will occur whenever one person, X, promises another person, Y, that she will do something with or to some physical object not connected to Y. I promise you that I will mow a patch of grass. Kyle promises Eva that he will say a prayer at the Vietnam Memorial when he visits Washington, D.C. Vinita promises Matt that she will visit the Musée de Cluny when she goes to Paris. While many rights are exercisable, many are not.

The fifth objection holds that there is a problem with the justified-constraint theory's view of immunity rights. This objection takes several forms. One form asserts that rights are necessarily things that can be violated and that one cannot violate an immunity. From this it would follow that immunities are not rights. On the other hand, the view that immunities are not rights is implausible on its face. Paradigm cases such as the right to free speech indicate that one can violate an immunity. Many people hold that the U.S. government has, at various times in history, violated the immunity of its citizens to having their liberty to say certain things removed.

Some believe that the U.S. laws passed in the wake of September 11 violated their immunities. In Hohfeldian terms, these laws assert that certain triggering acts performed by certain government officials remove certain previously held liberties and claims. Some believe that the First Amendment of the U.S. Constitution implies that these triggering acts do not remove the relevant liberties and claims. In this important sense, some believe that the laws passed after September 11 violate their immunities to having these liberties and claims extinguished. Of course, it is a matter of constitutional law as to whether the assertions of violations of the right to free speech are true or not. Many countries seem to violate moral free speech immunities on a regular basis.

Careful attention to Hohfeldian relations resolves this puzzle. If by "violate a right" one simply means "fail to perform the duty correlative to the right" then it immediately follows by definition that immunities are not rights. But the free speech case shows that this is an inappropriately narrow conception of violation. The objection overlooks two different senses of the term "cannot," the normative and the physical. Hohfeldian relations do not refer to physical relations. An immunity exists when, according to the rules of a normative rule system, one cannot change some relation. The "cannot" in the previous sentence is not the "cannot" of physical impossibility. Rather, it refers to what one can and cannot do according to the rules of a normative rule system. With this distinction in mind, one can see the broader sense of "violate" on which one can violate an immunity right. One does so by doing physical acts and asserting that those acts change Hohfeldian relations when in fact they do not. One asserts that a physical act is a triggering act that extinguishes a relation even though it does not. This is the sort of violation that occurs when governments violate free speech rights. A citizen has an immunity right to burn the flag. How would the President go about violating this right? The President would do some physical act and assert that the act extinguished the liberty to burn the flag. Then the President would punish those who burn the flag. There are two ways to violate a right. In the case of claim rights, one violates the right when one fails to perform the duty correlative to the claim. In the case of immunity rights, one violates the right when one does a physical act and falsely asserts that this act is a triggering act which extinguishes a relation.

Similarly, one might wonder what it means to enforce a disability. A disability is the lack of a power. So one might think that a disability cannot be enforced. It is true that one cannot enforce a disability in the way that one can enforce a claim that a person take or refrain from taking some action. If I have a legal claim that you paint my porch and you fail to do so, then I can seek the assistance of the state to force you to paint the porch and/or compensate me for your failure to paint it. One cannot enforce a disability in this sense. However, it can occur that a person has a disability and denies that she has it. Suppose that someone were to falsely assert that they had the legal power to create a legal claim that I pay them $500. I could then seek the assistance of the state for an authoritative declaration that the individual lacked this power. In this sense, a disability can be enforced.

Montague has offered a second form of the argument that there is a problem with the justified-constraint theory of immunity rights.

> Powers are typically characterized as abilities of a sort. If some X has a certain right, then X has the power—the ability—to affect the duties implied by his right. Immunities can be explained in terms of powers: X's immunity relative to another person Y is the absence of a power in Y relative to X. Hence both powers and immunities are clearly properties of persons rather than actions (2001, 263–264).

He then holds that rights are properties of acts, not properties of persons, and therefore that immunities are not rights.

The Hohfeldian analysis offered in Chapter 1 allows us to see why this objection is flawed. Immunities are not merely properties of persons. They are more complex than that. All immunities have a triggering act, the act that does *not* have the effect of causing the original relation to cease to exist and the resulting relation to come into being. In this sense, immunities are properties of acts. But this is not to deny that immunities are properties of persons. A person can have an immunity. An attempt to determine whether immunities are properties of persons or acts falls into the trap of a false dichotomy. Immunities are features of triggering acts done by people. In this sense, immunities are properties of persons and acts. The same is true of rights. A person has a right that another person perform an act. I have a right that you not strike me. One should not enter into a debate over whether this right is a property of me, a property of you, or a property of your act of hitting me. It is all of those things. Any attempt to force one to choose only one of these three as the unique feature of rights prevents an adequate understanding of rights in all their complexity.

A third form of the view that there is a problem with the justified-constraint theory of immunity rights rejects the view that an immunity, all by itself, can be a right. One might be tempted to try to imagine a situation in which a person had only an immunity. In this imaginary situation, there would only be one other relation, the disability correlative to the immunity. There would be no other claims, no other duties, etc. held by either the immunity holder or anyone else. One might then think that a person in such a situation would not have a right. However, this situation is logically impossible. An immunity is a second-order relation. The existence of an immunity necessitates the existence of an original relation and a resulting relation. One cannot have an immunity unless one has an original relation that cannot be changed into some resulting relation.

The fourth and final form of the view that there is a problem with the justified-constraint theory of immunity rights is the most complex and interesting. Hart has noted that:

> even in the loosest usage, the expression 'a right' is not used to refer to the fact that a man is ... immune from *advantageous* change; the fact that ... my neighbor has no power to exempt me from my duty to pay my income-tax, do[es]

not constitute any legal right for me. An individual's immunity from legal change at the hands of others is spoken and thought of as a right only when the change in question is *adverse*, that is, would deprive him of legal rights of other kinds . . . or benefits secured to him by law (1982, 191).

Hart has not pointed to some rare or odd feature of some rule systems. I cannot think of a non-imaginary rule system that does not contain disadvantageous immunities. The justified-constraint analysis of rights seems to imply that disadvantageous immunities are rights. In this way, it appears to depart in a significant way from normal English usage of "rights," and this seems to be a problem for the analysis.

The best response to this important objection cannot be presented until Chapter 5 because it relies on the theory of relational obligation defended in that chapter. However, there are four other responses to Hart's objection that can be presented now. First, Hart and many others have failed to note the importance of the distinction between having a right and having a right which one wants to mention, assert, or demand. Hart is correct when he says that "the expression 'a right' is not used to refer to the fact that a man is . . . immune from *advantageous* change." I cannot think of a situation, other than one in which one wanted to make the philosophical point that I am currently making, in which one would mention, assert, or demand one's disadvantageous immunities. Indeed, one would have every reason to hope that others did not notice one's disadvantageous immunities and, far from pointing them out, one has reason to conceal them. Disadvantageous immunities are not mentioned and people do not use the expression "a right" to refer to disadvantageous immunities. But many unmentioned things exist, so the fact that "the expression 'a right' is not used to refer to the fact that a man is . . . immune from *advantageous* change" does not imply that disadvantageous immunities are not rights. One could explain the fact that disadvantageous immunities are not referred to as "rights" on the grounds that, even if they are rights, people have reasons of self-interest not to mention them.

Second, rights are, to a large extent, something like the umpires of a baseball game. If the umpires make good calls and are not challenged, then one hardly notices that they exist. Although they are on the field for all to see, one does not notice them until someone thinks that they have made a mistake. Similarly, rights are frequently unmentioned until and unless they are violated or threatened with violation.[9] I recently went to a restaurant and had a catfish poor-boy sandwich. After I ordered the sandwich but before I paid, the owner of the restaurant had a legal right that I pay for it. No one thought of this right. I was deep in philosophical discussion with a friend and mechanically left a ten on the table. The owner was dealing with the lunch rush. Neither of us brought to mind the existence of this right. The right was unnoticed because it was respected. If, on the other

---

[9]   This point was brought to my attention by Karen Mazner.

hand, I had tried to leave without paying my bill, the owner certainly would have thought of his rights. This provides another possible explanation for the fact that disadvantageous immunities are not referred to as rights. They simply are not mentioned because they are unreflectively respected. In the normal course of events, my immunity that my neighbor not exempt me from paying my income taxes will be respected without me or my neighbor ever even thinking of the matter. The nature of the disadvantageous immunity implies that they will almost always be unreflectively respected, and therefore they might be rights and yet go unnoticed as rights.

Third, the view that all rights are advantageous is implausible. One could assert that one has a right if and only if one has an advantageous claim or an advantageous immunity. But the examples of disadvantageous rights presented above show that this is not correct. These examples were my duty right to pay my debts and my duty right to grade my students' papers. It is easy to think of more cases of disadvantageous rights. Suppose that a friend dares me to let you hit me on the nose. He promises to pay me $200 if you hit me on the nose. I want the $200, so I ask you to promise me that you will hit me on the nose. You make the promise. Then my friend passes away. I will no longer get $200 if you hit me on the nose. But, because of your promise, I still have a claim that you hit me on the nose. This is a disadvantageous claim. I have a right that you hit me on the nose.

Fourth, the view that all rights are advantageous leads one into the tangle of determining when a relation is advantageous and when it is not.[10] At first glance, it seems that whether or not an immunity is advantageous depends on the psychological state of the subject of the immunity. One person might find an immunity advantageous while another person might find an immunity with an identical content to be disadvantageous. A religious ascetic might regard the fact that his neighbor cannot remove his duty to pay his income tax as an advantageous immunity while most people would regard this as a disadvantageous immunity. If one made advantageousness part of one's analysis of rights, one would seem to be led to the conclusion that this immunity was a right for the ascetic but not for others. There are many possible situations in which an immunity thought by most to be disadvantageous is thought by some to be advantageous. Suppose that one has a divorce agreement which ties one's payments to one's former spouse to one's own post-tax income. The agreement specifies that all post-tax income above a certain amount must be given to the former spouse. If a person feels the way that many do about making payments to a former spouse and her income is approaching the threshold amount, she might be glad that she has the immunity to the tax relief that Hart discusses.[11] There are ways that one might try to avoid these problems with the view that rights are necessarily advantageous, but consideration of them is best left until Chapter 4 and a discussion of the views of Raz.

---

[10] This point was brought to my attention by Elise Marchetta.
[11] Simmonds (Kramer et al., 1998, 152–154) offers a nice discussion of this point.

Taken together, these four points do much to diminish the force of Hart's objection. But much of its force remains. It would be better if one could show that the justified-constraint theory does not imply that my immunity to my neighbor's removing my duty to pay my income taxes is one of my rights. That can be shown, but not until Chapter 5.

5. MARTIN: SOCIALLY RECOGNIZED NORMATIVE DIRECTIONS

In *A System of Rights*, Rex Martin argues that rights are "ways of acting or ... of being treated" which are "socially recognized," and provide "normative direction" to the actions of others (1993, 42, 51, 31).[12] Martin's concept of normative direction has much in common with the concept of normative constraint discussed above. It is therefore natural to discuss Martin's view at this point. While there is much to be learned from Martin's theory of rights, it is inadequate. The central problem with Martin's view is the claim that social recognition is a necessary condition for the existence of rights. Martin's theory is the most subtle and sophisticated version of a view on the relationship between rights and social recognition that goes back at least to Bentham. Bentham considered the claim that "there are such things as rights anterior to the establishment of government" and famously announced that it was "nonsense upon stilts" (1987, 52–53).

Let us use "internalism" to refer to the view that social recognition is not a necessary condition for the existence of rights and "externalism" to refer to the view that social recognition is a necessary condition for the existence of rights.[13] These terms are natural because the externalist holds that something external to the right-holder (i.e., social recognition) is necessary for the right-holder to be a right-holder. The internalist, on the other hand, denies this claim.

Before turning to the social recognition issue, let us briefly consider a general evaluation of Martin's theory of rights. A good way to do this is to examine the parts of the quote in the first sentence of this section. What, according to Martin, is a way of acting or of being treated? He presents his view with a central example.

> A group of people live in an out of the way place, a forest perhaps. In that place is a pond and the people there are used to going to the pond to fish. There are several well-worn paths by which they can go to the pond .... One day a fence

---

[12] This is not Martin's complete analysis of rights. He also holds that rights must be "determinate" (p. 25) and "individuated" (p. 26). These issues need not concern us here. In a later (2005) article, Martin revises his view. This revision is fairly substantial. A complete analysis of the changes in Martin's view would be time-consuming. Because *A System of Rights* (1993) remains the canonical statement of his view and because I believe that the revisions found in 2005 article do not allow Martin to avoid the objections outlined in this section, I will focus on *A System of Rights*.

[13] I borrow these useful terms from Darby (2004). I do not use them in precisely the way Darby does.

is put across one of the paths and the people are told that the path is closed. One of them responds that this cannot be. They are going to the pond to fish and it is their right to do so and they have taken this path and it is their right to do so; the fence maker should remove the fence . . . (1993, 24–25).

In this case, the way of acting in question is taking the particular path to the pond. More generally, a way of acting is anything that a person does. Walking down a path, giving a speech, and writing a note are ways of acting. Ways of being treated are acts that one person does to another. Being hit, being given $100 and being ignored are ways of being treated. On Martin's view, a right is always a right for the right-holder to act in a particular way or a right for the right-holder to be treated in a particular way.

As noted by Kramer (Kramer et al., 1998, 14) a right is always, strictly speaking, a passive right, a right that another do or not do a certain act. Active rights should be analyzed as a set of Hohfeldian relations that include a liberty plus claims and immunities that protect that liberty. Strictly speaking, only claims and immunities are rights. This analysis is preferable to Martin's because it allows us to account for some rights that Martin's does not. Recall my right that you stick your feet in Squam Lake. You promised me that you would do this when you went to New Hampshire. This clearly is a right, but your sticking your feet in Squam Lake is not a way I act. Unless one stretches the notion of being treated, your sticking your feet in Squam Lake is not a way of treating me. It is a way of treating your feet and the lake. I am the right-holder but my right is a right that you do something, not a right that I act in a certain way or a right that I be treated in a certain way. Rights are not ways of acting or ways of being treated. The justified-constraint view avoids this problem because your promise to me generates my claim, my right, that you stick your feet in Squam Lake. Of course, Martin could reply that he intended "treat" to be used in a broad sense according to which your sticking your feet in Squam Lake is a way of treating me. He might point out that your sticking your feet in Squam Lake is a way of keeping your promise to me and, in that non-physical sense of "treating," it is a way of treating me. If he makes this reply, then I have no objection to Martin on this point. In that case, it turns out that we hold the same view. Hereafter, let us use "ways of acting" to refer to "ways of acting and ways of being treated."

What does it mean to say that rights provide normative direction to the actions of others? Martin's analysis of normative direction is similar to the justified-constraint analysis of normative constraint. Martin begins by noting that duties direct one's actions. He also notes that disabilities direct one's actions as well. He and I agree that duties direct/constrain by specifying an act that one may not do while disabilities direct by specifying an act that one cannot do. The term "constrain" is preferable to the term "direct" because duties and disabilities direct one's actions by *limiting* one's options. The term "constrain" brings out this feature of the normative direction that duties and disabilities imply.

Martin holds that "any genuine right must involve some normative direction of the behavior of persons other than the holder, for example, direction of the sort given by the Hohfeldian relations mentioned earlier (duty, disability, liability)" (1993, 31). Martin explicitly states that liabilities provide normative direction, and the phrase "for example" suggests that there may be other Hohfeldian relations that, on Martin's view, provide normative direction. However, he does not provide examples of any relations besides duties and disabilities, which provide normative direction. He merely asserts, without providing an example, that liabilities provide normative guidance. This implies that powers, the correlative of liabilities, are rights. As argued above, this is not correct. Only duties and disabilities constrain one's action, and therefore only claims and immunities are rights. So, although Martin correctly holds that duties and disabilities are normative constraints, he incorrectly holds that other relations are normative constraints.

Martin's general theory of rights has two flaws. First, the Squam Lake case shows that rights are not best thought of as ways of acting or of being treated. Second, Martin is wrong to hold that relations other than duties and disabilities impose normative constraints.

This brings us to the central point of contention, whether social recognition is a necessary condition for the existence of rights. We need to begin with a detailed presentation of Martin's view. He tells us that a way of acting is socially recognized when it is "backed up" or has an "appropriate social ratification" (1993, 27, 36).

> [Social recognition] could take the form, if the right were a legal one, of official recognition, if it were a conventional or customary one, of common acceptance . . . (1993, 36).

The pond example is a case of a conventional right. The past practice of many people using the path gives social recognition to this way of acting.

> How, then, does the person whose action has been challenged make good a rights claim? Certainly that person could do so, for example, by drawing forth an acknowledgment that the action was indeed his or her practice and the practice of others . . . (1993, 26).

In the case of a legal right, a way of acting is legally recognized when there exist "practices of governmental promotion and protection" (1993, 59) of the way of acting. In the most obvious case, my typing at my desk (a way of acting) is promoted and protected by the legal duties of non-interference that the government enforces with the threat of punishment.

Martin provides two other examples to help clarify the notion of social recognition. The first concerns the victims of Aztec human sacrifice rituals (1993, 78). Martin holds that the victims in Aztec human sacrifice rituals did not have a right not to be killed and that the priests who performed these rituals had no duty not to kill their victims. Because there was no social recognition of the rights of the victims of human sacrifice, they had no rights. The other example concerns the right to travel.

> Let us imagine the case of innocent travel. Suppose that we were able to formulate matters fairly precisely here: we could distinguish travel from emigration; we could exclude some obvious cases of unlawful travel; we were able to add a reasonably good exceptions clause.... Not only this; we could show also a decisive moral endorsement of travel so conceived....
>
> Citizens the world over might declare for it. Pronunciamentos are issued, editorials written, sermons preached. [...] The idea of a liberty to travel enters the reflective consciousness of humankind as something morally endorsed and well grounded.... The claim is valid: the liberty in question has an impeccable moral title, is widely practicable, the relevant duties are in place, etc.
>
> It would seem that there is a human right to travel. But the guard at the border or the ticket agent at the airport counter says no.
>
> Now, clearly, what the balky official was doing did not satisfy the claim. But that would not detract from the integrity of the claim; it would still be a valid one. Even if everyone acted as these officials did, the claim would still stand; there would be no defect in the claim, as a claim, on that account. [...]
>
> But the matter stands differently with a right: the right to travel would be vitiated *as a right* if it were not protected or promoted at all. In such a case the right would be a merely nominal one, a right that existed in name only but not in fact. [Nominal rights] are rights only on paper.
>
> To be sure, nominal rights are rights. The point is, though, that we regard the total absence of promotion and maintenance as making a right infirm, as rendering it defective. [...] Such a right, when merely nominal, has failed in a crucial respect. It represents at best a marginal and precarious example of a right. It is a degenerate case (1993, 82–83).

Martin's view, and all versions of externalism, have two implications worth noting. First, externalism implies that it is logically impossible for there to be rights that no one knows about. A way of acting can only be socially recognized if some people know that it is. Furthermore, because one society may recognize a way of acting while another does not, externalism implies that all rights are relative to a society. There are no rights *tout court*. All rights are the rights of some society, the society that socially recognizes that way of acting. Many would regard these implications of externalism as objections to the view. On the other hand, externalists may regard them as virtues of their view.

On Martin's view, the social recognition of a way of acting can be morally justified or morally unjustified. Whether the social recognition of a way of acting is morally justified depends on whether the way of acting is a "means to or part of accomplishing some interest or perceived benefit or other good (or desirable) thing" (1993, 27). In this way, Martin incorporates a version of the interest theory of rights into his view. But the incorporation of the interest theory of rights is not a necessary part of Martin's account. One could replace his analysis of whether social recognition is morally justified with a choice theory according to which whether social recognition of a way of acting was justified depended on whether the way of acting protected an agent's choices. So the interest theory of rights is a "module" in Martin's theory that we can "unplug" without damage to the rest of the theory. To focus on the social recognition of rights, let us "unplug" this "module" of Martin's view. We will consider the interest theory in Chapter 4.

Martin does not hold that social recognition is a necessary condition for the existence of moral requirements in general. He goes out of his way to make it clear that, while rights require social recognition, moral requirements do not. The above quote concerning the right to travel illustrates this feature of Martin's view. He also states the same view in the following quote.

> Now, suppose we were able to say for a particular right-to-be that it has all the rights-making features I identified in the previous chapter: it ... had social recognition, afforded normative direction to the conduct of others, etc. And it could be said ... to be fully justified. Let us say for simplicity here that it was fully justified morally. Then it would be a right, specifically, a moral right.
>
> Suppose next that it had all the rights-making features but one. It lacked social recognition. It ought to have social recognition, no doubt about that. For its being socially recognized *would* be justified, we can say without cavil, whether that recognition actually occurred or not (1993, 52).

The phrase "it ought to have social recognition" reveals that Martin thinks that social recognition is not a necessary condition for the truth of moral assertions in general. On Martin's view, although the Aztec priest had no duty not to kill his victim, he ought not kill his victim. The victim ought to, but does not, have the right not to be killed.

We are now in position to evaluate Martin's externalism. The first thing to note is that Martin's discussion of social recognition is not as clear as one would like. There are two clarity problems. First, the phrase "To be sure, nominal rights are rights" seems to imply that Martin does not hold that social recognition is a necessary condition for the existence of rights. He seems to hold that social recognition is merely a necessary condition for the existence of non-nominal, non-degenerate, non-vitiated rights. On the other hand, Martin explicitly attacks Feinberg's view that rights are merely justified claims (with no social recognition requirement). This seems to imply that social recognition is a necessary condition for the existence of rights *tout court*. Sometimes Martin seems to hold that nominal, degenerate, vitiated rights are not rights at all and so social recognition is a necessary condition for the existence of rights *tout court*. Sometimes Martin seems to hold that nominal, degenerate, vitiated rights are rights and so social recognition is not a necessary condition for the existence of rights *tout court* but merely a necessary condition for the existence of non-nominal, non-degenerate, non-vitiated rights. Fortunately, we need not get bogged in resolving this issue. Social recognition is not a necessary condition for the existence of non-nominal, non-degenerate, non-vitiated rights. Whichever view Martin holds, it is flawed. Because it makes the language of this chapter simpler, let us assume that Martin holds that nominal, degenerate, vitiated rights are not rights at all. But the arguments below apply, *mutatis mutandis*, to the view that without social recognition, rights are merely nominal, degenerate, or vitiated.

The second clarity problem concerns non-governmental social recognition. As far as governmental recognition of a way of acting, it seems that social recognition can be divided into two types. Sometimes, the government recognizes a way of acting by requiring people to perform actions. For example, the government requires us to pay taxes and refrain from killing others. In Hohfeldian terms, the government can recognize the doing of A by imposing a duty to do A. In other cases, the government grants and protects the liberty to do A. In some cases, this is done explicitly. The U.S. Constitution explicitly grants and protects my liberty to speak freely. In other cases, it is done implicitly. Although there is no right to look over one's garden fence explicitly acknowledged in any legal text, the collection of rights granted by the U.S. legal rule system has the effect of granting and protecting my liberty to look over my garden fence. We can draw from Martin's comments a clear analysis of governmental recognition.

This issue is not so clear when it comes to non-governmental social recognition. When has a society recognized a way of acting in the absence of governmental recognition? Martin seems to be of two minds on this point. In the pond example, he takes it to be clear that people have a right to use the path that is blocked by the fence. So here it seems that the actions of one individual (in this case, the one who built the fence) do not cause a right to cease to exist. But when it comes to the right to travel, Martin seems to hold that the actions of one individual (the border guard) are sufficient to cause a right to cease to exist. This conflict leaves the concept of non-governmental social recognition unclear in a crucial way.

Let us assume that these clarity problems can be resolved. What are Martin's arguments for his view? Martin's central positive argument for externalism begins with the claim that one can have a duty only if one is aware or is able to be aware that one has the duty. "One cannot have an obligation (or a duty) of which one literally cannot be aware" (1993, 78). Martin claims that for a person to have a duty, the duty must be "reflectively available" to the individual.

> A ... duty ... is reflectively available when it can and reflectively unavailable when it cannot, arise in the context of and cohere with the overall set of moral beliefs and other important beliefs people have (1993, 79).

From the claim that one cannot have a duty of which one literally cannot be aware, it is arguable that externalism follows. The argument is a bit complex. To simplify its presentation, let us ignore immunity rights. The correlative of a claim is a duty. Therefore, one cannot have a claim unless someone else has a duty. If X cannot have a duty of which she literally cannot be aware, then Y cannot have a claim against X of which X literally cannot be aware. Rights are claims. If X cannot have a duty of which she literally cannot be aware, then Y cannot have a right against X of which X literally cannot be aware. Therefore, if Y has a right against X, then X can be aware of it. The only way to assure that X is aware of Y's right is for society to recognize this right. This seems to imply that social recognition is a necessary condition for the existence of rights.

Note that Martin's example of the right to travel is at odds with his analysis of reflective availability. He claims that the mere fact that the border guard refused to let one pass implied that a person trying to pass did not have the right to pass. Martin never said that the border guard's duty to let people pass must be reflectively unavailable to him. The mere refusal to let people pass (no matter what the state of the guard's mind) was held to imply that one did not have the right to pass. Let us assume that, in light of the above comments, Martin would revise the border guard example.

It is not obvious that the only way to assure that X is aware of Y's right is for society to recognize this right. It seems at least possible that one could come to be aware of a right by one's own reflection on the situation. But let us put this matter aside because the central problem with Martin's view is elsewhere. One can have a duty of which one literally cannot be aware.

Martin seems to provide two arguments for the view that one cannot have a duty of which one literally cannot be aware. First he offers the following argument.

> Moral beliefs... should... exhibit intellectual coherence and should be coherent... with other important, high-order beliefs. A certain duty... is... reflectively unavailable when it cannot arise in the context of and cohere with the overall set of moral beliefs... people have. It follows that people cannot, when their beliefs are true to the standards of intellectual coherence, have duties that are reflectively unavailable to them... (1993, 79).

This argument is not convincing. Let us grant that our moral beliefs should exhibit intellectual coherence. Suppose that my moral beliefs should, but do not, exhibit coherence. It does not follow that I have no duties that are reflectively unavailable to me. At most, Martin has argued for the conditional conclusion that if our beliefs are coherent, then we will be aware of all our duties. It does not follow that if our beliefs are not coherent, then we do not have certain duties. Martin admits as much.

> One might reply that this matters little. If someone holds beliefs that cannot be made to cohere with critical moral principles..., so much the worse for that person (1993, 79).

He then asks:

> But can anyone really hold the position implicated in this response? This brings me to the second consideration: that reflective availability is a necessary condition for a detail of morality... to count... as properly moral (1993, 80).

Martin's first argument rests on the second, and he really has only one argument for the view that one cannot have a duty of that one literally cannot be aware.

This second argument calls on the Kantian distinction between acting from duty and acting in accord with duty.

> People cannot be acting dutifully (as distinct from merely acting according to moral duty) unless ... they perceive or can come to perceive that they are required to act that way by a moral principle ... which ... they accept or can accept (1993, 80).

It is true that one cannot act from duty unless one is aware of one's duty. Indeed, reflective availability is too weak a requirement for acting from duty. A person cannot act from duty unless she actually and currently believes that she is doing something which she has a duty to do. Mere availability is not enough. But from this it does not follow that one cannot act in accord with duty without knowing that one is doing so or, most crucially, that one cannot have a duty that is reflectively unavailable.

The view that one can have a moral duty which is reflectively unavailable is supported by the fact that people clearly have legal duties that are reflectively unavailable to them. This becomes most clear when different cultures clash. Some immigrants to France come from cultures in which the ritual removal of a woman's clitoris is a common practice. This practice is illegal in France. Under French law, a woman's consent is not a valid defense to a charge of violating the law banning this practice. Some women very much want to undergo this ritual. They often regard it as an important part of their cultural heritage. The view that one has a duty not to undergo or perform the ritual removal of a clitoris cannot cohere with the important moral and cultural beliefs of these women. Yet it is clear that these women have, when they move to France, a legal duty not to undergo or perform this ritual. This case also serves as a powerful example of a group of people having a moral duty that is reflectively unavailable to them. Everyone has a duty not to undergo or perform this ritual, whether they are able to make that belief a coherent part of their belief system or not.

Having considered Martin's positive argument for externalism, let us turn to his arguments against internalism. The first of these four arguments is the claim that if one holds that social recognition is not a necessary condition for the existence of rights, then one is committed to the counter-intuitive view that social recognition is not a necessary condition for the existence of legal rights.

> The fatal flaw in the theory of rights as grounds of justified duties ... is the suggestion that practices of recognition and enforcement in law are dispensable in the case of legal rights (1993, 70–71).

Martin claims that internalists are committed to holding that social recognition is not a necessary condition for the existence of legal rights. His argument is as follows:

1. Internalists hold that having a claim is a sufficient condition for having a right.
2. Having a claim is not a sufficient condition for having a legal right. Social recognition is also required.
3. Therefore, internalism is false.

This argument is invalid. There is no contradiction between the claims that (a) having a claim is a sufficient condition for having a right *tout court* and (b) having a claim is not a sufficient condition for having a *legal* right. One could hold that social recognition is a necessary condition for legal rights but not for all rights. The assertion "X has a right if and only if X has a claim" is a compact way of saying that "X has a legal right if and only if X has a legal claim," "X has a moral right if and only if X has a moral claim," and "X has a Georgia State University right if and only if X has a GSU claim," etc. where the terms "legal," "moral," "GSU," etc. are replaced with a reference to a rule system. Let us assume for the sake of argument that externalism is true with regard to legal rights. It does not follow that social recognition is a necessary condition for the existence of a right *tout court*.

Martin is aware of and responds to this objection to his argument.

> It might be said in response that the institutional features I have identified, recognition, [etc.], are characteristic features of a legal system and hence, derivatively so, of legal rights; but its does not follow that these are characteristic features of rights per se. But I have shown that one cannot bridge directly from legal rights to valid claims or to valid arguments without leaving out features, perhaps the most important features, of legal rights. Accordingly, we cannot contend that it is especially revelatory to treat (valid) claims as the genus to which legal rights stand as a species (1993, 71–72).

It is true that "one cannot bridge directly from legal rights to valid claims . . . without leaving out features . . . of legal rights." On the other hand, it is revelatory to treat claims as the genus of which legal rights are a species. It reveals what is common to all rights, a certain normative position. This is revelatory even if one declines to offer a theory of what legal, moral, etc. constraints are. What is a legal right? A legal claim. What is a legal claim? A legal normative constraint. What is a legal normative constraint? With this question we move out of theories of rights and into theories of law. The justified-constraint view is neutral on this question. What is a moral right? A moral claim. What is a moral claim? A moral normative constraint. What is a moral normative constraint? With this question we move out of theories of rights and into meta-ethics. The justified-constraint view is neutral on this question. The parallels between legal rights and moral rights are significant and revelatory. (This argument assumes that there are moral rights. This assumption will be defended in Chapter 3.)

Martin's second argument against internalism takes the form of an attempt to provide a counterexample. The purported counterexample is the right to travel presented above. Here Martin and I are reduced to a clash of intuitions. I do not find his attempted counterexample convincing. This example strikes me as a straight-forward case in which someone (the guard) is *violating* someone's existing rights, not a case of causing someone's rights to cease to exist.

Martin's third argument against internalism is that, according to Martin, it commits one to the view that the word "claim" has a different sense in the phrase "legal claim" than it does in the phrase "moral claim." As Martin correctly notes,

> internalism supposes that legal rights differ significantly from human [i.e., moral] rights on the point at issue: the existence of appropriate mechanisms of recognition and promotion (1993, 84).

He thinks that this supposition is implausible because it

> suggests ... that "claim" does not have the same sense in the one case [legal rights] as it does in the other [moral rights] (1993, 85).

Internalism does not imply that "claim" in "legal claim" is used in a different sense than it is in "moral claim." In both cases, "claim" is analyzed in terms of normative constraints. To use a biological metaphor, moral claims and legal claims are species of a clearly defined genus, claims. The version of internalism defended here is neutral on deeper questions of the nature of legal and moral normative constraint. These questions are not part of a theory of rights but belong to the philosophy of law and meta-ethics.

Martin's arguments for externalism are weak. So are his objections to internalism. However, we have yet to examine any argument for internalism. Derrick Darby holds that

> a general justification, and arguably the primary justification, for postulating a class of rights that exist prior to or independently of human invention has been a political one, namely that doing so is politically instrumental for condemning, as immoral or unjust, oppressive social practices and institutions (2003, 53).

Darby calls this the "political justification" for the view that social recognition is not a necessary condition for the existence of rights. While I will not argue the point here, the political justification is not, as a historical matter, the primary justification for internalism. Moreover, even if this argument were the primary justification for internalism, that would be irrelevant to its strength.

Defending the thesis of this book requires no more than noting that I do not adopt this argument for internalism. However, let me very briefly (and without giving a complex matter its due) indicate why I take this route. The adoption or rejection of a theory cannot be justified on the grounds that it would allow or disallow one to make certain kinds of political arguments. Politics is not this closely tied to justification. For example, it is no strike against some theories of personhood that it would prohibit those seeking to make U.S. law more pro-choice (and less pro-life) from making certain politically effective arguments. On the other hand, it is a strike against a theory if it implies views with which the reader disagrees. If a theory of personhood implies that fetuses are not persons and a reader thinks that fetuses are persons, then that reader has a reason to reject the theory. If one thinks that human infants have rights and an analysis of rights implies that they do not, then one has reason to reject that analysis. But whether a view is or is not "politically instrumental for condemning, as immoral or unjust, oppressive social practices and institutions" is irrelevant to the question of whether the view is true.

The central argument for internalism is that it is more in accord with the ordinary language of rights than externalism. David Lyons puts the point well.

> Some rights are thought to exist independently of social recognition and enforcement. This is what I think we usually mean by "moral rights." [. . .] Moral rights . . . do not depend on social recognition or enforcement, as is shown by the fact that they are appealed to even when it is not believed that they are enforced or recognized by law or by prevailing opinion (1994, 149).

Lyons is correct to argue for internalism by pointing to the way people talk about rights and what they believe about rights. The way people talk about rights obviously reflects what they believe about rights. (Raz (1984) agrees with Lyons.) Martin asserts that internalism and externalism are both equally well supported by standard talk of rights.

> There appears no clear reason to accept my version . . . (where it is the fact of social recognition that is the essential rights-making feature) over the alternative version (where it is the *justification* for such a state of affairs . . . that is the rights-making feature). At least there appears no clear reason in the way we ordinarily talk about rights, for each version can be found in the way we ordinarily talk. Thus, although my account up to now had depended heavily on facts about rights as found in ordinary parlance and in the history of rights, it cannot depend on these facts to carry it through this pass; for here the relevant record supports both accounts (1993, 53).

This is not an accurate statement of the content of ordinary rights talk and the history of rights. It is notable that Martin does not provide any examples of ordinary rights talk that support externalism. Were externalism true, such examples would be easy to provide for the difference is an easy one to state in ordinary language. All one needs to do is find a situation in which people feel that they are being treated immorally. Then one would examine the record to see whether these people say things such as "my rights are being violated" or if they say things such as "I want some rights I don't now have." The situation is slightly complicated because one must be careful to distinguish legal rights (which, according to most, do have social recognition as a necessary condition for their existence) from moral rights (which, according to internalism, do not). It is easy to find cases which support internalism.

Perhaps the most famous historical counterexample to Martin's claim that externalism is as well supported in ordinary rights talk as internalism is the U.S. Declaration of Independence.

> We hold these truths to be self-evident, that all men are created equal, that they are endowed by their Creator with certain inalienable Rights, that among these are Life, Liberty, and the pursuit of Happiness. That to secure these rights, Governments are instituted among Men, deriving their just powers from the consent of the governed. That whenever any Form of Government becomes destructive of these ends, it is the Right of the People to alter or to abolish it and to institute new Government, laying its foundation on such principles and organizing its powers in such form, as to them shall seem most likely to effect their Safety and Happiness.

The Declaration holds that a function of government is to "secure," not create, rights. It also holds that the people have the right to abolish the government. It is hard to see how such a right could be socially recognized. If Jefferson had held Martin's view, this paragraph could have easily been rewritten in something like the following manner.

> We hold these truths to be self-evident, that all men are created equal, that Governments ought to create certain inalienable Rights, that among these are Life, Liberty, and the pursuit of Happiness. That to create these rights, Governments are instituted among Men, deriving their just powers from the consent of the governed. That whenever any Form of Government fails to create these rights, the People have the liberty to alter or to abolish it and to institute new Government, laying its foundation on such principles and organizing its powers in such form, as to them shall seem most likely to effect their Safety and Happiness.

The actual Declaration provides a powerful counterexample to externalism. Other classic documents such as the French Declaration of the Rights of Man and the United Nation's Universal Declaration of Human Rights also provide powerful counterexamples to externalism. Further examples that favor internalism over externalism can be found in a search of any major U.S. newspaper. A search of the *Atlanta Journal Constitution* for the phrase "human rights" returns hundreds of documents. In the first 50 of them, there are many that contain assertions that governments are violating the rights of their citizens, that the failure to recognize socially certain ways of acting violates people's rights. There are none that contain assertions that societies should create new moral rights. On the day that I am writing this, the *New York Times* contains a story entitled "Secretive Colombian Courts Survive Protests Over Rights."

> For a decade, terrorism and drug trafficking cases in Colombia have routinely been sent to special tribunals that allow judges, prosecutors, and witnesses to remain anonymous.

The controversial system had been scheduled to expire on June 30. But new legislation, approved by the Colombian Congress last week and about to be signed by President Andres Pastrana, renews the faceless courts for another eight years and modifies, but does not eliminate, many of the procedures that have been most criticized as denials of fundamental rights.

Like the old law, the new one infringes on citizens' rights to due process, an effective defense, a fair and speedy public trial, and the presumption of innocence, according to an analysis published by the United Nations Commission on Human Rights.

"We are in a state not of absolute normality but of atrocious violence and massacres and so normal procedures are insufficient," the Minister of the Interior, Nestor-Humberto Martinez, said in an interview this week. "That means we have to find an equilibrium between the rights of the accused and those of the entire society, which is the real victim of that violence (Rohter, 1999)."

This article contains the assertion that governments are *violating* the rights of their citizens, that the failure to socially recognize certain ways of acting violates people's rights. Externalism is at odds with this common way of speaking about rights. If externalism were true, these articles would assert that some rights that do not now exist should be brought into existence. That is not what they assert. They assert that rights that currently do exist are being abused, denied, or violated.

No one can examine each use of the term "rights" to see whether it better accords with internalism or externalism. More examples that accord with internalism would risk boredom. If one considers the language heard in debates over such issues as abortion, animal rights, and gun control, one can recall more examples. No doubt there are some texts that accord with externalism better than internalism. But they are few and far between. Contrary to Martin's claim, there is a "clear reason in the way we ordinarily talk about rights" to accept internalism. Martin's externalism is at odds with ordinary rights talk, and internalism is in accord with it. This is a powerful argument in favor of internalism. Although certain species of rights, such as legal rights, do require social recognition, the genus does not. The justified-constraint theory is correct to omit any reference to social recognition.

There is a history of philosophical analysis that seeks to find a Hohfeldian structure common to all rights. Sumner holds that

We are ... inevitably drawn to hypotheses which treat most (or all) rights as packages of Hohfeldian normative advantages. But which packages of which advantages? Since liberties, claims, powers, and immunities admit of innumerable different combinations and permutations, it would be fruitless to embark on an exhaustive inventory of the possible structures of a right (1987, 45).

It is true that Hohfeldian relations "admit of innumerable different combinations." The number of combinations is even larger than Sumner imagines because there are also duty, disability, no-claim, and liability rights. This chapter shows that Sumner was wrong to conclude that "it would be fruitless to embark on an exhaustive inventory of the possible structures of a right." We have discerned a pattern, a structure, in each of the innumerable combinations of Hohfeldian relations that is a right. One has a right when one has a claim or an immunity.

3. Deontic and Alethic Concepts

One might be content to formulate an analysis of rights in purely Hohfeldian terms. Hohfeldian vocabulary has much to recommend it. Hohfeldian terms allow one to clearly distinguish different sorts of rights and so to see the differences and similarities between them. Moreover, as will be discussed in Chapters 4 and 5, they highlight the relational character of rights. However, Hohfeldian vocabulary is cut off from other normative concepts central to rights. When one discusses rights in Hohfeldian vocabulary, terms such as "forbidden" and "obligatory" are remarkable by their absence. Surely, my right to drive my pickup imposes some obligations on others. Surely, rights have some relationship to obligations. What is the relationship between claims/immunities and obligations? This is a question that one cannot answer in purely Hohfeldian terms. This chapter shows that we can better understand Hohfeldian relations by explaining them in terms of the deontic modal triad and the alethic modal triad. Concepts are understood by the company they keep. The explication of Hohfeldian relations in terms of the deontic and alethic triads allows us to better see the strengths and weaknesses of various theories of rights. It also allows us to understand the relational nature of rights. It provides a better understanding of rights conflict, of what things can have rights, and of the rights of past and future generations.

I am not the first to attempt this project. Anderson (1962), Fitch (1967), Kanger (1981), Lindahl (1977), Porn (1970), Robinson et al. (1983), Ross (1968), Stoljar (1984), and Sumner (1987) have all done important work on the formalization of Hohfeldian relations. I have learned something from each of these authors. It would be tedious to point out my agreements and disagreements with each of them. Moreover, pointing out the agreements and disagreements would require a sustained foray into formal logic. In order to reach a wider audience, this book does not require a background in formal logic. Finally, apart from Sumner (whose views are considered throughout this book), these authors have not focused on offering an analysis of rights. For these reasons, I will merely say that I do not believe any of these authors' explications of Hohfeld is fully adequate.

1. Some Fundamental Normative Concepts

As we did in Chapter 1, let us begin with a basic presentation of the deontic and alethic concepts and then fill in some important details. As this chapter proceeds, parallels between the normative concepts and the Hohfeldian relations will become obvious. Therefore, certain points can be made more quickly than they were made in Chapter 1.

Let us consider four imaginary normative rule systems, R1 through R4. Each of these normative rule systems will be complete as stated. There will be no statements in the rule systems other than the ones explicitly indicated. These four normative rule systems will be ridiculously simple. Actual normative rule systems are much more complex than R1 through R4. Simple normative rule systems will serve to bring out the properties of more complex ones. The four normative rule systems will also be odd ones. Odd normative rule systems allow us to keep the properties of any possible normative rule system separate from the properties of actual normative rule systems.

(R1) It is forbidden to wash any person, X, unless X has signed a red piece of paper, in which case washing X is obligatory.

Any normative rule system, including R1, has implications for the normative status of acts. The normative status of an act is forbidden, permitted, obligatory, impossible, possible, and/or necessary. Normative rule systems have two different types of implications—deontic and alethic. The deontic modal triad classifies acts as forbidden, permitted, or obligatory. The alethic modal triad classifies acts as impossible, possible, or necessary. Suppose that Tamara has not signed a red piece of paper. In that case, R1 implies that the act of washing Tamara is *forbidden*. This is a deontic implication. R1 also implies that it is *possible* for Tamara to change the normative status of the act of washing Tamara. According to R1, if Tamara signs a red piece of paper, then washing Tamara is obligatory. This is an alethic implication of R1.

(R2) It is forbidden to wash people.

This normative rule system has the alethic implication that it is *impossible* for anyone to change the normative status of acts of washing people. According to R2, it is forbidden to wash people and there is no way to make acts of washing people permitted or obligatory. Another way of saying the same thing is that R2 has the alethic implication that *not* changing the normative status of washing people from forbidden to permitted or obligatory is *necessary*.

The baseball rule system implies that hitting a pitched ball is permitted and that hitting the umpire is forbidden. These are deontic implications. This rule system also implies that if there is no batter in the batter's box and no other runner on the base paths, then it is impossible to change the normative status of a runner with his foot on a base. Such a runner is permitted to remain on that base and there is no way for a member of the opposing team to change the normative status of the act of remaining on the base. This is an alethic implication. If a runner leaves the base, which is permitted according to the rule system, then it is possible for members of the opposing team to change the normative status of the runner. If they touch her with the ball, then she is forbidden to return to a base. If they do not, then she is permitted to remain on base.

According to typical legal rule systems, most killings of people are forbidden, as are such things as leaving the scene of an accident, infringing a patent, and burning down another's house. A great many acts, such as walking, playing a guitar, and watching a sunset, are permitted. Some acts, such as paying taxes and stopping at red lights, are obligatory. These are deontic implications of typical legal rule systems. These rule systems also imply that Joshua's changing the normative status of Joshua's driving Evelyn's car by stating, "I hereby give myself permission to drive Evelyn's car," is impossible. Typical legal rule systems imply that Joshua's driving Evelyn's car is forbidden. If Joshua said, "I hereby give myself permission to drive Evelyn's car," this would not change the fact that Joshua's driving Evelyn's car is forbidden. This is an alethic implication of typical legal rule systems. On the other hand, it is possible for Evelyn to change the normative status of Joshua's driving Evelyn's car. All she has to do is say, "Joshua, you may drive my car," and Joshua's driving Evelyn's car will become permitted.

With this quick overview behind us, let us consider some details. It is useful to begin by stipulatively defining some terms. A "normative statement" is a statement that asserts that an act is forbidden, permitted, obligatory, impossible, possible, or necessary. Here are some examples.

(1) Jasmine has an obligation not to hit Gary.
(2) It is possible for Dick to relieve Marcella of her obligation not to enter Dick's house.
(3) If Sheila promises Lee that she will meet him for lunch, then she has an obligation to meet him for lunch.

I am using "normative" in a stipulative manner. It is somewhat unusual to refer to a statement that a particular act is impossible, possible, or necessary as a normative statement. As we will see at the end of this section, this stipulative usage avoids certain confusions.

A "normative rule system" is a unified set of normative statements. There are many normative rule systems. Probably, the most obvious is the legal system. The legal normative rule system of a country is the set of all true statements about what is legally forbidden, legally permitted, legally obligatory, etc. There are many other normative rule systems. Organized sports, companies, clubs, and other social organizations often create normative rule systems.[1]

Like "normative statement," "rule system" is used stipulatively. There is a broader sense of "rule system" on which a legal rule system is much more than the set of all true statements about what is legally forbidden, legally permitted, legally obligatory, etc. As used here, a "rule system" only governs acts but on the broader sense many "rule systems" have implications for the evaluation of agents. There is an important sense in which agents are part of rule systems. Judges, lawyers, and other officials are part of the legal system of a country. If one uses "rule system" in

---

[1] What is it that unifies a set of normative statements? This is an interesting question. It might be the pedigree of the rules. It might be some kind of rule of recognition. As nothing in this book turns on this question, I will set it aside.

this broader way, the set of all true statements about what is forbidden, permitted, obligatory, etc. by the rules of a state, company, or club is only part of that organization's rule system. There is a sense in which it would be more accurate to say that the set of all true statements about what is forbidden, permitted, obligatory, etc. by a rule system is a description of part of that rule system. On the other hand, this way of speaking would lead to long complex phrases in much of what follows. As long as the stipulative nature of "rule system" as used in this book is clear, there is no harm (and some stylistic benefit) to using "rule system" to refer to the set of all true statements about what is forbidden, permitted, obligatory, etc.

It is natural to speak of a person having one member of the deontic triad. One has an obligation. One does not naturally say that a person has a permission, a forbidden, an impossibility, a possibility, or a necessity. There is no substantive corresponding to the adjectives "permitted," "forbidden," "impossible," "possible," and "necessary." This is not surprising. English often lacks the terminology philosophers need. This feature of English would hinder clarity throughout this book. At the cost of doing some violence to the English language, I will fix the problem by stipulating the meaning of "to have an impossibility, forbidden, etc." and thus create the grammatical substantives corresponding to the adjectives. These substantives will be defined analogously to the phrase "to have an obligation."

To say that a person has an obligation is to make a statement about a person's position under a normative rule system. Tamara has an obligation when a normative rule system implies that an act open to Tamara is obligatory. In R2, Donald has an obligation to refrain from washing Tamara. In other words, it is obligatory for Donald to refrain from washing Tamara. One has an obligation if and only if a normative rule system implies that an act one can do is obligatory. The adjective "obligatory" refers to a feature of an act under a rule system. The substantive "obligation" refers the position of an agent under a rule system. Because acts are necessarily performed by agents, there is a one-to-one correspondence between obligatory acts and the obligations of agents. We can use a parallel one-to-one correspondence to stipulatively define substantives corresponding to the rest of the modal adjectives.

Donald has an impossibility when a normative rule system implies that it is impossible for Donald to change the normative status of an act. In R2, Donald has an impossibility to change the normative status of the act of washing Tamara. One has a forbidden if and only if a normative rule system implies that an act one can do is forbidden. One has a necessity if and only if a normative rule system implies that one's changing the normative status of some act is necessary. In R2, Donald has a necessity not to change the normative status of washing Tamara. One has a possibility if and only if a normative rule system implies that one's changing the normative status of some act is possible. Let us refer to the person who has the obligation, impossibility, etc. as the *subject* of the obligation, impossibility, etc. Let us refer to the act with respect to which they have the obligation, impossibility, etc. as the *content* of the obligation, impossibility, etc. If Donald has an obligation to refrain from washing Tamara, then Donald is the subject of this obligation and "to refrain from washing Tamara" is the content of this obligation.

We are missing the notion of an object of the deontic and alethic concepts. Without this notion, there is no hope of analyzing Hohfeldian relations with these concepts. With respect to obligations, the notion of an object is part of ordinary thinking about moral matters. Assume that one has an obligation to repay one's debts and that those who are relatively wealthy have an obligation to give to charity. There is an important difference between these two obligations. The obligation to pay the debt has an object, the creditor. The obligation to give to charity is the standard example of a non-realtional obligation because this obligation does not have an object. What is it to have an obligation/impossibility *to* someone? What is the difference between relational and non-relational obligations/impossibilities? Chapters 4 and 5 are entirely devoted to answering this complex and crucial question. Pending the results of those chapters, let us assume that it makes sense to talk of relational and non-relational permissions, forbiddens, possibilities, impossibilities, and necessities. "To" is a convenient preposition with which to refer to the object of the relational versions of all the deontic and alethic concepts.

With these stipulative definitions laid out, let us turn to some provisional assumptions that will allow for a more orderly presentation of various issues. We have provisionally assumed that it makes sense to talk of the relational and non-relational versions of the deontic and alethic concepts. Let us also assume that there is a moral normative rule system (hereafter "moral rule system"). This assumption is defended in Section 4 of this chapter. The moral rule system is the set of all true statements that some act is morally forbidden, morally permitted, morally obligatory, etc. For example, I think that the following statement is part of the moral rule system: "Under normal circumstances, if a person, X, promises another person, Y, that he will do act A, then X has an obligation to do A." A moral rule system cannot be a complete moral code because a complete moral code must also evaluate agents. A moral rule system must be distinguished from the conventional morality of a certain culture. Anthropologists study the moralities of different cultures. They study conventional morality. Philosophers study true, valid, or appropriate moral rule systems. On certain philosophical views, a true, valid, or appropriate moral rule system is identical to the morality of a culture (such as the culture of the territory one happens to be in). This work assumes neither that such views are false nor that they are true.

Let us use typical adult humans in all of our examples. It may be that there are restrictions on what sort of things can be the subject and object of a deontic and/or alethic concept. However, pending the results of Chapter 7, we will bracket that issue.

The above stipulative definitions and provisional assumptions allow us to reconsider the deontic and alethic concepts in order to make them more precise and to avoid possible misunderstandings. The concept of permission is a stipulative, technical, and weak one. An act is permitted if and only if it is not forbidden. The fact that X is permitted to do A does not imply that Y is forbidden from attempting to stop X from doing A. Suppose that Joshua's driving Evelyn's car is permitted. This does not imply that she is forbidden to cut off his hand to prevent him from driving. It does not imply that she is forbidden to blow up her car or his house to prevent him from driving her car. It implies *nothing more or less* than that his driving her car is not forbidden.

Because the sense of "permission" is a technical and weak one, inanimate objects are permitted to do things. An act is permitted if and only if it is not forbidden. Consider the stapler on my desk. It, like all inanimate objects, is not forbidden to do anything at all. Therefore, it is not forbidden to staple the papers in the office next to mine. Permission is defined in terms of something not being the case—it is not the case that doing something is forbidden. One way for it to be true that a thing is not forbidden to do an act is for that thing to be the sort of thing that cannot be forbidden to do acts. An act is possible if and only if it is not impossible. Possibility is also defined in terms of something not being the case, so it is possible for inanimate objects to do things.

This use of the terms "permission" and "possibility" is odd. However, it is appropriate to use these terms in this weak sense at this stage of this book. In Chapter 7, we will consider the question of whether inanimate objects can have rights. If we did not use "permission" and "possibility" in this weak sense, we would risk begging the question against those who think inanimate objects have rights.

The weakness of the notion of permission used here can also been seen in the fact that one can have permission to do something because one is not subject to a particular rule system. I have no legal obligation to pay French income tax. I have a legal obligation to pay U.S. income tax. I have permission not to pay French income tax. It is also impossible for the French government to give me a legal obligation to pay French income tax by sending me a letter saying that I owe them taxes. Nothing the French government could do would give me such an obligation. The laws of France apply only to the individuals subject to those laws and I am not such an individual.

It can be possible for someone to do something that is forbidden for her to do.

(R3) It is forbidden to wash any person, X, unless X has signed a red piece of paper and this paper is extant, in which case washing X is obligatory. It is forbidden to destroy signed red papers.

R3 has the deontic implication that burning signed red papers are forbidden. This implies that one possible way of changing the normative status of an act is forbidden. It is forbidden for Donald to change the normative status of washing Tamara from obligatory back to forbidden. R3 does not imply that it is impossible for Donald to make such a change. Such a change is forbidden *and* possible. Normative rule systems R1 and R2 imply that changing the normative status of washing people other than oneself is impossible. R3 implies that such changes are possible but forbidden.

Possible but forbidden changes occur in actual normative rule systems. The case of a mayor's appointment powers in Chapter 1 can be used to illustrate this point. The mayor of a town has the power to appoint the members of the zoning commission. It is possible for the mayor to appoint members of the zoning commission. There are no qualifications for being a member of the zoning commission; so it is possible for the mayor to appoint anyone. The laws of the town are then changed to say that if the mayor appoints someone under the age of 21 years, then that person is a full member in good standing of the zoning commission, but the mayor will be fined $1,000. This gives the mayor an obligation not to appoint someone under 21 years but leaves the mayor with the possibility of appointing someone under 21 years. If the town's laws were changed to say that the appointment of someone under 21 years is a legal nullity, then it would no longer be possible for the mayor to appoint someone under 21 years. The odd law that says that someone under 21 years who is appointed is a member in good standing but it is illegal for the mayor to make such an appointment (on penalty of a $1,000 fine) creates a situation in which there is a possible but forbidden change.

In general, "Xly impossible" means "counter to the laws of X." My leaping over a tall building in a single bound is physically impossible, and my leaping over a tall building in a single bound is counter to the laws of physics. My desk being round and square at the same time is logically impossible, and my desk being round and square at the same time is counter to the laws of logic. This simple analysis of impossibility will not do when it comes to normative rule systems. There are two ways that an action can be counter to a normative rule system.[2] An act, A, could be something that, according to the rules of the system, one may not do. Alternatively, A could be something that, according to the rules of the system, one cannot do. When discussing the legal system, lawyers use "illegal" to refer to the former and "legal nullity" to refer to the later. One of the seminal features of Hohfeldian vocabulary is that it brings out this important distinction. One could draw this distinction in the moral rule system by introducing the term "moral nullity" and contrasting it with "immoral."

Normative rule systems often have implications concerning the possibility of one person changing the possibility of another person changing the normative status of an act. This is a form of nesting.

> (R4) It is forbidden to wash any person, X, unless X signs a red piece of paper *that has been signed by another person*, Y, in which case washing X is obligatory.

R4 is identical to R1 except that it includes the restriction that another person must sign the red piece of paper in order to make it possible for Tamara to change the normative status of washing Tamara. R4 implies that it is possible for Donald to make it possible for Tamara to change the normative status of washing Tamara. R1 implies that this change is impossible. This sort of nesting—that Y can change the

---

[2]   Reina Hayaki brought this point to my attention.

abilities of X to change the normative status of an act—could obviously continue. We can imagine a normative rule system that implies that Estelle can change the abilities of Donald to change the abilities of Tamara to change the normative status of an act. There is no theoretical reason that this sort of nesting would ever have to end. The only limits on this kind of nesting are practical.

In typical legal rule systems, it is possible for Tamara to change the abilities of Donald to change the normative status of Donald's walking onto a certain piece of land. Suppose Tamara owns a certain piece of land and has posted "No Trespassing" signs. It is forbidden for Donald to walk on that land. It is impossible for Donald to change the normative status of this act. It is possible for Tamara to change the abilities of Donald to change the normative status of Donald's walking on the land. If Tamara signs a contract of sale and sends it to Donald, this does not make it permissible for Donald to walk on the land. It does make it possible for Donald to make it permissible for Donald to walk on the land. If Donald signs the contract and fulfills its terms, then it will be permissible for Donald to walk on the land.

The full description of any alethic implication of a rule system must include mention of a triggering act. When it is possible for someone to change the normative status of an act, the triggering act is the act that has the effect of causing the normative change. When it is impossible for someone to change the normative status of an act, the triggering act is the act that does *not* have the effect of causing a normative change. The full description of an alethic implication of a rule system must also include mention of the normative status, which will cease to exist and the normative status, which will come into being. The full description of the fact that it is possible for Evelyn to make it cease to be the case that Joshua is forbidden to drive her car and make it true that Joshua is permitted to drive her car must include reference to what is possible for Evelyn, the pre-triggering act normative status of Joshua's driving Evelyn's car and the post-triggering act normative status of Joshua's driving Evelyn's car. The situation is more clearly presented as follows:

> It is possible for Evelyn to
> change
> > It is forbidden for Joshua to drive Evelyn's car
> into
> > It is permitted for Joshua to drive Evelyn's car
> by saying "You may drive my car."

Let us refer to the first of the three alethic implications here as the *primary* implication. Let us call the second implication the *original* implication and the third implication the *resulting* implication.

Having focused on the notions of permission and possibility, let us turn to some points about the nature of all six fundamental normative concepts. First, the normative positions created by a rule system need not be explicitly stated in the normative rule system. A legal rule system might state that destroying another person's will is illegal. This would imply that destroying another person's will is forbidden. Because one can destroy a will in many different ways (shredding, burning, etc.), the legal rule system would imply that it is forbidden for Jon to put Ellen's will in a washing machine and run the machine. This is true even though the law explicitly says nothing about the washing of wills.

Second, the deontic modalities and the alethic modalities are interdefinable. Any member of one of these two modal triads is equivalent to another member of its triad plus a negation. Washing Tamara is forbidden if and only if not washing Tamara is obligatory. Washing Tamara is permitted if and only if washing Tamara is not forbidden. Changing the normative status of washing Tamara from forbidden to obligatory is impossible if and only if not changing the normative status of this act from forbidden to obligatory is necessary. It is possible for Tamara to change the normative status of the act of washing Tamara if and only if it is not impossible that Tamara change the status of that act. Moreover, a statement using any member of the alethic triad is logically equivalent to a conditional statement using only members of the deontic triad. The following two statements about R1 are logically equivalent:

(1) By signing a red piece of paper, Tamara has the power to change the normative status of washing Tamara from forbidden to obligatory.
(2) If Tamara signs a red piece of paper, then the act of washing Tamara is no longer forbidden and is obligatory.

Third, if a normative rule system implies that one has an obligation or an impossibility, then one's actions are normatively constrained. In typical legal rule systems, Joshua has an obligation to refrain from torturing people and an impossibility to make his driving Evelyn's car permissible. This obligation and this impossibility restrict Joshua's acts. They restrict or constrain his acts of torturing people and changing the normative status of driving Evelyn's car. Joshua's obligation to refrain from torturing people is an example of a deontic normative constraint. There is some act that Joshua *may not* do. Joshua's impossibility to change the normative status of his driving Evelyn's car is an example of an alethic normative constraint. According to typical legal rule systems, Joshua's saying, "I hereby give myself permission to drive Evelyn's car" has no effect. There is some act that Joshua *cannot* do.

Normative rule systems create normative, not physical or logical, constraints. Suppose that a normative rule system implies that washing humans is forbidden. In that case, Donald has an obligation to refrain from washing Tamara. This does not change Donald's physical ability to wash her or refrain from washing her. Similarly, if a normative rule system implies that it is impossible for Donald to change the normative status of washing Tamara, this does not change Donald's physical abilities. It, like the deontic implication, imposes a normative constraint on Donald's action. Suppose that Hyoung has been injured and it is physically impossible for him to sign his name. Under R1, it is normatively possible for

Hyoung to make washing Hyoung obligatory. He cannot perform the triggering act, but that does not imply that it is not normatively possible.

One might object that my use of the alethic concepts is not normative and, therefore, that my use of normative possibility, normative impossibility, and normative necessity is incoherent. There are standard uses of "possible," "impossible," and "necessary" that are clearly non-normative. There is nothing normative about the assertion that it is physically impossible for me to leap a tall building in a single bound. In this work, the alethic terms are not used in this way. As used here, the alethic terms are normative in a crucial sense. They refer to what is possible, impossible, and/or necessary according to the rules of a *normative* rule system. An act is normatively impossible in a certain normative rule system when, according to the rules of the system, a certain triggering act has no normative effect. An act is normatively possible in a certain normative rule system when, according to the rules of the system, a certain triggering act has a certain normative effect. A triggering act has a normative effect when it changes someone's normative relation. Although this use of "normative" is different from other usages, it is clear, coherent, and useful.

2. HOHFELDIAN AND NORMATIVE ANALYSIS

Hohfeldian rule systems can be analyzed in terms of normative rule systems. Some parallels between them should be obvious at this point. I hope that the reader has a sense of déjà vu. The first-order Hohfeldian relations can be analyzed in terms of the deontic implications of normative rule systems. Claims and duties are correlatives. Therefore, statements of claims are logically equivalent to statements of duties. Evelyn has a claim that Joshua not drive her car if and only if Joshua has a duty not to drive Evelyn's car. Joshua also has an obligation to Evelyn not to drive her car. The following three statements are logically equivalent:

(1) X has a claim against Y that Y do A.
(2) Y has a duty to X that Y do A.
(3) Y has an obligation to X that Y do A.

Joshua buys a liberty pass from Evelyn. This pass states that Joshua has no duty to Evelyn not to drive Evelyn's car but does not impose on Evelyn a duty to refrain from interfering with Joshua's driving her car. Joshua has a liberty to drive Evelyn's car if and only if Joshua has a permission to Evelyn to drive her car. The correlative of a liberty is a no-claim. The following three statements are logically equivalent:

(1) X has a liberty against Y that X do A.
(2) Y has a no-claim against X that X do A.
(3) X has a permission to Y that X do A.

The second-order Hohfeldian relations can be analyzed in terms of the alethic implications of normative rule systems. One has a power when one can change some Hohfeldian relation. In R1, Tamara has the power (by signing a red piece of paper) to change the claim that Tamara has against Donald that Donald refrain from washing Tamara into a claim against Donald that Donald wash Tamara. Tamara has a possibility to Donald to change Donald's obligation to refrain from washing Tamara into an obligation to wash Tamara. Liabilities are correlative to powers. The following three statements are logically equivalent:

(1) X has a power against Y that X do A.
(2) Y has a liability with respect to X that X do A.
(3) X has a possibility to Y that X do A.

The act, A, in the case of powers, liabilities, and possibilities must be an act of changing an agent's normative positions.

Evelyn has an immunity against Joshua to Joshua's giving Joshua a liberty to drive Evelyn's car by stating "I hereby give myself the liberty to drive Evelyn's car." Joshua has an impossibility to Evelyn to make Joshua's driving Evelyn's car permissible by stating, "I hereby give myself permission to drive Evelyn's car." The correlative of an immunity is a disability. The following three statements are logically equivalent:

(1) X has an immunity against Y that Y do A.
(2) Y has a disability with respect to X that Y do A.
(3) Y has an impossibility to X that Y do A.

In this case, the act, A, is one that Y is unable to do.

In Chapter 2, we saw that X has a right if and only if X has a claim or an immunity. In this chapter, we have seen that X has a claim if and only if Y has an obligation to X and that X has an immunity if and only if Y has an impossibility to X. It follows that

X has a right against Y that Y do A if and only if
(1) Y has an obligation to X that Y do A, or
(2) Y has an impossibility to X that Y do A.

One has a right if and only if someone else has an obligation or impossibility to one.

At this point, one might wonder if the material in Chapters 1 and 2 was a useless diversion. Why present Hohfeldian terminology if one can use the deontic and alethic triads instead? Would it not have been simpler to ignore Hohfeld and proceed immediately to analyzing rights using the deontic and alethic concepts presented above? Is there any reason, other than an interest in the scholarship of jurisprudence, to discuss Hohfeld? Hohfeld's work is of sufficient historical importance and intellectual power that it is worthy of study for its own sake. On the other hand, it would indeed have been simpler (if by "simpler" one means "uses fewer concepts") to analyzing rights only in deontic and alethic terms. However, simplicity is not the only virtue of a theory. Connection to the history of work in the area is another. At this point in the history of thinking about rights, we stand on the shoulders of Hohfeld. Any serious theory of rights must come to terms with Hohfeld and the authors who use Hohfeldian analysis. One must relate one's theory to those of scholars such as Hart, Wellman, Feinberg, and Raz. Since they use Hohfeldian analysis, others must do so as well. There is also a matter of acknowledging one's intellectual debts. The justified-constraint analysis sprang from Hohfeld. Chapters 1 and 2 were not a useless diversion because, in addition to satisfying an intrinsic interest in Hohfeld, they allow the justified-constraint theory to connect to theories offered by others and to acknowledge its intellectual debts.

The deontic and alethic modalities (forbidden, permitted, obligatory and impossible, possible, necessary) are interesting and useful moral concepts. They are not the only such moral concepts. Our moral concepts are much more varied than that. They are so varied that we cannot consider all of them here. It is worth a brief and seriously incomplete digression to quickly consider how the deontic and alethic modalities are related to a few other moral concepts.

It seems that the deontic modalities can be analyzed in terms of what is wrong. An act is forbidden if and only if it is wrong. Stabbing an innocent person to death and not paying one's taxes are forbidden. An act is permitted if and only if it is not wrong. Drinking a Dr. Pepper and paying one's mortgage are permitted. There are at least two kinds of permitted action—the merely permitted and the obligatory. An act is merely permitted if and only if doing it is permitted and not doing it is permitted. Drinking a Dr. Pepper is merely permitted. An act is obligatory if and only if doing it is permitted and not doing it is not permitted. Paying my mortgage is obligatory. (The class of obligatory acts can be divided into the perfectly obligatory and the imperfectly obligatory, but this distinction need not concern us here. For more on this issue, see Rainbolt (2000).)

This analysis of merely permitted action must be modified to distinguish it from supererogation. An act is merely permitted if and only if doing it is permitted, not doing it is permitted, doing it is not good and not doing it is not good. Following Mellema (1991) and Heyd (1982), let us say that an act is supererogatory if and only if doing it is permitted, not doing it is permitted and doing it is good. James is on a boat when Tynisha falls overboard. If diving in and attempting to rescue her involves a substantial risk to his own life, then diving in is supererogatory. Diving in is permitted, failing to dive in (and throwing her a life preserver instead) is permitted and diving in is good.

Because there is a use of "right" that means "not wrong," one can rework the analyses above in terms of rightness. There are many other moral terms that are close synonyms of "forbidden." One might use "ought not" or "should not." One ought not stab an innocent person. One should not stab an innocent person. But these terms are not perfect synonyms. They carry slightly different shades of meaning. "May not" and "should not" do not carry as much condemnatory force as "ought not," and "forbidden" carries more condemnatory force than any of the other three. When one is discussing morality (as opposed to legal or other institutional systems), the terms "moral" and "immoral" are used as adjectives to described actions. "Immoral" is roughly synonymous with "forbidden" and carries about the same condemnatory force. "Moral" ambiguously refers to any act that is not forbidden—merely permitted, obligatory, or supererogatory.

While there are many terms, one can use to refer to the deontic implications of rule systems, I can think of only two other terms used to refer to alethic implications—"can" and "must." One's act is impossible if and only if one cannot do it. One's act is necessary if and only if one must do it. The alethic implications of rule systems can be analyzed in terms of what one must, can, and cannot do. This is obviously an incomplete and inadequate analysis of moral concepts. Nothing has been said, for example, about such concepts as principled, meritorious, honest, trustworthy, virtuous, praiseworthy, desirable, etc.

3. FEINBERG: VALID CLAIMS

It is quite possible that more people have begun their study of rights with Feinberg's "The Nature and Value of Rights" (1980, 143–155) than with any other work. I began there and it is a very good place to begin. Feinberg provides a theory of rights by relating Hohfeldian terms to other moral concepts. In particular, Feinberg attempts to analyze rights with a particular conception of a claim. It is useful to compare Feinberg's influential theory of rights to the justified-constraint theory. His theory of rights as valid claims is suggestive and powerful but inadequate.

Feinberg holds that "a right *is* a kind of claim" (1980, 149). He correctly notes that one can fall into the trap of asserting that rights are claims and then, when asked what claims are, asserting that they are rights. One falls into an unilluminating circle. The justified-constraint analysis avoids this trap by providing an analysis of claims and other Hohfeldian relations in terms of the fundamental normative concepts just explicated. Feinberg attempts to avoid the circle by providing a different analysis of claims. According to Feinberg, we must distinguish making claim to, claiming that, and having a claim.

Making claim to is an activity we perform when we "petition or seek by virtue of some right, to demand as due" (1980, 149–150). I can make claim to the shirt that I left at the cleaners this morning. I do this by presenting the claim check and asking for my shirt. Making claim to something can be done only by the person who has a right to the object in question. Anyone can claim that my shirt is theirs, but only I or my representatives can make claim to the shirt. Making claim to something is performative in the sense that it creates a duty for someone to give the claimant the thing to which claim was made.

On the other hand, claiming that is not performative. To claim that something is the case is merely to assert that it is true. I can claim that the Earth is flat or that I teach philosophy. My claiming that something is true does not make it true. One can claim or assert that anything is true. In particular, one can claim that one has certain rights. This can easily lead people to confuse making claim to with claiming that.

"The Nature and Value of Rights" was first published in 1970. At that time, Feinberg held that "having a claim consists in being in a position to claim, that is, to make claim to or claim that" (1980, 151, emphasis omitted). In his 1973 work *Social Philosophy*, Feinberg revised his view. "[H]aving a claim consists in being in a position to claim in the performative sense, that is, to make claim to" (1973, 65, emphasis omitted). The evidence that one has a claim is often a receipt, claim check, IOU, or other piece of paper. However, this is merely the evidence. If I lose the claim check for my shirt, I do not lose the claim to the shirt. I merely lose the ability to show that I have a claim to the shirt. Although anyone can claim that anything is true, only some are in a position to make claim to something. To be in such a position, one must be able to provide some reasons for the view that one has a right to the thing in question. One must have at least a case meriting consideration.

Many individuals might have a claim to something and might have a case meriting consideration. However, according to Feinberg, the only person who has a right to it is the person who has the best or strongest case. Thus, in the final analysis, Feinberg holds that rights are valid claims. If one has a valid claim then one has the claim for which the best or strongest case can be provided.

> To have a right is to have a claim against someone whose recognition as valid is called for by some set of governing rules or moral principles. To have a claim in turn, is to have a case meriting consideration, that is, to have reasons or grounds that put one in a position to [make a claim or claim that] (1980, 155).

There are three crucial problems with Feinberg's analysis of rights. First, his view cannot account for immunity rights. There are eight different kinds of rights: claim rights, immunity rights, liberty rights, power rights, duty rights, disability rights, liability rights, and no-claim rights. Feinberg obviously has an account of claim rights. Can Feinberg's theory be extended to provide a plausible account of non-basic rights? Perhaps, each of the non-basic rights contains a claim; so he might argue that each of these sorts of rights is a right because it contains a claim. In each case, a claim protects the relation after which the right is named. On the other hand, Feinberg cannot provide a plausible analysis of immunity rights. Feinberg's theory is entirely focused on claims. Feinberg holds that "a right *is* a kind of claim." No account of rights can be plausible unless it can account for the immunity rights found in such central documents as the U.S. Bill of Rights. Feinberg has overlooked the fact that two Hohfeldian relations imply constraints on others. Feinberg notes that duties, the correlative of claims, constrain others. "A duty, whatever else it be, is something *required* of one. That is to say ... that a duty ... is something that *obliges*" (1980, 136). The justified-constraint analysis uses the term "constrains" in place of Feinberg's "obliges" or "required of one," but both are referring to the same feature of duties. Feinberg fails to notice a crucial similarity between duties and disabilities. This leads him to formulate a theory that cannot account for immunity rights. Another way to make the same point is to say that Feinberg has overlooked the fact that in addition to actions that rule systems tell us we *may not* do, there are actions that rule systems tell us we *cannot* do.

One might think that this objection is unfair to Feinberg. Perhaps Feinberg only intended to provide a theory of claim rights. Rather than overlooking the distinction between what we may not do and what we cannot do, he may simply have decided to focus on the former. There would be nothing wrong with such a decision. Claim rights provide plenty of grist for the philosophical mill. However, this response, if accurate, only shows that Feinberg does not overlook an important distinction. It does not show that Feinberg's theory is an adequate and complete theory of rights. Even if Feinberg chose to focus only on claim rights, the project of this book is broader. We seek a theory of rights that accounts for all the many sorts of rights. So Feinberg's theory, even if it were adequate for Feinberg's project, is not adequate for ours.

The second problem with Feinberg's view is that it has no theory of the relational nature of rights. Feinberg is aware that some obligations are to others while others are not. A substantial portion of his article "Duties, Rights, and Claims" is devoted to enumerating the cases in which obligations are relational. He holds that "indebtedness is the clearest example of one person *owing* something to another; and owing, in turn, is perspicuous model for the interpretation of that treacherous little preposition 'to' as it occurs in the phrase 'obligation *to* someone'" (1980, 130). However, Feinberg's discussion of making claim to, claiming that, and having a claim does not provide any clue as to why the obligations and disabilities correlative to rights are relational. Feinberg cannot answer the question "Why are the obligations correlative to a right obligation to the right-holder?"

The final problem with Feinberg's view is that it provides an insufficiently detailed analysis of the link between rights and non-Hohfeldian moral concepts. Feinberg analyzes rights in terms of claims and then distinguishes three kinds of claims and claiming. This provides a link between rights and duties because one can analyze claims in terms of duties. His theory is an important step forward. Duty is a key normative concept. Moreover, there is clearly some link between duties and obligations. Feinberg is of course aware of this link and provides some discussion of it in his "Duties, Rights, and Claims." However, Feinberg does not purport to be providing a detailed discussion of the link between duties and obligations. He set that question aside with some suggestive but incomplete remarks and some references to the work of others. So, Feinberg does not tell us how rights relate to non-Hohfeldian moral concepts such as those discussed above. How does claiming relate to obligation? How does claiming relate to what one may not or cannot do? Feinberg's theory is incomplete because it does not provide fully developed answers for these important questions.

4. MORAL RIGHTS

We have been assuming that there are moral rights. It is now time to examine that assumption. Before we can discuss whether or not there are moral rights, we must consider what moral rights are. A moral right is a right implied by the moral rule system. A legal right is a right implied by a legal rule system. A legal right and a moral right can have the same subject, object, and content. If one holds that people have the *legal* right to be given what they have paid for and that people have the *moral* right to be given what they have paid for, then one holds that these two rights have the same subjects, objects, and contents. (For a useful collection of work on the questions discussed in this section, see Wellman 2002, vol. 4.)

This usage of "moral rights" is far from universal. Some authors use "human" or "natural" to refer to what I call "moral" rights. Some, such as Feinberg (1973, 84–85 and 96–97), use "human" and "natural" to refer to subclasses of moral rights. In other cases, the term "human" is reserved for a subclass of legal rights established by international law. In still other cases, "human" rights are those moral rights that all humans have. Suppose that if I give the person at the popcorn stand a quarter and that is the advertised price of a bag of popcorn, then I have a moral right to a bag of popcorn. This is not a right that all humans have. Only those who have given the person at the popcorn stand a quarter have a moral right to a bag of popcorn. All humans might have the moral right to be given what they pay for, but only those humans who have paid for a bag of popcorn have a moral right to a bag of popcorn.

The term "natural rights" has a wide variety of meanings. Some, such as Feinberg (1973, 84), define natural rights as those moral rights that a being has in virtue of its biological nature. When used in this way, the adjective "natural" indicates not only that a certain right is a moral right, but also that the right is a moral right which a being has because of its biological constitution. Others use the term "natural rights" to refer to those moral rights one would have in a state of nature. Still others use this term to refer to those moral rights that are implied by the natural law. (For a discussion of the various sorts of natural rights, see Finnis 1980.)

Sumner (1987) holds that moral rights are rights that ought to be part of a legal or other non-moral rule system. Some think this view of moral rights is incorrect. Feinberg (1992, 197–221) argues this view cannot account for a great deal of our discussion of rights. Suppose that in some country there is a beach that is reserved, by law, for whites. On Sumner's view, those black people who claim that they have a moral right to use the beaches are asserting that the government has a moral obligation to give them the legal right to use the beaches. Consider the statements that might be made by a group of protestors who occupied a beach reserved by law for whites. They might well assert that they are exercising their moral right to use the beach. Those who hold that moral rights are nothing more than morally justified legal or other non-moral rights cannot account for such assertions. They must hold that the people on the beach who claim to be exercising their moral rights are speaking nonsense. This is a strike against Sumner's view. The view that moral rights are rights that ought to be part of a legal rule system seems to be open to other counterexamples. Many people hold that children have a moral right not to be struck as a form of punishment and that the government should not pass a law forbidding parents from striking their children as a form of punishment. A couple with whom I talk at a local park is of the view that children have a moral right to be prevented from watching television. They do not allow their children to watch television and believe that all parents have a moral duty to prevent their children from watching television. One of them told me that letting your children watch television is a form of child abuse. I asked them if they favored a law requiring parents to prevent their children from watching television and they quickly responded that they did not. They were correct to think that their view was consistent. The law is a blunt instrument that is costly to use. The law must be relatively general and enforcement costs money. Therefore, it seems possible for someone to have a moral right which ought not be a legal right.

We need not settle the issue between Sumner and Feinberg. Both views are compatible with the justified-constraint theory of rights. The view that moral rights are rights that ought to be part of a legal or other non-moral rule system is compatible with the view that moral rights are moral obligations to the right-holder. One merely needs to hold, as Sumner clearly does, that moral obligations are obligations that ought to be part of a legal or other non-moral rule system. Some think that moral rights are those rights set down by God. This view is also compatible with the justified-constraint theory of rights. One merely needs to hold that moral obligations are obligations set down by God. One could accept the justified-constraint analysis of rights and hold that there are no rights and/or that there are no moral rights. One would merely need to hold that there are no moral obligations or no relational moral obligations.

A right with a particular subject, object, and content might exist in one rule system but not in another. Consider the assertion that if one is 16 years and has passed the driver's exam, then one has a right to drive. This assertion is true in some legal rule systems and false in others. Some jurisdictions allow driving at 16 years while others require that individuals wait until they are 17, 18, or 21 years. France requires that one be 18 years in order to have the right to drive. So one could have a right to drive under the U.S. legal system without having a right to drive under the French legal system. Rights are created by rule systems and are relative to those rule systems. We need to incorporate this feature of rights into the justified-constraint analysis.

X has a right under S against Y that Y do A if and only if
(1) Y has an obligation under S to X that Y do A, or
(2) Y has an impossibility under S to X that Y do A.

The "S" is replaced by the name of the rule system that implies the right. It takes values such as "Georgia law," "French law," "the statutes and bylaws of Georgia State University," etc. (The rights of different rules systems can overlap and influence each other. For an excellent discussion of this, see Wellman 1997, 40–41.)

A particular right R exists under S if and only if (a) there is a rule system S and (b) S implies R. Philosophers have the habit of discussing the legal rules of Erehwon but they all know there is no such legal system. It is an imaginary, non-existent rule system. No one doubts the existence of the Georgia legal system. However, under this rule system, there is no right for a 6-year-old to drive. The justified-constraint analysis tells us a great deal about whether a rule system implies a right. A rule system S implies that X has right if and only if S implies that Y has an obligation or an impossibility under S which is to X. The notions of obligation and impossibility have been clarified above. The notions of obligation and impossibility *to* someone will be clarified in Chapters 4 and 5. On the other hand, the justified-constraint analysis tells us little about whether a rule system exists. When does a legal system exist? When does an institution such as a club or university have a rule system? When does the moral code of a society form a rule system? The possible answers to these sorts of questions are complex and interesting. They have been much discussed by philosophers and legal scholars. They are outside the scope of a theory of rights and we will not discuss them here.

The comments in the preceding paragraph apply to moral rights. A moral right M exists if and only if (a) there is a moral rule system and (b) it implies M. The justified-constraint analysis tells us a great deal about whether a moral rule system implies a particular right. X has a moral right against Y that Y do A if and only if Y has either a moral obligation to X to do A or a moral impossibility to X to do A. Chapters 4 and 5 will focus on the question: What are moral obligations/impossibilities *to* individuals? On the other hand, because the justified-constraint analysis has little to say about the existence conditions of rule systems in general, it has little to say about the existence of a moral rule system in particular. What are moral obligations/impossibilities *tout court*? What is true when someone morally may not or cannot do some act? These questions require a brief detour into metaethics. (For the remainder of this chapter, let us simplify matters and ignore impossibilities.)

The vast majority of metaethical views leave space for moral rights. Let us adopt, with only minor changes, the classification of metaethical views suggested by Sayre-McCord (1988). All metaethical views can be divided into two categories—those which hold that moral statements are literally true or false and those which hold that moral statements are not literally true or false. A moral statement is literally true or false if and only if it is true or false in just the same way that non-normative statements about the physical world, statements like "The cat is on the mat," are true or false. I deliberately decline to specify what this "same way" is. This vague definition of literal truth is good enough for our purposes. Let us call the view that moral statements are literally true or false "cognitivism." Let us call the view that moral statements are *not* literally true or false "non-cognitivism." Emotivism and prescriptivism are versions of non-cognitivism. Cognitivist views can be divided into those that hold that all moral statements are false and those that hold that some moral statements are true. The former are error theories. Mackie (1977) is an error theorist. The latter are success theories. Utilitarians are success theorists.

Success theories can be divided according to their view of the truth conditions of moral statements. Objectivist theories hold that the truth conditions of moral statements make no reference to the mental states of people. If one holds that there is a non-natural property of goodness and that acts which maximize the amount of this property are right, then one holds an objectivist view. Subjectivism is the view that the truth conditions of moral statements refer to the mental states of people. Here are three of many possible subjectivist views:

(1) A is good if and only if A is approved of by the majority of people in the world.
(2) "A is good" spoken by X is true if and only if X approves of A.
(3) A is bad if and only if A causes a person pain.

The third sort of view is often not classified as a version of subjectivism. For our purposes, it will be clearer to classify the view this way. The second and third sorts of subjectivism illustrate a final metaethical distinction. Relativism is the view that the truth conditions of moral statements refer to mental properties of the judger. (This definition does not cover cultural relativism—the view that different cultures have different conventional moralities. I think this is appropriate because cultural relativism is not a metaethical view.) Absolutism is the view that the truth conditions of moral statements do not refer to mental properties of the judger. Because judgers must be people, all relativists are subjectivists. The view that "A is good" spoken by X is true if and only if X approves of A is a relativistic subjectivist view. The view that A is bad if and only if A causes a person pain is an absolute subjectivist view.

Much more could be said about various sorts of metaethical views, but we have enough for our purposes. We can now ask which metaethical views allow space for moral rights. The answer is that *only* error theories and ethical particularism do not allow such a space. All other metaethical views are compatible with the existence of moral rights. The discussion of ethical particularism requires consideration of the relation nature of rights and so it must be postponed until Chapter 5.

The error theorist thinks that all moral statements are literally false. Typical error theorists hold this view because they think that the truth conditions of moral statements refer to properties that do not exist. An error theorist might hold that the statement "Acts which maximize the amount of the non-natural property of goodness are right" would be literally true if there were such a non-natural property. She also thinks that there is no such non-natural property. Therefore, she thinks that the statement is false. Because the error theorist holds that all moral statements are false, she is committed to the view that there are no moral rights.

On the other hand, non-cognitivism is compatible with moral rights. The non-cognitivist who thinks that there are moral rights will hold that the statements of relational obligation that are logically equivalent to statements of rights are not literally true or false. Relativistic subjectivism is also compatible with moral rights. The relativistic subjectivist will hold that the statements of relational obligation that are logically equivalent to statements of rights are true or false depending on the views of people (e.g., the majority). The relativistic subjectivist is not committed to the view that there are no moral rights. She is only committed to the view that whether or not there are moral rights is determined by the views of people.

The general conclusion from these cases is clear. Any metaethical view which holds that some moral statements of relational obligation and impossibility are

81

appropriate, valid, or true will be compatible with moral rights. Statements of moral rights are logically equivalent to statements of relational moral obligation and impossibility. This is true no matter what metaethical view one adopts. No matter what metaethical interpretation one gives of statements of relational moral obligation and impossibility, statements of moral rights will simply inherit that interpretation.

We are now in position to present a simple and powerful argument for moral rights. Moral rights are logically equivalent to moral obligations and moral impossibilities. Therefore, if there are moral obligations and/or moral impossibilities, then there are moral rights. One is free to deny the antecedent of the conditional. In this sense, this argument does not show that there are moral rights. Rather, it shows that taking the position that there are no moral rights has a high intellectual cost.

At least since Bentham (1987), one of the main sources of moral rights scepticism is the view that moral rights have implausible ontological implications. One might think that rights are created by rule systems and that rule systems must be the rule systems of some society or institution. On this view, moral rights cannot exist for there is no moral institution to enact the moral rule system. Some seem to have held that moral rights imply that there is a ghostly rule system in the sky. Moral rights have no greater ontological implications than the relational obligations and impossibilities to which they are logically equivalent. Moral obligations, moral impossibilities, and moral rights are all created by moral rule systems. So if one thinks that there are moral obligations and impossibilities in the absence of institutions, one is committed to the view that there is a moral rule system even if no human institution enacts it. One cannot then consistently object to moral rights because they imply the existence of a moral rule system. Of course, one might consistently hold the view that all moral statements, even obligation and impossibility statements, must be enacted by some human institution. However, one cannot consistently hold that there are relational moral obligations and impossibilities in the absence of institutions and object to moral rights on the grounds that they have implausible ontological implications.

Just as the justified-constraint theory of rights is metaethically thin in the sense just noted, it is also normatively thin in the sense that many (but not all) normative moral theories are compatible with moral rights as analyzed here. Any normative moral theory which is compatible with the view that there are obligations to individuals is compatible with the view that there are moral rights. There are some normative moral theories (e.g., consequentialist moral theories) that imply that there are no obligations to individuals. The defense of this assertion must wait until Chapter 5 when justified-constraint theory or relational obligation has been explicated.

Some hold that moral rights are superfluous. Frey claims that

> not even a practical advantage is gained by positing some moral right based upon agreed upon moral principles, since I as a moral man, implementing and following my principles, will behave the way you want me to *even without the right*. (1980, 12)

On the justified-constraint analysis, statements of moral rights, like all statements of rights, are logically equivalent to statements of relational obligation. There is a sense in which statements of all rights, not just moral rights, are superfluous. Statements of rights are superfluous in the sense that there is a logically equivalent statement of relational obligation to replace any statement of rights.

If this sort of superfluity is worrisome, then we ought to stop using all statements of rights, not merely statements of moral rights. One can make the exact same point against legal rights that Frey has made against moral rights. One can argue with equal plausibility that not even a practical advantage is gained by positing some legal right based upon agreed legal principles. This reflects the fact that statements of legal rights are logically equivalent to statements of relational legal obligations just as statements of moral rights are logically equivalent to statements of relational moral obligations. Yet Frey (1980, 10) holds that talk of legal rights is not superfluous. Given his criticism of moral rights, this is inconsistent.

This sort of superfluity is not worrisome. Chapter 5 will defend the view that statements of rights point out an important difference among obligations. Some are relational and some are not. Some are grounded in the features of individuals and some are not. It is extremely useful to have a term that refers to relational obligations. Therefore, the existence of statements of rights is not superfluous. Statements of rights point to an important area of normative discourse with special features. Noting the area of normative discourse allows one to avoid conceptual muddles and solve practical problems.

The normative and metaethical thinness of the justified-constraint analysis of rights is a virtue of the theory. A theory of what it is to have a right should exclude as few normative and metaethical views as possible. Thinness is an argumentative virtue because when a theory of rights excludes some normative or metaethical view, then a full defense of the theory must defend the non-excluded view against the arguments made by those who hold the excluded view. Neutrality allows one to avoid battles. Metaethical thinness is also a virtue because it coheres with a notable feature of the metaethical debate—it has not involved a discussion of the nature of rights. In the vast literature on metaethics, those who defend one of the views noted above have not argued that their view is superior because it allows for the existence of rights while opposing views do not. The metaethical thinness of the justified-constraint theory of rights provides an explanation for this feature of the literature on metaethics. It does not include a debate on rights because almost all metaethical views are compatible with rights.

4. The Relational Nature of Rights

In the previous chapter, an interest in smooth exposition led us to set aside the important and difficult question of what it is to have an obligation, permission, etc. *to* another. An essential feature of rights is that they place normative constraints on another. Another essential feature of rights is that *these constraints are owed to the right-holder*. What is a normative constraint owed to someone? The justified-constraint theory's answer builds on the work of Raz, Hart, and Wellman. Therefore, in this chapter we will consider their theories of rights. The next chapter will present the justified-constraint theory's view of the relational nature of rights.

1. RELATIONAL OBLIGATIONS

There is an important difference between failing to respect someone's rights and failing to fulfill an obligation that is not part of a right. Consider the difference between failing to pay a debt and failing to give to charity. Assume that one has an obligation to pay the debt and that, if one has attained some relatively high level of financial resources, one has an obligation to give to charity. There is an important difference between these two obligations. In failing to pay the debt, one *wrongs* the debt-holder. In failing to give to charity one does something wrong, but one does not wrong anyone. In general, if one violates another's right, then one has wronged him. The verb, as opposed to the adjective, "wrong" is used to indicate that one has failed to meet an obligation that one owes to the right-holder. These cases indicate that rights are relational. Rights are relational in the sense that the obligations and impossibilities implied by rights are owed to the subject of the right.

We can multiply the cases. Suppose that I promise that I will meet you for lunch. Then it seems that, not only do I have an obligation to meet you for lunch, this obligation is *to* you. My obligation is not to my son. You also have a right that I meet you for lunch. Suppose that I lend you a book. It seems that, not only do you have an obligation to return the book, this obligation is *to* me. Your obligation is not to my son. I have a right that you return the book. Assume that I have an obligation not to hit you. It seems that this obligation is *to* you and that you have a right that I not hit you. Again, my obligation not to hit you is not to my son.

Cases like these give us reason to explore a conception of rights in terms of obligations and impossibilities owed *to* someone, in terms of relational obligations and impossibilities. We have reason to see if Raz was correct to assert that "a duty is toward a certain person if and only if it is derived from his right" (1984). But the notions of relational obligation and relational impossibility require an explication. For convenience, we can focus on relational obligations. The discussion will apply, *mutatis mutandis*, to relational impossibilities.

Obligations to should not be confused with obligations regarding. Suppose that I promise Madeline that I will take out the trash this evening. Madeline has a right that I take out the trash. I have an obligation to her to take out the trash. But my obligation is regarding the trash. It is the trash that must be taken out, not Madeline. An obligation can be to and regarding the same person. If I promise Madeline that I will kiss her then my obligation to kiss her is both to and regarding her. In third-party beneficiary cases the distinction between obligations to and obligations regarding is controversial. If I promise Fred that I will give Jane $10, is my obligation to Fred, to Jane, regarding Fred, regarding Jane or some combination of these options? This issue will be discussed in Chapter 5.

The distinction between relational and non-relational obligations must not be conflated with the distinction between rights *in personam* (a.k.a. special rights) and rights *in rem* (a.k.a. general rights). In Chapter 1, we saw that a right *in rem* is a right that holds against everyone. The classic example is the right not to be assaulted. A right *in personam* is a right that holds only against a particular individual. The classic example is the right of a creditor to repayment from his debtor. If I lend you $20, then I have a right *in personam* that you give me $20. Both your obligation not to assault me and your obligation to give me $20 are relational obligations. The distinction between *in personam* rights and *in rem* rights does not correspond to the distinction between relational and non-relational obligations. Both rights *in personam* and rights *in rem* imply relational obligations.

One reason philosophers and legal scholars have found analyzing rights in Hohfeldian terms attractive is that Hohfeldian relations are defined so that they always relate two people. The relational feature of Hohfeldian terms insures that if one analyzes rights in Hohfeldian terms, one will include the relational nature of rights in one's analysis. However, Hohfeldian analysis also conceals the need for an analysis of the relational nature of rights. If one restricts oneself to Hohfeldian analysis, the relational nature of rights is automatically incorporated into one's analysis through the relational aspect of Hohfeldian relations. One might not even notice that a theory of this aspect of rights is needed.

2. PROTECTION AND JUSTIFICATION: THE INTEREST AND CHOICE THEORIES

Much of the debate over rights is framed by the interest and choice theories of rights. According to the interest theory of rights, rights are to benefits. On this view, rights are necessarily in the interest of the right-holder. According to the choice theory of rights, rights are to choices. On this view, rights necessarily allow the right-holder to make a choice. Each of these theories comes in two versions, the protection version and the justification version.

On the protection version of the interest theory, rights protect the interests of the right-holder. Kramer holds that

> Necessary but insufficient for the actual holding of a right by X is that the right, when actual, *protects* one or more of X's interests (2001, 28, emphasis added).

This view has also been defended by Lyons (1994) and MacCormick (1977). There are rights that fit this model. My right that you not hit me clearly protects my interest in not being in pain.

On the justification version of the interest theory, the obligations correlative to rights are justified by the interests of the right-holder. This theory also provides a plausible analysis of my right that you not hit me. It seems that my right is correlated with your obligation not to hit me and that your obligation is justified by my interest in not being in pain. If one were to ask: "Why does George have a right not to be hit?" an obvious answer would be that being hit causes pain and people have an interest in being free from pain. In a moment, we will examine in detail an instance of the justification version of the interest theory, Raz's theory of rights.

On the protection version of the choice theory, rights protect the choices of the right-holder. There are rights that fit this model. My right to drive my pickup truck clearly protects my choices as to whether or not to drive my pickup. Although there are some interpretational issues, it seems that Hart holds the protection version of the choice theory. In a moment, we will examine Hart's view in detail.

On the justification version of the choice theory, the obligations correlative to rights are justified by the choices of the right-holder. This theory also provides a plausible analysis of my right to drive my pickup truck. It seems that my right is correlated with your obligation not to interfere with my choices regarding my pickup and that your obligation is justified by the importance of my being able to make choices about matters such as when to drive my truck. If one were to ask: "Why does George have a right to drive his pickup?" one plausible answer would be that my being able to make choices regarding driving my truck is morally important and so justifies my right. (Interestingly, no one I know of has defended the justification version of the choice theory. This is somewhat odd because, as we will see below, justification theories are in some respects superior to protection theories.)

Both versions of the interest theory and both versions of the choice theory have an important strength that any other theory must match. All can provide plausible accounts of the relational nature of rights. Consider the protection version of the interest theory. It contains an implicit theory of relational obligation. If Julia has a right, why, on this view, is the obligation implied by that right an obligation *to* Julia? Because it is Julia's interest that is the protected by the obligation. The right does not protect Steve's interests or the interest of some other person. On the justification version of the interest theory, the obligations correlative to Julia's right are justified by one of her interests. The reason for the obligation is not one of Steve's interests or the interests of some other person. The reason for the obligation is not some other feature of the world. The obligation implied by the right is *to* Julia. Similarly, the protection version of the choice theory can account for the relational nature of rights by asserting that the obligation correlative to Julia's right is *to* Julia because the right protects one of Julia's choices and not the choices of some other person. Finally, the justification version of the choice theory can assert that this obligation is justified by the importance of Julia's choice. One reason that many have found the interest and choice theories to be plausible is that they can account for the relational nature of rights.

3. RAZ: INTERESTS THAT JUSTIFY DUTIES

Raz holds that

> X has a right if and only if X can have rights and, other things being equal, an aspect of X's well-being (his interest) is a sufficient reason for holding some other person(s) to be under a duty (1986, 166, quotation marks omitted).

This analysis "aims to encapsulate the common core of all rights" and is a "definition of rights *simpliciter*" (1986, 167). In other words, Raz proposes an analysis of all rights—legal, moral, institutional, etc. Raz's use of "duty" is equivalent to "obligation" as it is used in this work. We will consider the issue of what can have rights in Chapters 7 and 8. Therefore, for the moment, let us ignore the phrase "X can have rights." In light of these two comments and altering his language to match the conventions used in this book, we may reformulate Raz's analysis as follows:

> X has a right if and only if other things being equal, an aspect of X's well-being (his interest) is a sufficient reason for holding some other person to be under an obligation.

This view is an influential instance of the justification version of the interest theory. Raz holds that the "reason," the justification, of X's rights is X's well-being. At first glance, this theory of rights seems to be open to obvious counterexamples. First, Raz's view seems to imply that all rights must be in the interest of the right-holder. As he puts it, "rights are to benefits" (1994, 32). But there are many rights that are not in the interest of the right-holder. I might inherit some property that is literally more trouble than it is worth. Suppose that the property in question is bound up in complex legal proceedings that prevent its sale but require my time and attention. Imagine that it is far from my home and generally of no use to me. Consider my liberty right, under U.S. law, to cut off my little left toe. This right is of no benefit to me. I have no desire to cut off my little toe. Theo is very allergic to peanuts. If he eats one, he will die. Since peanuts tend to be in processed food products without being adequately labeled, he would be better off if it were illegal to produce peanuts and no one had a right to eat them. Theo's parents are afraid that he will unintentionally eat a peanut at a friend's house so they wish that peanuts were illegal. Theo has a liberty right under U.S. law to eat peanuts. Not only is this right of no benefit to him, but a case could be made that it sets back his interests.

Second, Raz's view seems to imply that rights must be justified by the interests of the right-holder. But there are cases in which rights are not justified by the right-holder's interests but by the interests of others. In typical legal rule systems, the duty rights of public officials are justified in this way. A judge has a duty right to impose sentence. In most instances it is in the judge's interest to impose sentence.

(A judge who consistently failed to impose sentence would, in most legal systems, be removed from office.) But it is not the judge's interest in imposing sentence that justifies his right to do so. This right is justified by the interests of other individuals in having criminals punished. There are cases in which the person who has a right has explicitly said that it is not in his interest to have the right. Congress decided that the chairman of the Federal Deposit Insurance Corporation (FDIC) was to have a large set of rights concerning the disposal of the property owned by failed savings and loans. The chairman of the FDIC, William Siedman, opposed being granted these duty rights. He felt that he already had too many rights and that someone else ought to be appointed to dispose of the property. Congress gave Siedman these rights in spite of his objections.[1] The "sufficient reason" for these rights is not to protect Siedman's interests but to protect the interests of other individuals (e.g., taxpayers).

Raz is aware of these potential problems with his theory of rights and attempts to respond to them. He makes two attempts to respond to the first objection.

> What one can have a right to may be in one's interest to have in some respect but not in others. One may have a right to some valuable property which may make one a target for criminals or for temptation. It may be in one's overall interest not to have it, but as having the property is in one's interest in some respect one can have a right to it (1992, 129, footnote 2).

It would have been clearer if Raz had replaced "an aspect of X's well-being (his interest)" in his analysis with "an aspect of X's well-being (*one of* his interests)."

To account for cases such as my right to cut off my little left toe, Raz draws a distinction between core and derivative rights. A derivative right is a right grounded on another right. A core right is a right that is not a derivative right. Right X is derivative on right Y if and only if the statement that right X exists is a conclusion of a sound argument whose premises include a statement that right Y exists. Derivativeness is a matter of justification. Suppose that, in a series of transactions, I buy each and every house on the street. I have a right to the street as a whole. But my right to a particular house does not derive from my right to the street as a whole. The right to a particular house is not derivative. Suppose that I inherit the whole street from my grandfather. In that case, my right to a particular house is derivative on my right to the whole street. Raz would argue that my right to cut off my little left toe is derivative of my right to personal liberty. Raz claims that only core rights need be in one's interest. Sometimes derivative rights are in one's interest and sometimes they are not (1986, 168).

These qualifications significantly weaken the link between rights and interests. Raz frequently says things that would indicate that the link between rights and interests is very strong. Consider the claim that "the fundamental role of rights [is] representing concern for the interest of the right-holder sufficient to hold another

---

[1]   Here I recount an interview broadcast in July of 1989 on the MacNeil/Lehrer News Hour. I am unable to discover the exact date.

subject to a duty" (1986, 188). He often says things such as: "An individual has a right if an interest of his is sufficient to hold another to be subject to a duty" (1984, 14). If one considers the distinction between an interest of a person and that person's overall interest as well as the distinction between core and derivative rights, it turns out that many, perhaps even most, rights are not in the right-holder's overall interest. Many rights are quite troublesome and so not in one's overall interest. Consider the many annoying rights that typically come with one's job. Moreover, there are probably more derivative rights not in one's interest than there are core rights in one's interest. Consider all the rights to do things that one will never have any desire to do.

The distinction between an interest and overall interest as well as the distinction between core and derivative rights are not adequate responses to the first objection to Raz's theory. Imagine a country, Erewhon, with a legal system that is very much like the ones found in western industrialized countries. Erewhon has executive, legislative, and judicial offices. It has enforcement systems that involve courts and prisons. It has statutory and case law that is used by the courts. Imagine that Erehwon has as developed a system of making and enforcing laws as any actual country on earth. However, now imagine that Erehwon makes a new set of laws that is radically different from any actual country's. A law is passed (following all the procedures for making valid law) that states that any act not specifically permitted or obligatory is forbidden. The law continues with a list of acts that are permitted and there only six acts on this list: talking, walking, severing one's little left toe, making Erehwonian law, interpreting Erehwonian law, and enforcing the Erehwonian law. Under Erehwonian law, others are under an obligation to refrain from interfering with another's severing of his little left toe because all acts that are not specifically permitted or obligatory are forbidden. This rule system contains a right to sever one's little left toe. This is a right that is in hardly anyone's interest. The vast majority will not avail themselves of this right because it is not in their interest to have it. This is not a right that is "in one's interest to have in some respect but not in others." For the vast majority of people, excepting people such as those who have a serious disease of the little left toe, this right is not in their interest in any respect. Nor will the core/derivative distinction solve the problem, because in Erehwon each of the seven rights is a core right. None of them is justified by reference to another right.

At this point one might think that Raz would deny that Erehwon has a legal system. This raises the complex issue of Raz's theory of the nature of law. Fortunately for the purposes of this book, we may ignore much of that complexity. The feature of Raz's theory of the nature of the law that is relevant in this context is his view that a necessary condition for the existence of a legal system is that the rules of the legal system must function as "a system of practical reasoning." "To say of the law that it is a system of practical reasoning is . . . to claim that it consists of rules some of which justify some of the others" (1984, 6). Raz then explains how it is that one rule justifies another.

The statement 'It is the law that P' legally justifies the statement 'It is the law that R' just in case 'It is the law that P' is true and there is a set of true statements (legal or non-legal), such that it is the law that P state a complete reason to believe that R . . . (1984, 7–8).

One might argue that the laws of Erehwon are not a system of practical reasoning. Erehwon has, on this view, merely a fragment of a legal system, not a genuine one. Because only seven acts are permitted, some might think that Erehwon does not have a genuine legal system as Raz conceives of a legal system.

This response to the objection to Raz is flawed. The laws of Erehwon are a system of practical reasoning. It is Erehwonian law that any act not specifically permitted or obligatory is forbidden and that only seven acts are permitted. This statement follows from, is justified by, the Erehwonian rules about the making of law and the fact that the law in question was made according to those rules. Raz's theory of law does not require that the legal system must be beneficial to the citizens of the state. Therefore it is possible, on Raz's view, for there to be a legal system that does not serve the interests of its citizens. Raz's view of rights and his view of legal systems are in tension. Raz holds that (core) rights, including (core) legal rights, are justified by an interest of the right-holder. He also holds that a legal system may fail to serve the interests of citizens. These two theses are in tension. If a legal system fails to serve the interests of its citizens, then, on Raz's theory of rights, it must fail to create rights. One must either reject the view that a legal system may fail to serve the interests of citizens or the view that (core) legal rights are justified by an interest of the right-holder. Cases like Erehwon are possible. It follows that a legal system may fail to serve the interests of the citizens and that one must reject Raz's theory of rights. Raz's theory implies that rights that do not protect interests, what one might call useless rights, are impossible. He thinks that rights are obligations justified by the fact that they protect the right-holder's interests. This is incorrect.

There is another response to the Erehwon case that can serve to bring out another feature of Raz's theory of rights. Up to this point, I have ignored one part of Raz's view. He holds that "every legal right is a legally recognized pre-existing moral right" (1984, 15). So Raz might assert that the Erehwon counterexample fails to bite because the six Erehwonian rights are not moral rights. This line of argument is implausible. It is implausible to hold that there is no moral right to talk, no moral right to walking, and no moral right to severe one's little left toe.

For the purposes of this book, this is all that needs to be said to defend the Erehwon case as a counterexample to Raz's view. But Raz's view that every legal right is a legally recognized moral right merits a brief digression. Raz is aware that many will object to his view of the relationship between legal and moral rights and considers some possible objections.

One kind of case which creates a problem for Raz's view that every legal right is a legally recognized moral right occurs when a person has a legal right to something which cannot exist without a legal system. Suppose that Ward fills out all the proper forms, pays all the proper fees, and meets all the legally specified conditions for obtaining a building permit. It would seem that Ward has a legal right to a building permit but that this cannot be a legally recognized pre-existing moral right because a right to a building permit cannot exist in the absence of a legal system. In reply, Raz argues that the law changes a person's interests. It can create new interests where none existed before. In Ward's case, Raz thinks that the law gave rise to a new interest (the interest in having a building permit) and then this interest was the sufficient reason for a moral right (the moral right to a building permit) which the law then recognizes and so creates Ward's legal right. Raz has adequately responded to this objection.

Another kind of case which creates a problem for Raz's view that every legal right is a legally recognized moral right occurs when a legal system creates a legal right to do wrong. The classic cases here would be those in which a legal system creates a right to harm members of a group. The Jim Crow laws which at least seemed to create a legal right for shop owners to refuse to serve blacks is one example. Let us assume that there is no moral right for shop owners to refuse to serve blacks. On that assumption it would seem that Raz is committed to denying that Jim Crow laws created legal rights. If one holds some relatively robust version of legal positivism, one will think that this view is implausible. (Roughly speaking, legal positivism is the view that "it is in no sense a necessary truth that laws reproduce or satisfy certain demands of morality, though in fact they have often done so" (Hart, 1994, 185–186). It is not clear that Raz's view on legal rights is consistent with his version of positivism but we need not enter that debate here.)

Raz considers this objection and it is best to reproduce his response in his own words.

> Suppose that in a certain country Parliament enacts a legal right to use contraceptives. Some people believe that there is no moral right to use contraceptives ... They recognize of course that Parliament in granting this legal right assumes otherwise. But they do not agree. Yet they think that Parliament's authority carries such moral force as to entail that once the legal right is granted people are morally bound to respect it and not to stop others from using contraceptives. On my account, strictly speaking this is not a case of a moral right. One's moral duty not to prevent the use of contraceptives which is the consequence of the law is not based on the interest of the right-holder, but on respect for the authority of Parliament. But since this is respect for Parliament's mistake about moral rights, and since its moral consequences are to give individuals all they would have had, had they a right to contraceptives, it is a natural extension of the concept to regard such legislation as conferring a (legal) right (1984, 17–18).

In the Jim Crow case, Raz would presumably hold that the Jim Crow laws did create legal rights because most people obeyed these immoral laws, the laws served the interests of white shop owners, and the laws gave the white shop owners "all they would have had, had they a right to" discriminate against blacks. So Raz holds that, strictly speaking, the Jim Crow laws did not create legal rights but it is a natural extension of the concept of legal rights to regard Jim Crow laws as conferring legal rights.

Many, including myself, will find this analysis of the Jim Crow case to be implausible. Many will think that it distorts the nature of these and many other immoral laws to hold that "every legal right is a legally recognized pre-existing moral right" (1984, 15). I know of no other interest theorist who adopts this part of Raz's view. Every interest theorist I know of holds the more straightforward view that Jim Crow laws create legal rights because the (immoral) interests of white shop owners serve to justify these laws or that these laws protect these (immoral) interests. But this is a weak criticism of Raz because he obviously accepts this view. Sometimes resolution of a philosophical problem becomes difficult because one person explicitly accepts implications of a view which others find implausible. One person's modus tollens is another person's modus ponens.

Leaving this disgression behind us, let us turn to consider the second objection to Raz's view. It seems to imply that rights must be justified by the interests of the right-holder. There are cases in which rights are not justified by an aspect of the right-holder's interests but by the interests of others. It is not plausible to hold that the judge has a right to impose sentence if and only if the judge's interest in imposing sentence is a sufficient reason for others to have a duty. It is the public's interest (or perhaps the interest of the victim of the crime) that justifies the judge's right to impose sentence.

As with the first objection to his theory of rights, Raz is aware of and responds to this second objection to his view. He notes that:

The rights of journalists . . . to protect their sources are normally justified by the interest of journalists in being able to collect information. But that interest is deemed to be worth protecting because it serves the public. That is, the journalists' interest is valued because of its usefulness to members of the public at large (1986, 179).

Another useful example offered by Raz is the right to a child benefit.

I, as a parent, have, in English law, a right to a periodic payment known as child benefit, which I receive because I am a parent and because benefiting me is a good way of benefiting my child. The right [to a child benefit] is justified by the fact that by serving the interest of the right-holder it serves the interest of some others . . . (1992, 133).

But, according to Raz, there are restrictions on this sort of justification of a right.

Other people's interests count for the justification of [a] right only when they are harmoniously interwoven with those of the right-holder, i.e., only when benefiting him is a way of benefiting them, and where by benefiting them the right-holder's interest is served (1992, 134).

93

In the case of the judge, Raz would hold that it is in the judge's interest to impose sentence. That imposing sentence is in the interest of the judge is a result of the way we have set up the office of judge and the penalties the legal system would impose on a judge who refused to impose sentences. It is also in the interest of other people that the judge impose sentence. To put the point another way, Raz's view is that it is the interest of the judge *as a judge* that grounds her right to impose sentence (even though, as noted above, it may not be in her overall interest), but what makes this interest important enough to impose one or more duties on others is the public interest in a system of judges that have and perform the duty to impose sentences. All of this seems plausible if a bit recherché. But it does not seem to be compatible with Raz's theory. According to Raz, X's well-being must be a *sufficient* reason for holding some other person to be under an obligation. It is not plausible to hold that the judge's interest alone, in the absence of the general public's interest, would justify the judge's right to impose sentence. Imagine that it was not in the public interest for judges to impose sentence. In that case, one would not set up a legal system that made it in a judge's interest to impose sentence. A judge's interest in imposing sentence is not a sufficient reason for the right to impose sentence.

Raz himself seems to acknowledge this in his discussion of group rights. He notes that Yassir Arafat has an interest in Palestinian self-determination. But he continues:

> Arafat does not have a right to Palestinian self-determination. Self-determination is a typical collective good. Its satisfaction imposes far-reaching demands on the life of whole communities. Arafat's interest by itself does not justify imposing such far-reaching duties on so many other people. So he does not have it, [i.e., the right to Palestinian self-determination] (1986, 207).

Neither Arafat's interest in self-determination nor a judge's interest in imposing sentence is sufficient to justify imposing duties on others. The same line of argument applies to Raz's examples of journalists and the child benefit. (Raz might also attempt to defend his theory by arguing that one must distinguish between the judge's overall interest and his interest as a judge. This is a version of the first response to the first objection to Raz's theory. This response was considered above.)

A defender of the interest theory might argue that the entire line of argument against Raz is flawed because it fails to appreciate a distinction between two ways of using the term "protect" when speaking of one relation protecting another.[2] This distinction was noted in Chapter 2. The example used there was the assertion that "a claim protects a liberty." This assertion could refer to

(i) a claim that protects the doing of the action which is the content of the liberty,

or it could refer to

(ii) a claim that protects the liberty itself.

---

[2] This objection was made by an anonymous reviewer.

94

The case discussed was "Laural has a claim against Gene that protects her liberty to go swimming." This could mean (i) that Gene has a duty not to do things which would interfere with Laural's swimming (e.g., draining her pool). On the other hand, it could mean (ii) that Gene has a duty not to extinguish Laural's liberty itself. Gene might have the power to extinguish the liberty, but it might be illegal for him to exercise this power. In this work, "a claim that protects a liberty" refers to (i).

Let us focus on the Siedman example above to illustrate how a defender of the interest theory might use this distinction to respond to my argument. Congress gave Siedman, in his role as chairman of the FDIC, a large set of rights concerning the disposal of the property owned by failed thrifts. Siedman did not want these rights because he felt that his rights and duties as chairman of the FDIC were already onerous. I asserted that the sufficient reason for the rights given to Siedman was not any of his interests but the interests of the public at large and therefore this case was a counterexample to Raz. One might argue that I assumed that the rights in question protect the powers themselves (i.e., the powers to dispose of the property) when in fact they protect the ability to exercise those powers (i.e., the ability to do the triggering acts of the relevant powers).

This objection is not persuasive. First, I have consistently used "protects" in sense (i) noted above. So I have argued that Siedman believes that he does not have an interest in exercising the powers Congress gave him. Second, noting this distinction is of no help to the interest theorist because neither Siedman's interest in protecting his ability to exercise the powers nor his interest in protecting the powers themselves is a plausible sufficient reason for the existence of the claims and powers that (together with other Hohfeldian relations) constituted his right to dispose of the property of failed thrifts. It is surely not either of these interests that justified Siedman's rights but rather the interests of the many people who stood to benefit from the orderly disposition of this property and the stability of the U.S. banking system. The same line of argument applies to the other examples discussed above. Reconsider my right, under U.S. law, to cut off my little left toe. I have neither an interest in the claim to cut off my little left toe nor an interest in cutting off my little left toe. The distinction between an interest in the doing of the action that is the content of a relation and an interest in the relation itself is of no help to an interest theorist.

Although he defends a protection version of the interest theory, Kramer has offered two arguments which might be used to defend Raz against the objections made above. First, he has argued that:

> a right . . . is *normally* advantageous. From that fact that a right is normally beneficial, however, we should not conclude that it is *invariably* so. On the one hand, each right protects some aspect of welfare or freedom that is usually desirable. On the other hand, some instances of the protection which a right provides can redound to the detriment of this or that particular right-holder (Kramer et al., 1998, 93).

Kramer might argue that Raz's distinction between an interest and overall interest and his distinction between core and derivative rights are unnecessary because an interest theorist need not hold that rights are invariably justified by the interest of the right-holder. Kramer might argue that the examples given above all fail because they are examples of exceptions the existence of which an interest theorist need not deny.

It is not clear that rights are normally advantageous. Although there are many advantageous rights, the analysis in Chapter 2 indicated that disadvantageous rights are a common, banal part of most rule systems. Recall cases such as my right to pay my debts and my right to grade my students' papers. In addition, it is not clear that the quote above from Kramer is consistent with his views stated in other places. As noted above, Kramer holds that

> Necessary but insufficient for the actual holding of a right by X is that the right, when actual, protects one or more of X's interests (2001, 28).

If protecting one or more of X's interest is *necessary* for the existence of a right, then it follows that rights invariably protect interests. However, one should not make too much of this interpretational issue. Kramer says that the quote above is a terse and approximate summary of the interest theory, so perhaps his final view is that the protection of interests is not necessary for the existence of a right.

However this interpretational issue is resolved, Kramer's view has implications that at least some will find to be counterintuitive. He holds that minimum wage laws create rights even if they have an adverse impact on some workers, those who would be employed at a rate lower than the legal minimum but whose skills are such that they are not employed when the minimum is enforced. This seems plausible. But Kramer then considers the case in which the minimum legal wage is set so high that it works against the interests of most workers. In this case, Kramer holds that the minimum wage law creates no rights. "When putative rights are generally detrimental to the people who hold them, they ought not be classified as rights at all" (Kramer et al., 1998, 95). Some will find this an odd implication of Kramer's view. Suppose that there is a minimum wage law that is generally beneficial. Angie is employed and is paid the minimum wage. On Kramer's view, she has a right to this wage. But then the law is changed in only one way—the specified wage is raised so high that the new policy is "generally detrimental" to most workers. Angie's skills (and/or luck) are such that she remains employed. Kramer's view is that she no longer has a right to the new higher wage. Her right vanished when it became based on a generally detrimental law. This is implausible. It is not plausible to hold that the changing of one number in a minimum wage law can cause the rights of those who remain employed to vanish. Angie's case is another example that shows that it is possible for rights to be generally detrimental to the people who hold them. Those who agree with me will see this as a reason to reject Kramer's view. However, because Kramer accepts this implication of his view, it will have no argumentative power against him.

There are two other problems with Kramer's view. First, some of the examples given above are rights that are generally useless and only exceptionally advantageous. The right to sever one's little left toe is such a right. This right is not normally advantageous. It is normally useless. Second, the claim that rights are normally but not invariably advantageous leaves the interest theorist open to the charge of making *ad hoc* exceptions merely to respond to apparent counterexamples. The claim brings the interest theorists very close to saying that rights are advantageous except when they are not. To avoid this line of attack, the interest theorist must do as Raz has done and present a theory of principled distinctions that explains how the apparent counterexamples to the view that rights are always advantageous can in fact be understood within a sophisticated version of the interest theory. Raz's distinctions, although unsuccessful, are the correct sort of move to make in this debate. Consider a choice theorist who, when confronted with the apparent counterexamples to the choice theory that will be discussed below, responded that a right *normally* protects the right-holder's choices but that from that fact that a right normally protects choices we should not conclude that it *invariably* does so. Surely an interest theorist would not be convinced by this line of thought. She would correctly argue that this move is *ad hoc* and that the choice theorist owes us a principled explanation of the apparent counterexamples.

Kramer's second response to the arguments made against Raz is similar to but distinct from Raz's core/derivative distinction. Suppose that there is someone, Alex, with odd preferences who asserts a legal right to be tortured. Alex asserts that legal system under which he lives gives him a legal claim that others not interfere with the voluntary acts of those whom he has authorized to torture him. Suppose that Alex is correct that these claims exist. Even in this case, Kramer asserts that an assertion of this right is "so deeply counter-intuitive as to seem ludicrous" (2001, 87). Kramer thinks that instead of calling this situation

> a gratuitously jolting and rather misleading fashion as a 'right-to-be-tortured', we can and should designate it as a 'right-to-be-unimpeded-in-pursing-a-voluntary-and-harmless-[to-others]-activity-even-if-that-activity-of-submitting-oneself-to-being-tortured-is-repugnant-to-most-people' (2001, 87).

Kramer thinks that all rights can be relabeled in this way. He thinks that "there is no canonical way of individuating or specifying the contents of any Hohfeldian elements" (2001, 86). He might well use this technique to try to respond to some of the objections raised above. He might say that the right to severe one's little left toe can be relabeled as (perhaps) the right to severe one's body parts. This right, he might argue, does protect interests, for there are cases in which severing one's body parts is in one's interest. Most people have an interest in cutting their finger nails every now and then. Chapter 5 will argue that there is one correct way to individuate rights and Hohfeldian elements. But even before that case is made, one can see that Kramer's views on his matter are flawed. First, it is not clear that Alex's assertions are deeply counterintuitive. Alex's preference structure is very different from that of most people. But if the claims asserted by Alex are indeed part of a legal system, then one might well hold that Alex has the right to be tortured. In fact, it would seem that such a right exists under the laws of most U.S. states. Another interest theorist might well argue that Alex does have a right to be tortured because it is in his interest to be tortured. Second, the move that Kramer makes in the quote above has one of the same problems found in Kramer's previous response to my objections—it renders his view *ad hoc*. Unless Kramer can follow Raz and provide a principled way to pick out the correct description of a right, then he is open to the charge that he simply picks a description for no other reason than that it allows him to avoid objections to the interest theory.

The arguments of this section lead to the conclusion that rights need not be justified by or protect the interests of the right-holder. Even if there were no actually disadvantageous rights, this would not show that they are impossible. But there are disadvantageous rights. Rights that are not in the interest of the right-holder are a common part of actual rule systems. Most people (everyone?) in the United States have legal rights which they would rather not have. Duty rights are probably the most common type of disadvantageous rights. It is possible to impose rights on an individual for the public good, even if it is not in her interest. A rule system can give a person a right that it is not in any of her interests. This would not, in general, be a practical way to set up an effective rule system. It would lead to unhappy right-holders and a mismatch between the right-holder's interest and the public interest. It would be an invitation to corruption and poor job performance. But these contingent and practical facts should not obscure the point that rights can be justified by things other than the interests of the right-holder.

The fundamental problem for any interest theory of rights is that there clearly are many rights that are not in the interest of the right-holder. All over the world there are rule systems which have grown bizarrely over centuries. These rule systems have layered rules over rules over rules and thus have created bizarre rights. Many rule systems are so complex that they create rights completely unanticipated by those who set up the rule systems. The U.S. tax code is only one of many examples. The rule systems of sports, clubs, corporations, universities, and other institutions are often so badly designed that many of the rules do not serve the interests of those who are subject to them. Many rule systems are designed by evil people who are intent on lining their own pockets and/or hurting those they dislike. In the face of this, it would be a miracle if all the rights set up by all these rules systems were all in the interest of all the right-holders. Interest theorists are thus driven to a series of more and more complex qualifications to their view. At a certain point, one should step back from these qualification and admit that the interest theory distorts the nature of rights.

4. HART: PROTECTED CHOICES

One influential theory of rights is the protection version of choice theory proposed and then partially retracted by Hart. Other versions of the choice theory have been proposed by others such as Montague (1980) and Steiner (1994), but Hart's version remains the classic. The objections noted below apply to Hart and all other choice theories. Hart's paradigm right is one we have considered before—a person's right to look over his fence at his neighbor's yard.

> [A] man has a right to look over his garden fence at his neighbor; he is under no obligation not to look at him and under no obligation to look at him. [The neighbor] has certain legal obligations or duties ... which preclude some, though not all forms of interference (1982, 166).

Using this right as a model, Hart suggests that rights are protected choices. I have a right to look over the fence at my neighbor's yard because I have a choice (the liberty to look over the fence and the liberty not to look over the fence) that is protected by duties not to interfere with these liberties. Because he suggests that rights are protected choices, he thinks it initially plausible to hold that every right contains a bilateral liberty—a liberty to do or not to do A.

Hart sees power rights as liberty rights of a special sort. They are liberty rights in which what one has the liberty to do is to change or not to change an Hohfeldian relation. Evelyn has the power right to change Joshua's duty not to drive her car into a liberty to drive her car because she has (1) the power to effect this change (by saying "You may drive my car."), (2) the liberty to effect this change, (3) the power not to effect this change, and (4) the liberty not to effect this change. She also has (5) claims against interference that protect these powers and liberties.

Hart sees claim rights as composed of claims and powers. On his view, one has a claim right when one has a claim and a power that give one control over the actions of others. In the paradigm case, according to Hart, one has (a) the power to extinguish the duty correlative to the claim, (b) the power to enforce the duty correlative to the claim by taking legal action, and (c) the power to extinguish the duty to compensate that arises from the failure to perform the duty correlative to the claim.

On Hart's view, three relations are necessary and sufficient for the existence of a right: (1) a liberty to do A, (2) a liberty not to do A, and (3) at least one claim that protects these liberties. The liberties give the right-holder a choice and the claim protects this choice. This theory is an interesting and plausible analysis of many rights. Hart has given the correct Hohfeldian analysis of liberty rights. On the other hand, Hart has not given the correct Hohfeldian analysis of claim rights. The arguments provided in Chapter 2 show that the other components of what Hart refers to as a "claim right" are part of a rights package that we often refer to as a single right.

One might think that Hart's theory is flawed because it cannot account for immunity rights in general. The point of an immunity is not necessarily to protect one's choices. It may well be to protect other things that a person wants. Suppose that you promise me that you will return one of my books to the library. Let us assume that I have a claim that you return the book and an immunity to your extinguishing this claim. It does not seem that any choice of mine enters into the Hohfeldian description of this situation. The point of my right that you return the book is not to protect any choice of mine but to protect other things I value—my good name among library personnel and my wallet (for I would have to pay a fine if you do not return the book).

Simmonds (Kramer et al., 1998, 227) and MacCormick (1977, 195) have noted that immunity rights are not counterexamples to Hart's view. Hart thinks that claim rights are power rights of a special sort. On his view, one has a claim right when one has a claim and a power right that give one control over the actions of others. Immunities are the alethic parallels to the deontic claims. It would, therefore, seem reasonable for Hart to have held that one has an immunity right when one has an immunity and a power right that give one control over the actions of others. In the paradigm case, he could have held that one has (a) the power right to extinguish the disability correlative to the immunity, (b) the power right to enforce the disability correlative to the immunity, and (c) the power right to extinguish the duty to compensate that arises from attempts to violate the immunity.

Hart himself thought that a choice theory would be unable to provide an account of certain specific immunity rights.

> The notion of a legally respected individual choice ... cannot be taken as exhausting the notion of a legal right: the notion of individual benefit must be brought in ... to supplement the notion of individual choice. Unless this is done no adequate account can be given of the deployment of the language of rights ... in the constitutional law of many countries by Bills of Rights, which afford to the individual protection even against the processes of legislation (1982, 189).

Hart cites examples such as "freedom of speech and of association, freedom from arbitrary arrest, security of life and person, education, and equality of treatment in certain respects" (1982, 190). Consider the disability of the legislature to remove certain procedural protections found in the criminal law, e.g., the right not to be subject to double jeopardy. Hart thought that a choice theory cannot account for this right. I have an immunity to the U.S. Congress removing my immunity to being prosecuted twice for the same crime. Furthermore, I have no choice in the matter. I cannot alienate this right. There is no act that I could do that would remove these two immunities.

Hart's theory is more powerful than he recognizes. Note that he held the elements (a), (b), and (c) are present in the paradigm cases of typical immunity rights. But, as Hart himself notes, there can be non-paradigm cases. He says that "the fullest measure of control [i.e., choice]" exists when (a), (b), and (c) are present but that "the right-holder will have less than the full measure of control if... he is unable to ... extinguish the duty" (1982, 183, quoting from the main text and from footnote 85). So Hart thinks there are some cases in which (a) is not present. In the case of the right against double jeopardy, I retain element (b), the power right to enforce the disability correlative to the immunity by taking legal action. Here is a choice that I have. The link between the choice and the right against double jeopardy is a weak one. Perhaps this link is too weak for Hart's liking. On the other hand, this may be a way for a choice theory to provide some account of the rights, which Hart thought could not fit into a choice theory.

However, the issue of immunity rights is resolved, there are several other problems with the view that rights are protected choices. First, as Wellman (1985, 65) has noted, Hart is unable to account for duty rights. He thinks that rights necessarily contain a bilateral liberty but duty rights contain only a unilateral liberty. A duty right occurs when a duty is protected by a claim. Consider the duty right to vote (which exists in those countries in which failing to vote is illegal). There seems to be no choice protected by the duty right to vote. If one has a liberty right to vote, as those in the United States do, then there is clearly a choice which the liberty right protects. In the U.S. legal rule system one has a permission to vote and a permission not to vote. These permissions are protected by claims. In the United States, one's choices concerning voting are protected by rights. In those countries where one has a duty right to vote, one's choices concerning voting are not protected. One has a duty to vote, and it is this duty, not a choice, that is protected by claims. Hart was aware of duty rights.

> Thus a policeman ordered to arrest a man might be asked "What right have you to arrest him?" and might well produce his orders as showing that he had a right to arrest (1982, 174).

Unfortunately, this right is a counterexample to his own theory. He never considers this possible objection to his view.

What might he say in response to the charge that duty rights are counterexamples to his theory? He might, of course, retract the police officer example and argue that there are no duty rights. He might argue that duty rights are merely obligations that we mistakenly call rights because many people want to perform these duties. But, as argued in Chapter 2, duty rights are rights in the most straightforward sense. They have exactly the same structure as liberty rights, power rights, etc. Duty rights are not aberrations. They are perfectly typical. It is implausible to deny that they are rights.

Another problem with Hart's theory is that it cannot account for disability rights. In Chapter 2, I argued that there are disability rights. One example was the disability right that you had (if you were a first-year faculty member) not to hold the office of tenure-giver. Here the right does not protect a choice but protects you from having to make choices you do not want to make. You do not demand this disability right because you have a choice you want to make. Rather, you have no choice.

THE CONCEPT OF RIGHTS

As a first-year faculty member you have a disability to give anyone tenure. This is true whether you want to give someone tenure or not. The waters are muddied because you would probably not demand this disability right if you wanted to sit on the tenure committee. Suppose you wanted to sit on the committee and someone, mistakenly thinking that you were a second-year faculty member, asked you to do so. You would be tempted to ignore the fact that you lack the power to give tenure and try to fake it. That you can attempt to deceive others into thinking that you have a power does not mean that you have a power. The fact remains that you have a disability to give tenure. Disability rights do not protect choices for there is no choice to be protected. Therefore, Hart cannot account for these rights.

A third problem with Hart's view is that it implies that those who violate the criminal laws of the United States do not violate the legal rights of their victims. Wellman's view has the same implication and is therefore open to the same objection. Both Hart and Wellman are aware that their views have this implication. Here is Wellman.

> Although the state's claim against the would-be rapist that he not rape a woman is a legal advantage to the woman confronting a potential rapist, it cannot stand at the center of any right of the woman not to be raped, because the law does not confer upon her any dominion concerning the criminal duty not to rape.[3]

The reason that the criminal law does not grant a woman a right not to be raped is that it is the state, not the woman, who has the power to file a charge of rape. If a woman is raped and the prosecutor refuses to file charges against the rapist, the woman cannot step in and file those charges herself. She could, on the other hand, file civil charges against her attacker. On Wellman's view, while civil law grants people rights against would-be attackers, criminal law does not.

This view is counterintuitive. Let us imagine a country whose legal rule system contains only criminal law. All legal actions in this imaginary country are between an individual and the state. Individual citizens as such have no power to bring legal actions. There is no civil law. On Wellman's view, such a legal rule system grants no legal rights. Pretheoretically, it is more plausible to hold that the legal rule system of this country does create legal rights.

The same point can be made by considering the actual U.S. legal system. Pretheoretically, it is odd to hold that the criminal law implies no right of a woman not to be raped. Consider how natural it would be for a woman to say of her attacker: "He violated my rights." One could hold that she is merely saying that the attacker violated her moral rights and/or her civil law rights. But that seems forced. It is more natural to hold that the woman turns to the criminal law and asks the prosecutor to file charges to uphold her right, *under criminal law*, not to be raped. This

---

[3]   *Real Rights*, p. 00.

description of the legal situation created by the criminal law is more plausible than Wellman's description.

Steiner considers the criminal law objection to the choice and will theories. He argues that "this criticism ... suffers from severely disabling circularity inasmuch as it simply presupposes the truth of the Benefit Theory ..." (1994, 66). Steiner is incorrect. The arguments in the previous two paragraphs do not presuppose the interest theory. The argument is that the ordinary language of rights favors the view that criminal legislation can create rights. On this issue, the interest theory is more in line with the ordinary language of rights than the choice or will theories.

The most serious problem with Hart's view is that if one holds that rights necessarily protect choices, then it seems that beings that cannot choose cannot have rights. If one assumes, as seems plausible, that human infants cannot choose, this implies that infants cannot have rights. If Hart's theory implies that infants do not have rights, this is an extremely serious objection to the theory. Suppose I kill two people—one an adult and the other an infant. It would be odd to hold that in killing the adult I violated a right that I did not violate in killing the infant. Moreover, we clearly do quite naturally speak of the rights of infants—an infant's right to a certain amount of food, to be free from abuse, etc. (MacCormick (1982) has pressed this objection.)

Hart holds that infants have rights but that their rights are exercised by others.

"Where infants or other persons not *sui juris* have rights, [the] powers [associated with the right] and the correlative obligations are exercised on their behalf by appointed representatives ..." (1982, 184, footnote 86).

On this view, X can have a right against Y that Y do A but the powers (a), (b), and (c) noted above are held by some other person, Z, who acts for X. In the case of infants, it would usually be the parents who act for the child.

This move comes at a great cost to Hart. It means that he must give up the theory of relational obligation noted above. On the view suggested to Hart, if X has a right against Y, Y's correlative obligation is an obligation to X because it is X's choices that are protected by the obligation. But if X is an infant who cannot make choices but rather has choices made for her by Z, then it seems that it is Z's choices that are protected by the right, not X's. So it would seem that parents have the right to make choices for their infants but that infants do not have rights. This is implausible.

A more straightforward problem with Hart's attempt to account for the right of infants is that it is perfectly possible for there to be an infant who has no one to act as her representative. (This shocking situation may actually exist for many infants in the developing world.) There is nothing that requires that every legal system assign a guardian to every infant. Hart's view implies that if a legal system were not to appoint a guardian for infants, then infants would not have any rights. That is implausible. The basic problem for Hart is that the structure of the rights of infants seems to be identical to the structure of rights of adults.

Before turning to Wellman's view, it is worth a brief pause to note that the interest theory has an implication structurally parallel to the choice theory's implication concerning what beings can have rights. The choice theory at least seems to imply that beings that cannot choose cannot have rights. The interest theory at least seems to imply that beings that do not have interests cannot have rights. The interest theory at least seems to imply that a human child born without a brain cannot have rights.

The hedging phrase "at least seems" is necessary for two reasons. First, a sophisticated version of the interest theory might have the resources to deny the apparent implication that a being without interests cannot have rights. For example, Kramer (2001, 48–49) holds that interest theory allows, but does not necessitate, that a being that lacks interests cannot have rights. Very briefly, he holds that membership in a species of right-holders allows a being to have rights even if it has no interests. We need not consider whether this argument is sound because it would turn on issues regarding species membership outside a theory of rights. Second, the interest theory is not fully complete unless it is supplemented with a theory of what it is to have an interest and which things can have interests. As Feinberg uses the word "interests," only beings with a conative life can have interests. But one can speak of something being in the interest of a plant, a building, an ecosystem, a species, and many other things. Some might hold that a certain amount of water is in the interest of a plant and that the pollution that turns historic buildings black is not in the interest of those buildings. We need not consider the issues surrounding the determination of the correct theory of interests.

5. WELLMAN: ADVANTAGED WILLS

Over the last fifteen years, Wellman has defended an extremely interesting version of the will theory of rights. Wellman's basic view is that:

> A ... right ... is a complex ... advantage to which the right-holder can appeal in the event of some possible confrontation with one or more second parties. It is [an] advantage, not necessarily because its possession is beneficial to the right-holder, but in the sense that it favors the right-holder's will vis-à-vis the opposing will of any second party (1985, 91–92).

Sumner suggests a similar theory of rights.

> In singling out liberties, claims, powers and immunities as normative advantages we are not of course denying that possession of them can make us worse off on particular occasions ... Instead, we are pointing to the fact that occupying one of these positions means having the rules ... on one's side *vis-à-vis* the occupant of the correlative position. [...] Whatever rights may be, everyone agrees that they too are normatively advantageous. Thus we may limit the materials out of which they are constructed to those Hohfeldian positions which are advantages (1987, 32).

Sumner incorrectly holds that rights must be constructed out of only liberties, claims, powers, and immunities. The packages of Hohfeldian relations that are rights may contain any of the relations. The view was defended in Chapter 2. The police officer's right to make a court-ordered arrest cannot be plausibly analyzed without a reference to the officer's duty to make the arrest. Sumner was also incorrect to assert that "everyone agrees" that rights are advantageous. On the other hand, Sumner notes that he is not using "advantageous" in the way that interest theorists do. His use of "advantageous" follows Wellman.

Philip Montague has developed another version of the will theory of rights.

> I am equating moral rights to morally significant permissions... This line of thinking is certainly similar in spirit to Wellman's "dominion" and Sumner's "autonomy within a domain" (2001, 271).

Although one can see the initial plausibility of providing an analysis of active rights in terms of morally significant permissions, such an analysis cannot provide an account of passive rights. Consider my right that you not hit me or my right that you stick your feet in Squam Lake. Attempting to fit passive rights into the model of morally significant permissions leads to philosophical contortions. It would be time-consuming to enter into a detailed discussion of the subtle differences between these three fascinating views. It is better to make a hard choice and focus on one of the three. Because Wellman has a greater body of work, we will focus on his view.

We can get a good picture of Wellman's theory by discussing his quote above in some detail. By saying that a right is a "complex" advantage Wellman indicates that he believes that only a set of Hohfeldian relations can be a right. No single relation by itself is sufficient to be a right. (His argument for this view was discussed in Chapter 2.) Wellman believes that every right is a set of Hohfeldian relations that may be broken down into two parts—the core relation(s) and the associated elements. The core relation "is logically central to the complex right because it and it alone, defines the essential content of the right" (1985, 81). Wellman holds that "to change the core in any way is to extinguish the old right and create a new and different right" (1985, 81). The core, therefore, serves to individuate rights. The core also determines whether the right in question is a claim right, a liberty right, a power right, etc. For example, if a claim is the core relation of a right, then the right is a claim right. The core of my right that Georgia State University pays my salary is a claim that Georgia State University pays my salary.

On Wellman's view, every right is complex because, in addition to its core, it contains some associated relations. These relations are associated with the core because they "distribute some sort of freedom or control to the possessor of [the] core" (1985, 93). The associated elements, taken as a group, give the right-holder freedom or control over the core relation. If the core of the right to look over one's fence at one's neighbor is a liberty to look over the fence, then the associated elements are those relations that give freedom and control over looking over the fence to the holder of this liberty. The associated elements in this right would include claims against interference, immunities to the extinguishing of the core liberty, and powers to seek damages if the core liberty is not respected.

Wellman's theory of an advantage is intended to avoid the problems that plague the choice and interest theories. Wellman, like Sumner and Montague, does not assert that a relation is advantageous when it is beneficial to the holder of the relation. Wellman agrees that there are rights that are not in the interest of the right-holder. Wellman does not assert that a relation is advantageous when it gives its holder a choice. He agrees that there are rights which do not protect choices. Instead, Wellman holds that a relation is advantageous when it favors the holder's will *vis-à-vis* the opposing will of a second party. This allows Wellman to account for duty rights. He offers the example of the right to scratch one's head. Let us assume that I have a duty right to scratch my head. I have the liberty to scratch my head but no liberty not to scratch my head. This duty right contains such associated relations as

> claims against others that they not prevent me from scratching my head..., powers to waive these claims, bilateral liberties of exercising or not exercising these... powers and my... immunity against other individuals that they not extinguish my liberty to scratch my head... (Wellman, 1997, 239).

These elements give me the freedom to scratch my head and control over the scratching of my head. They give me an advantage in a possible conflict of wills. I have an advantage in the event that I want to scratch my head and someone else wants me not to scratch my head. Wellman refers to having this combination of freedom-control, this way of being advantaged in a possible conflict of wills, as having "dominion" because the freedom and control that the right-holder possesses give one the power of governing, to a limited extent, the actions of others. A similar line of argument allows Wellman to account for disability rights.

Wellman conceives of the conferring of an advantage as something that necessarily involves a third-party. So every right has three parties—the right-holder, the person against whom the right holds, and a third-party to whom the right-holder can appeal to intervene if there is a conflict of wills between the right-holder and the person against whom the right holds. Wellman thinks that every right has three parties because for a right to exist there must be a third-party to whom the right-holder can appeal to for intervention if there is a conflict of wills. The right-holder is the person whose freedom or control is increased by the right. The person against whom the right holds is the person whose freedom or control is decreased by the right. The third person is the person to whom the right-holder can appeal to intervention if the person against whom the right holds fails to meet the obligations implied by the right. In contrast, Hohfeld and the justified constraint view hold that a right requires only two parties—the right-holder and the person against whom the right holds. The justified constraint view does not deny that many rights packages include a reference to a third party to whom the right-holder can appeal to for support in the case of a rights violation. But it sees this ability to appeal to a third party as a power distinct from the claim/obligation which is the right.

Wellman has developed a detailed and explicit theory of relational obligations. He claims that

> the concept of a relative duty [i.e., a relational obligation] is complex; it can and should be defined in terms of a duty together with the power of some second party to claim the performance of that duty (1999, 218).

According to Wellman, I have an obligation to you if and only if I have an obligation and you have the power to claim performance of that obligation. In the phrase "claim performance" the word "claim" is not used in the Hohfeldian sense. What then is it to claim performance of an obligation? According to Wellman, one claims performance when one "requests or demands performance of the duty [i.e., the obligation] and presents title to the duty-bearer [i.e., the obligation-bearer]" (1999, 218). Wellman's example concerns a colleague who wishes to move into a new office. Wellman promises to help his colleague move, but when moving day arrives, he decides that he would rather play golf. She claims performance and presents title by saying to him, "I insist that you help me . . . as you promised" (1999, 219). Because of his promise, Wellman has an obligation to help his colleague move. On his view, his obligation is to his colleague because she has the power to claim performance in this way. Claiming performance has moral force, on Wellman's view, because, although any breaking of a promise is the betrayal of a trust, the breaking of a promise after performance has been claimed also expresses contempt for the promise-holder.

In the next chapter, we will see that Wellman's theory contains several crucial insights. However, it also has several flaws. First, the idea of the core of a right is not sufficiently clear. As noted above, Wellman tells us that the core relation "is logically central to the complex right because it and it alone, defines the essential content of the right." Furthermore, "to change the core in any way is to extinguish the old right and create a new and different right." Consider once again a person's right to look over the fence at a neighbor's lawn. What is the core relation of this right? The liberty to look over the fence? The liberty not to look over the fence? The claim against the neighbor's interfering with attempts to look over the fence? The three relations appear to be individually necessary to having this right. The absence of any of these three relations would "extinguish the old right and create a new and different right." Indeed, Wellman himself seems to say as much. In his discussion of Hart's view, Wellman considers the right to look over the fence at a neighbor's lawn and claims that "neither an unprotected bilateral liberty nor a protective perimeter with no liberty to protect can properly be said to constitute a legal liberty-right" (1985, 64). Wellman agrees with Hart that "one must not ignore either the liberty or the perimeter" (1985, 63). Here it would seem that Wellman holds that the absence of either the claims (the perimeter) or the liberty would extinguish the right to look over the fence.

107

Wellman explicitly considers the issue of the identification of the core of a right. He claims that the problem of identifying the core "is *not* the problem of deciding which one of a given set of Hohfeldian [relations] constituting a right is the core of that right" (1985, 89). He believes that Hohfeldian relations do not come in predefined bundles from which one must pick out the core. Rather, rights are described and used in non-Hohfeldian terms and one must examine these situations in which rights are used to determine what the core is. He provides the example of the right to marry. One is never, in the law or in the actual use of the language of rights, given a list of Hohfeldian relations in this right and asked to pick out its core.

It is true that in the common use of rights one is never given a set of relations in a right and asked to pick out the core. However, it is appropriate, in the evaluation of a philosophical theory of rights, to ask for a clear understanding of a technical concept, in this case the concept of the core of a right. Picking out the core of a right is not something any lawyer will need to do. But, given that Wellman has introduced the concept of the core of a right, it is appropriate to ask if he has introduced a clear concept. The previous discussion shows that he has not. His appropriately stipulative definition of the phrase "the core of a right" does not clearly define the concept because it does not allow us to determine which of the set of relations in a right is the core. Because he is providing a philosophical theory of rights, Wellman must provide a solution to "the problem of deciding which one of a given set of Hohfeldian [relations] constituting a right is the core of that right."

A related problem with Wellman's theory concerns his answer to the question: Is the core of a right always one relation, or can the core be composed of more than one relation? This question is a natural one to ask as one seeks clarity concerning the concept of the core of a right. Wellman considers this question but his answer is not clear. He says that "the core is always a single Hohfeldian [relation], although sometimes a complexly defined relation" (1985, 84). In other places, Wellman asserts that set of relations can be at the core of a right. When considering a child's right to protection from harm, he asserts that "its core consists of a *set* of ethical claims ... "(1984, 446, emphasis added). Perhaps the answer to this puzzle is to be found in the notion of a "complexly defined relation." Unfortunately, Wellman never explicates this notion. He does provide an example. He thinks that the core of my liberty right to look over my fence is the bilateral liberty to look or not to look over my fence. This is confusing because a bilateral liberty is composed of two liberties—the liberty to look over the fence and the liberty not to look over the fence. Wellman follows Hohfeld on this issue. Consider his explicit definition of a legal liberty.

X has a legal liberty in fact of Y to some kind of act A if and only if X does not have a legal duty to Y not to do A (1985, 40).

Wellman, Hohfeld and the neo-Hohfeldian analysis all define "a ... liberty as the absence of a contrary ... duty" (1985, 40). He uses the singular article "a" in both these quotes. If *a* liberty is the absence of *a* contrary duty, then a bilateral liberty is a rights-package consisting of two unilateral liberties. Wellman needs a clear theory of the individuation of liberties. Is a bilateral liberty one relation or two? Sometimes Wellman holds that a bilateral liberty is one relation but in other places he holds views which imply that it is two. The lack of clarity about bilateral liberties leads to a lack of clarity in the notion of the core of a right.

Wellman also considers my right to scratch my head.

> My legal right to scratch my head now has at its core my legal liberty to scratch my head. The other half of Hart's bilateral liberty is not part of the core of *this* right, although it would belong in the core of my right to scratch or not scratch my head...(1997, 239).

On Wellman's view, at this moment I have three distinct rights. One of them, my right to scratch my head, has as its core a single liberty to scratch my head. The second, my right not to scratch my head, has as its core a single liberty not to scratch my head. The third right, my right to scratch or not to scratch my head, has as its core two Hohfeldian liberties. There is nothing strictly false in this description of the situation, but it is not as clear as the justified-constraint analysis of it. My liberty right to scratch my head is a package of Hohfeldian elements composed (at least) of two liberties and a set of claims.

A third problem with Wellman's view is that it implies that those who violate the criminal laws of the United States do not violate the legal rights of their victims. As we saw in the discussion of Hart's view, this is a serious problem for any theory of rights.

The final problem with Wellman's view is that it implies that infants do not have rights. Wellman is aware that his view has this problem.

> Now if...agency really is necessary for the possession of rights...and if infants lack agency, as scientific psychology and everyday observation attest, then infants, at least, cannot be...right-holders (1995, 113).

In addition to being aware of the problem, Wellman is aware of its seriousness.

> I recognize that this conclusion is highly counterintuitive. Indeed, when John Kleinig first pointed out to me that this is an implication of my conception of a right, I suffered a period of intellectual and emotional crisis. How could I avoid this monstrous conclusion? (1995, 113–114).

Wellman is also aware that infants are not the only human beings who, on his view, lack rights. He holds that the rights of those whose mental capacities, and therefore their agency, are diminished by age, disease or genetic abnormality have rights in proportion to their agency (1995, 130–132). Those whose mental capacities are diminished to the level of an infant lack rights entirely. One needs to be careful here. Wellman is *not* committed to the view that it is morally permissible to kill, assault, maim, etc. infants. Furthermore, he is *not* committed to the view that the relational obligation to an adult right-holder not to kill the adult right-holder is more morally important that the non-relational obligation not to kill an infant. He is merely committed to the view that killing, assaulting, etc. infants does not violate their rights. He is not committed to the view that killing, assaulting, etc. infants is morally any less serious than killing, assaulting, etc. an adult.

This view is counterintuitive for three reasons. First, the view that infants do not have rights conflicts with the settled law of all jurisdictions in the Anglo-Saxon world. "[I]t is manifest that [infants] have legal rights recognized and easily enforced by the courts" (Feinberg, 1980, 163). Second, the view implies that the moral reasons we have for not killing an infant are different from the moral reasons we have for not killing a typical adult. Wellman must assert that, although the reasons we have to refrain from killing an infant are just as strong as the reasons we have to refrain from killing a typical adult, the reasons are not the same. According to Wellman, we may cite the rights of an adult as a reason not to kill her but we cannot cite the rights of an infant as a reason not kill him. Third, the view that infants do not have rights is radically at odds with the ordinary language of rights. The over-whelming majority of competent speakers of English not only reject but recoil from the view that infants do not have rights.

How does Wellman respond this "monstrous" implication of his view? First, he holds that if we hold that infants have rights we

> lose much of the practical significance of rights. What is most important about right is the special status, legal or moral, that they confer upon their possessor in some potential confrontation with some second party (1997, 30).

In part, this response is dependent on Wellman's own theory. One who for independent reasons rejects the view that "what is most important about rights is the special status, legal or moral, that they confer upon their possessor in some potential confrontation with some second party" will not be moved. But the first part of the quote above provides a theory-independent reason to reject the view that infants have rights. If it were true that any theory of rights which implied that infants have rights also lost "much of the practical significance of rights," this would be a reason to hold that infants do not have rights. It might not be a weighty reason. One might feel that the view that infants have rights is so central to our moral experience that it would be better to hold that rights have no practical significance. In Chapters 5 and 7, we will see that the justified-constraint theory allows us to see the practical significance of rights and hold on to the view that infants have rights. We will see that the practical significance of rights is that they reflect the view that individuals are the source of obligations.

Wellman has another response to the "monstrous" implication of his view. He recognizes that a "moral theory must conform to those considered moral judgments that stand firm under criticism and must give way before any clear cases incompatible with it" (1995, 121). The evaluation of a moral theory is a comparative matter. One considers the defects of a view in comparison with the defects of alternative views and selects the view whose defects are the least serious. Wellman is in full agreement with this. Wellman believes that the defects of all other theories of rights are more serious than the defects, no matter how monstrous, of his view. Given the nature of Wellman's response to this objection, my response to it must wait until I have presented my own theory of relational obligation. I will argue that the defects of Wellman's view are more serious than the defects of the justified-constraint view. This argument can only be presented after the justified-constraint view is fully on the table.

6. SUMNER'S THEORY-BASED ARGUMENT FOR THE CHOICE/WILL THEORY

Sumner has offered a unique and interesting argument for the choice or will theory. Sumner considers the debate between the interest and choice/will theories of rights.

> How are we to decide between them? One obvious way of comparing them is in terms of their extension: what they include and exclude as genuine instances of rights. We might say, in general, that a conception of a concept is extensionally adequate when it includes every item which seems pre-analytically to be an instance of the concept and excludes every item which does not. It would then count in favour of a conception of a right that it draws the boundary between rights and other things on more or less the right place, and against a conception that it draws it in the wrong place (1987, 49–50).

(Sumner classifies Wellman's theory as a version of the choice theory.) Sumner then reviews the extensional adequacy of both the choice/will and interest theories. As we have, he notes that both theories seem to be open to counterexamples.

> It is evident from these disputes that for each of the competing conceptions there are both easy cases of rights which it can readily accommodate and hard cases which it can accommodate only by dint of some delicate manœuvring. [...] The result of these extensional skirmishes is therefore essentially a stand-off (1987, 51).

There is a great deal of truth in Sumner's views. This presentation of the concept of extensional adequacy is felicitous. Extension adequacy is indeed an important consideration in debates between alternative theories of a concept. We have relied heavily on extension adequacy in our discussion of alternative theories of rights. Sumner's discussion of the extensional adequacy of the choice/will and interest theories is flawed in some respects. But those flaws are minor and it would not be profitable to examine them. The essential point is that Sumner's final conclusion on this issue is correct. The extensional skirmishes between these two theories have led to a stand-off. However, Sumner overlooks the justified-constraint theory of rights. This theory is extensionally superior to both the choice/will and interest theories.

111

In the end, Sumner defends a Wellman-like version of the choice/will theory. Since he does not reach this conclusion on extensional grounds, he must defend his view in some other way. Sumner correctly notes that in addition to extensional adequacy there is another way to choose between competing conceptions of a concept.

> We ... have a further standard of theoretical adequacy in terms of which we can compare the merits of the two conceptions [of rights]. We are seeking a characterization of natural rights theories which, among other things, illuminates the important lines of division between them and our other theoretical options. Whereas the requirement that such theories contain some conception of rights is trivial, the selection of a particular conception may not be trivial. Since the two alternatives are not extensionally equivalent they are bound to yield different maps of the theoretical terrain. If one of these maps identifies more significant theoretical boundaries than the other, and if it seems advisable to use the concept of a right to mark these boundaries, then we will have good reason for preferring the conception which yields that map. Now it seems to me that the map generated by the choice conception does identify more important theoretical boundaries ... (1987, 96–97).

Theoretical adequacy is, for the reasons Sumner indicates, an appropriate standard by which to judge theories of concepts. However, there are two important caveats that Sumner overlooks.

First, theoretical adequacy is a criterion that is secondary to extensional adequacy. It would go too far to assert that extensional adequacy is lexically prior to theoretical adequacy. Intellectual matters are not that simple. However, a theory of rights that has serious extensional adequacy problems cannot be accepted even if its theoretical merits are numerous and important. Theoretical adequacy is a good reason to prefer one theory to another only if the competing theories are roughly comparable when it comes to extensional adequacy. If one does not give extensional adequacy a significant priority over theoretical adequacy, one runs the risk of ceasing to defend a conception of the concept in question and starting to create a concept for one's theoretical purposes. In this work we seek the best theory of rights. The best theory of rights must, in the main, be a theory of rights as they are ordinarily understood. There is no guarantee that rights as they are ordinarily understood will be as theoretically useful as philosophers would like them to be. Philosophers can certainly hope that rights as they are ordinarily understood are able to do theoretical work that is important to philosophers. But wishes do not make reality. Philosophers must remain open to the possibility that no extensionally adequate conception of rights is theoretically useful. For this reason, theoretical adequacy must give way to extensional adequacy in the evaluation of competing theories of rights.

Second, Sumner's characterization of theoretical adequacy is too narrow. Drawing important theoretical lines in appropriate places is an important part of theoretical adequacy but only a part. In addition to drawing appropriate theoretical lines, one analysis of a concept is theoretically superior to another to the extent that the former solves or illuminates theoretical problems which the later does not. In Chapter 6, we will see that the justified-constraint theory of rights allows us to understand the nature of rights conflict. In Chapter 8, we will see that it allows one to solve the problem of the rights of past and future generations. All else being equal, the justified-constraint theory of rights is superior to any other theory of rights that fails to illuminate the nature of rights conflict and the rights of past and future generations.

Why does Sumner think that the choice/will theory is superior to the interest theory in terms of his notion of theoretical adequacy? His argument moves in three steps. First, he holds that on the choice/will theory of rights the function of rights is to protect autonomy while on the interest theory the function of rights is to protect welfare.

> The basic difference between the two conceptions lies in the normative function which they assign to rights. On the interest conception that function is the protection of some aspect or other of the right-holder's welfare. [...] Thus, for example, certain basic interests of individuals might best be served by conferring on them claims to the protective services of others which they have no power to alienate, whether temporarily (by waiving them) or permanently (by relinquishing them). Since the interest conception will count such claims as rights, there are no internal connections on this model between rights and such values as autonomy, self-determination, and freedom (1987, 97).

(Sumner fails to note the distinction between the protection and justification versions of the interest and choice theories. While this makes his presentation less clear that it might have been, it does not weaken his argument.) Second, he asserts that the distinction between considerations of autonomy and considerations of welfare is an important theoretical line, a line worth drawing.

> Since it is possible to build a moral theory around either the value of individual welfare or the value of individual autonomy, it is also worth marking the boundary between these theoretical options in some emphatic way (1987, 98).

Finally, he argues that the best way to draw the line between considerations of autonomy and considerations of welfare is to use rights talk to refer to considerations of autonomy.

> If we adopt the model of rights as protected choices then we can assign a distinctive normative function both to rights and to those moral theories which, in one way or another, take rights seriously. We can say that to regard individuals as having certain moral rights is to regard them as being autonomous within the domains specified by the contents of the rights (1987, 98).

As Sumner notes, there is a problem with this argument. A defender of the interest theory will surely assert that if we adopt the model of rights as protected interests, then we can assign a different distinctive function to rights. A defender of the interest theory can hold that the function of rights is to protect interests. Sumner puts the matter very nicely.

> To see the ways in which our conceptual resources might be utilized consider the following three grounds for the imposition of constraints: (1) the protection of individual autonomy, (2) the protection of individual welfare, and (3) the general welfare. [...] On the interest conception of rights the duties in both (1) and (2) have corresponding rights while the duties in (3) do not. [...] On the choice conception, by contrast, the duties in (1) have corresponding rights while the duties in (2) and (3) do not (1987, 100).

On Sumner's view, if we adopt the interest theory of rights, then "we have no obvious resources for marking the distinction between (1) and (2)" (1987, 100). On the other hand, he holds that if we adopt the choice theory of rights and lump (2) and (3) together as far as rights are concerned, we have other conceptual resources to mark the distinction between (2) and (3). In particular, he argues that we have the concept of a relational duty, of an obligation *to* someone. He holds that we should use rights-talk to refer to (1), relational-obligations-talk to refer to (2), and utility/goals-talk to refer to (3). As we will see in the next chapter, the justified-constraint theory of rights, like the interest theory, holds that the duties in both (1) and (2) have corresponding rights while the duties in (3) do not. Sumner's objections to the interest theory are also objections to the justified-constraint theory.

There are several problems with Sumner's theory-based argument. The first problem is that the interest and choice/will theories are not extensionally equivalent. Although there are extensional problems with both theories, one particular problem with the choice theory is much more severe than any extensional problem with the interest theory. As Sumner acknowledges, the choice/will theory implies that human infants do not have rights (1987, 203–205). As Wellman noted, this implication is "monstrous." It is extraordinarily counterintuitive. The choice/will theory also implies that the criminal law creates no rights. This is also very counterintuitive. The interest theory is open to counterexamples such as rights to property that is literally more trouble than it is worth and a judge's right to impose sentence. These extensional problems with the interest theory are much less serious than the choice/will theory's problem with the rights of infants. As MacCormick (1982) has argued, implying that human infants have rights is almost a necessary condition for an adequate theory of rights. The view that the criminal law creates rights is very plausible.

To respond to this objection to his view, Sumner is obliged to do some of the "delicate manœuvring" in the theoretical realm that is similar to the extensional maneuvering that we see in the extensional arguments for and against the interest and choice theories. Sumner argues that while human infants do not have rights, we have obligations *to* infants. On Sumner's view, while my infant son has no right that I not beat him, I have an obligation to him not to beat him. The problem with this move is that there is no evidence to support it in our ordinary language of rights. It is extensionally inaccurate. In fact, Sumner is forced to draw a distinction that is explicitly denied in ordinary discussions of infants' rights. It is clear that my infant son would have a civil cause of action against me were I to beat him. Moreover, this action would be framed in terms of my violation of his rights. The distinction between rights and relation obligations would not be drawn. Any lawyer would hold simply that human infants have legal rights, but Sumner must deny that this is so. Sumner's argumentative move seems to be motivated only as a response to a problem with his theory of rights.

The theoretical maneuver of separating relational obligation and rights has other extensional costs. The cases with which we began this chapter show that in ordinary language relational obligations are thought to imply rights. Sumner is committed to the extensionally counterintuitive view that X can have an obligation to Y without Y having a right against X. Since Sumner correctly holds that claims are relational obligations, he is committed to the counterintuitive view that X can have a claim against Y that Y do A without having a right that Y do A. This flies in the face of the close link between claims and rights noted by many, including Hohfeld and Feinberg. We have seen that Feinberg's theory is flawed because it holds that having a claim is a necessary condition for having a right. But Feinberg's work shows that having a claim is a sufficient condition for having a right.

What of Sumner's claim that if we adopt the interest theory of rights "we have no obvious resources for marking the distinction between (1) and (2)?" (1987, 100) It is incorrect. It is easy to mark this distinction. In fact, Sumner admirably draws the distinction without the use of the term "rights." In the material quoted above he draws the distinction between "(1) the protection of individual autonomy, (2) the protection of individual welfare." To mark Sumner's distinction one can merely say that rights are justified in different ways. Sometimes they are justified on autonomy grounds while in other cases they are justified on the basis of individual welfare. In fact, Sumner acknowledges as much.

> Were we to adopt the interest conception . . . we would be unable to use this important concept [i.e., rights] to safeguard this important value. We would, of course, still be able to distinguish between protecting individual welfare and protecting individual autonomy. But the distinction would be drawn with the domain of rights rather than between that domain and its neighbors (1987, 98).

The theoretical benefits of adopting the choice/will theory are slim. One is allowed to use the concept of rights to mark a distinction that can easily be marked with other concepts. The corresponding theoretical costs of adopting the interest theory are also slim. One cannot use the concept of rights to mark the distinction between those normative constraints justified by an individual person's welfare and those justified by an individual person's autonomy. But, as the previous sentence illustrates, this distinction is easy to mark in other ways.

Sumner is correct that it would be somewhat useful for philosophers if the concept of rights were to allow us to distinguish between (1) the protection of individual

autonomy and (2) the protection of individual welfare. However, the examination of the choice theory above shows that ordinary rights talk does not do that work. An extensionally adequate theory of rights will not do the theoretical work that Sumner would like it to do. Fortunately for philosophers, the English language offers other resources with which one can easily do that work. The theoretical case for the choice/will theory is weak. If the choice/will and the interest theories were extensionally equivalent, then an ability to distinguish (1) and (2) would be a small reason to choose the former over the later. However, the choice/will and interest theories are not extensionally equivalent. The interest theory is extensionally superior to the choice theory. Moreover, the justified-constraint theory of rights is extensionally superior to both the interest theory and the choice/will theory. The theoretical costs of the justified-constraint theories are small. It is time to turn to a defense of the assertions made in the last two sentences.

5.   Rights, Reasons, and Persons

It is now time to draw on the insights of Raz, Hart, and Wellman to develop the justified-constraint theory of relational obligation. Raz's example of the justification version of the interest theory contains insights crucial to this development, so it is best to begin with his view.

1. REASONS AND RELATIONAL OBLIGATIONS

As noted above, Raz holds that

X has a right if and only if other things being equal, an aspect of X's well-being (his interest) is a sufficient reason for holding some other person to be under an obligation.

One can form a justification version of either the choice or the will theory by substituting choice or will for interest in Raz's justification version of the interest theory. A justification version of the choice theory holds that

X has a right if and only if other things being equal, the protection of one of X's choices is a sufficient reason for holding some other person to be under an obligation.

A justification version of the will theory holds that

X has a right if and only if other things being equal, advantaging X's will in a particular case is a sufficient reason for holding some other person to be under an obligation.

No one holds either of these two views, but the fact that one can form these alternative sorts of justification theories of rights illustrates that there are two independent parts of Raz's analysis. The first part is the claim that having a right is a matter of how obligations are justified. The second part is the claim that a particular aspect of a person, her interests, is the feature that does the justifying. The justification version of the choice theory and the justification version of the will theory show that one can agree with Raz regarding the first part of his analysis but disagree with him regarding the second part. One can form other Razian theories by holding that other aspects, other features, of people justify obligations. One could also reject Raz's view that only one aspect of people justifies obligations. One could hold a justification version of an interest *and* choice view.

X has a right if and only if other things being equal, an aspect of X's well-being OR protecting one of X's choices is a sufficient reason for holding some other person to be under an obligation.

117

Furthermore, one could develop a justification theory that declines to specify a particular feature or features of persons. The justified-constraint theory takes this form:

X has a right against Y if and only if a feature of X is a reason Y has an obligation (or an impossibility).

On this view, an obligation or impossibility is relational, is *to* someone, when a feature of that person is a reason another has the obligation or impossibility.

Y's obligation (or impossibility) is to X if and only if a feature of X is a reason Y has an obligation (or an impossibility).

A fully descriptive name for this view would be "the neutral justified-constraint theory of rights" because it holds that a certain sort of justification of obligations or impossibilities, independent of any particular feature or features, is the crucial feature of rights. The fully descriptive name is cumbersome. For that reason, I have chosen a name that is shorter, "the justified-constraint theory of rights."

Consider some of the parallels and differences between Raz's view and the justified-constraint theory. If Julia has a right that implies an obligation, why, on Raz's view, is the obligation implied by that right an obligation to Julia? Because it is Julia's well-being that is the sufficient reason for the obligation. If Julia has a right that implies an obligation, why, on the justified-constraint theory, is the obligation implied by that right an obligation to Julia? Because it is a feature of Julia that is the reason for the obligation. The reason for the obligation is not some other feature of the world.

Both Raz and the justified-constraint theory hold that a relational obligation/impossibility is an obligation/impossibility that has a certain sort of justification. The disagreement concerns the exact sort of justification required for a relational obligation/impossibility to exist. Raz thinks that the justification of a relational obligation/impossibility must be in terms of a single feature of the right-holder, the right-holder's well-being. The justified-constraint theory holds that, as far as the concept of rights is concerned, the justification may be in terms of any feature of the right-holder. On the justified-constraint view, the right-holder's well-being is only one of many features of the right-holder that can serve as the justification of a relational obligation/impossibility.

The justified-constraint theory is a development of W.D. Ross' suggestion that

to say that we have a duty to so-and-so is the same thing as to say that we have a duty, grounded on facts relating to them, to behave in a certain way towards them (1930, 49).

In Ross, the concept of a duty being "grounded on facts relating to" a person is unexplicated. The justified-constraint theory provides such an explication. It rejects Ross' view that obligations to someone must be obligations "to behave in a certain way toward them." As noted in the discussion of Martin (Chapter 2), the example of your promise to stick your feet in Squam Lake is a counterexample to this part of Ross' analysis. On the other hand, the justified-constraint conception of rights, like Ross and unlike Raz, holds that the concept of rights places no restrictions on the features of a person, the "facts relating to them," that can justify the obligation/impossibility correlative to a right.

As discussed later in this chapter, on the justified-constraint conception of rights the concept of rights places no restrictions on the features of a person that can justify a right, but there are substantive restrictions. If one adopts the justified-constraint theory of rights, then, as far as the concept of rights in concerned, any feature of persons can justify rights. But from a substantive perspective, the assertion that some features justify rights leads to preposterous conclusions. The justified-constraint theory of rights holds that concept of rights places no barrier to the assertion that brutal murderers have a moral right to be given $1,000 per month for life. The view that murderers have such a moral right is substantively absurd. On the justified-constraint theory, the concept of rights places no barrier to the substantively absurd assertion that I have a moral right that you drink at least 10 gallons of Dr. Pepper a day.

There are some other differences between Raz's view and the justified-constraint theory. For reasons discussed in Chapter 4, the theory adds an explicit reference to impossibilities. For reasons to be discussed in Chapter 6, it removes the phrases "other things being equal" and "sufficient" from Raz's analysis. Finally, it uses the word "feature" instead of "aspect." This is merely a semantic change. I find the term "feature" more natural. Any reader who wishes to may substitute "aspect" or "property" for "feature" in all of what follows.

We need to be more precise about the sort of justification crucial to rights. What does it mean to say that a feature of a person is a reason for an obligation/impossibility? Once again, Raz's view contains the seeds of the answer.

> An interest is sufficient to base a right on if and only if there is a sound argument of which the conclusion is that a certain right exists and among its non-redundant premises is a statement of some interest of the right-holder (1986, 181).

This is a natural analysis because one classic sort of reason, one classic sort of justification, is an argument. If I want to justify a claim, I attempt to provide an argument for it. Therefore, it is plausible to analyze reasons for obligations and impossibilities in terms of arguments. Following Raz, an initial version of the justified-constraint view is:

> A feature, F, of X is a reason for Y's obligation/impossibility if and only if there is a sound argument of which the conclusion is that Y's obligation/impossibility exists and among its non-redundant premises is a statement that X is F.

As will become apparent in Chapter 8, being more specific about the sound argument referred to in this analysis will allow us to solve the puzzle of the rights of the dead and future generations. The justified-constraint theory of rights holds that:

A feature of X is a reason for Y to have an S obligation/impossibility if and only if
there is a sound non-redundant instance of the following argument form:

1. X is F.
2. If X is F, then Y has an S obligation/impossibility to do A.
3. Therefore, Y has an S obligation/impossibility to do A.

Let us call the argument form above the "key argument form." From this view and the conclusion of Chapter 3, it follows that

X has an S right against Y that Y do A if and only if
there is a sound non-redundant instance of the following argument form:

1. X is F.
2. If X is F, then Y has an S obligation/impossibility to do A.
3. Therefore, Y has an S obligation/impossibility to do A.

On the justified-constraint theory, a right is an obligation or impossibility that is justified by a feature of a person. To see someone as a right-holder is to see them as a source of obligations and impossibilities. Hereafter, let us focus on obligations. The analysis will apply, *mutatis mutandis*, to impossibilities.

There is one respect in which the first version of the justified-constraint view is preferable to the second version. The first is more metaethically neutral than the second. On a certain metaethical view, ethical particularism, the second premise of the key argument form is always false. Ethical particularists hold that there are no moral rules. Here is Jonathan Dancy's statement of the view.

It is not the case that where my reasons for calling an action good are that it has properties *ABC* I am committed to calling any other action which has the properties *ABC* good (1981, 377).

Because ethical particularists hold that the second premise of the key argument form is always false, their view plus the justified-constraint analysis of rights implies that ethical particularists are committed to the view that there are no moral rights and no legal rights. For the reasons noted in Chapter 3, one generally would like one's theory of rights to be as metaethically neutral as possible. But the advantages of the second analysis (which will not become fully apparent until Chapter 8) are such that it is worth paying the cost in reduced metaethical neutrality. I have always found the usual objections to ethical particularism convincing, so I am not disturbed that the justified-constraint theory implies that one must reject either ethical particularism or rights. (For a good review of these objections, see Shafer-Landau (1997).)

A right exists when both premises of the key argument form are true. The truth of the first premise depends, in the usual way, on the facts about X, the subject of the right. On the other hand, the truth of the second premise is not determined by facts about X and Y. The "S" in the second premise of the key argument form indicates that the truth of the second premise depends on the rules of the rule system in question. Consider the following instance of the key argument form.

1. Tim is over 18.
2. If Tim is over 18, then the state has a legal obligation to provide him a minimum income.
3. Therefore, the state has a legal obligation to provide him a minimum income.

Whether or not the first premise is true depends on a fact about Tim, his age. The truth of the second premise does not depend on how old Tim is. It is the rule system S that determines whether the second premise of the key argument form is true or false. The second premise of this instance of the key argument form is true in some legal rule systems and false in others. Some European states have a minimum income law. The United States does not. This same point can be made without reference to a legal system. Suppose that Al is in fact male and Alice in fact has an obligation to meet Ben for lunch (because she promised him that she would). It does not follow that the second premise of the following instance of the key argument form is true.

1. Al is male.
2. If Al is male, then Alice has a moral obligation to meet Ben for lunch.
3. Therefore, Alice has a moral obligation to meet Ben for lunch.

Whether the conditional is true or false does not depend on the truth-values of the antecedent and consequent of the conditional but on the rules of the moral rule system. The second premise of the key argument form naturally leads one to wonder about complex matters in the philosophy of law. What does it mean to say that a rule is part of a normative system? What is a rule? What is the authority of a normative system? Many thinkers (such as Raz) have considered these questions but the answers to them will not have an impact on the issues under consideration in this book so we can set them aside.

Suppose that Sue promises Bob that she will give him $50 and that, ignoring many complications, the moral rule system contains the following statement:

If X promises to give Y $50, then X has a moral obligation to give Y $50.

Because of her promise, Sue owes Bob $50. Bob has a right that Sue pay him $50. A sound argument leading to the conclusion that Sue has an obligation to pay Bob $50 would look like this:

1. Bob is a person who was promised $50 by Sue.
2. If Bob is a person who was promised $50 by Sue, then Sue has a moral obligation to give Bob $50.
3. Therefore, Sue has a moral obligation to give Bob $50.

The first premise refers to a feature of Bob—that he was promised $50 by Sue. So Sue's obligation is *to* Bob and he has a right to $50 from her.

121

The undergraduate catalog of Georgia State University states: "Students will normally satisfy the curricular degree requirements of the catalog in effect at the time they enter Georgia State University . . . ." It then states: "Students may choose to satisfy the curricular degree requirements of a later catalog . . ." (2005, 67). There is a form that must be signed by the student's advisor for a student to change catalogs. Suppose that Cynthia goes to her advisor with a change of catalog form. According to the Georgia State rule system, the advisor has an obligation to sign the form. Here is a sound argument for this obligation.

1. Cynthia is a student at Georgia State.
2. If Cynthia is a student at Georgia State, then Cynthia's advisor has a Georgia State obligation to sign Cynthia's change of catalog form.
3. Therefore, Cynthia's advisor has a Georgia State obligation to sign Cynthia's change of catalog form.

The existence of this argument implies that the advisor's obligation is to Cynthia and that Cynthia has a right that the advisor sign the form. A case like this came to my attention when a particular advisor thought that it was not wise for a particular student to change catalogs. But, according to the Georgia State's rule system, a student has the right to change catalogs even if everyone thinks it is unwise to do so, and therefore, whether he thinks it is wise or not, the advisor has an obligation to sign the form. This is an implication of the rule that "students may choose to satisfy the curricular degree requirements of a later catalog." Of course, the student may well later regret her choice. The point of the form is not to gain the advisor's permission but merely to see that the advisor is informed of the change and that the student has been advised about the consequences of changing catalogs.

These examples might lead one to think that only features that relate two individuals can justify rights. Bob and Sue as well as Cynthia and her advisor have a relationship of one form or another. But this is merely an accidental feature of these two cases. Consider a country that passes a law which awards everyone with blond hair a monthly payment of $50. The feature of having blond hair is not one that relates two individuals but, in this odd legal system, this feature justifies a right.

Both the justification version of the interest theory and the justification version of the choice theory can be presented using the key argument form. The justification version of the interest theory would assert that the key argument form is:

X has an S right against Y that Y do A if and only if
there is a sound non-redundant instance of the following argument form:

1. X has an interest in I.
2. If X has an interest in I, then Y has an S obligation/impossibility to do A.
3. Therefore, Y has an S obligation/impossibility to do A.

The justification version of the choice theory would assert that the key argument form is:

X has an S right against Y that Y do A if and only if
there is a sound non-redundant instance of the following argument form:

1. X has a choice whether to do A1, A2 ... or An.
2. If X has a choice whether to do A1, A2 ... or An, then Y has an S obliga-
   tion/impossibility to do A.
3. Therefore, Y has an S obligation/impossibility to do A.

For the reasons noted in Chapter 4, neither of these theories is adequate. But it
is instructive to see that both of them are, in an important sense, variants of the
justified-constraint theory of rights.

Both the justified-constraint theory and Raz's theory contain the term "non-
redundant." The term is necessary because some features of individuals that do no
justificatory work can be artificially inserted into an argument for an obligation.
Jane negligently bumps into Fred and this causes him to fall and hurt himself.
Suppose that, according to the laws of the state of Georgia, Jane has a Georgia
legal obligation to compensate Fred for the injuries she caused. There is a sound
instance of the key argument form which refers to a feature of Fred.

1. Fred is a person who was injured due to Jane's negligence.
2. If Fred is a person who was injured due to Jane's negligence, then Jane has a
   Georgia legal obligation to compensate Fred for his injuries.
3. Therefore, Jane has a Georgia legal obligation to compensate Fred for his injuries.

So far, so good. But suppose that Fred has a grandmother, Mabel. The following
argument for Jane's obligation to compensate Fred is also sound.

1. Mabel is the grandmother of Fred, who is a person who was injured due to Jane's
   negligence.
2. If Mabel is the grandmother of Fred, who is a person who was injured due to
   Jane's negligence, then Jane has a Georgia legal obligation to compensate Fred
   for his injuries.
3. Therefore, Jane has a Georgia legal obligation to compensate Fred for his
   injuries.

Were it not for the term "non-redundant" the justified-constraint analysis would
imply that Mabel has a right that Jane compensate Fred. Mabel's features are
redundant in the sense that they are not essential to the justification of Jane's
obligation. The second argument also refers to a feature of Fred. The phrase "who
is a person who was injured due to Jane's negligence" refers to Fred. Mabel's
feature does no justificatory work. The statement of Mabel's feature is tacked onto
the front of the statement of Fred's feature. Suppose that Sutton was standing five
feet from Fred at a party the night before he was injured. One could construct
an argument like the one above which referred to this feature of Sutton. Sutton
is not unique. Everyone alive is some distance or other away from Fred. There is

no sound argument for Jane's obligation that does not refer to the fact that Jane negligently injured Fred. A redundant instance of the key argument form occurs when one inserts an additional true statement that a person has a feature in front of the feature that is doing the justificatory work. One can easily determine whether a feature is redundant by removing it from the argument and seeing if the argument is still sound. If it is, the feature is redundant.

The justified-constraint analysis of rights can be brought into sharper focus by considering a possible misunderstanding of it.[1] Suppose that Brian is a pedophile. The fact that he is a pedophile seems to be a very good reason for Jeffery not to leave his daughter, Vinita, alone with Brian. It seems clear that Vinita has a right that Jeffery not leave her alone with Brian. The justified-constraint theory holds that the concept of rights places no restrictions on the features of a person that can justify rights. It might seem that the justified-constraint theory is committed to the view that *Brian* has a right that Jeffery not leave Vinita alone with him. If the justified-constraint theory had this implication, it would be a fatal flaw. But it does not have this implication. It merely asserts that the concept of rights places no restrictions on the features of a person that can justify rights. As far as the concept of rights is concerned, one could write a set of laws that implied that pedophiles, far from being imprisoned, have a right to a government payment of $1,000 per month. As far as the concept of rights is concerned, a state could decide that murderers have a right to special honors not given to more mild-mannered citizens. The justified-constraint theory does imply that it is conceptually possible for Brian to have a right that Jeffery not leave Vinita alone with him. It does not imply that Brian actually has this right. The justified-constraint analysis only has this preposterous implication when combined with preposterous substantive views about what features justify obligations. It is much more substantively plausible to hold that Vinita has a right that Jeffery not leave her alone with Brian.

The pedophile objection makes two mistakes. First, it overlooks the way that the justified-constraint conception of rights draws the line between conceptual and substantive questions. Second, it overlooks the non-redundancy qualification. There is an instance of the key argument form that refers to a feature of Brian.

A. 1. Brian is a pedophile.
   2. If Brian is a pedophile, then Jeffery has a moral obligation not to leave Vinita alone with Brian.
   3. Therefore, Jeffery has a moral obligation not to leave Vinita alone with Brian.

There is also an instance of the key argument form that refers to a feature of Vinita.

---

[1] I am indebted to an anonymous reviewer for raising this issue and furnishing the useful example discussed in this paragraph.

B. 1. Vinita is a child who might be harmed if left alone with Brian.
   2. If Vinita is a child who might be harmed if left alone with Brian, then Jeffery has a moral obligation not to leave Vinita alone with Brian.
   3. Therefore, Jeffery has a moral obligation not to leave Vinita alone with Brian.

The most plausible substantive view is that Jeffery's obligation not to leave Vinita alone with Brian is justified by the fact that Brian might harm Vinita. The natural substantive view is that his case is parallel to typical cases of the right not to be assaulted that is justified (depending on one's substantive views) by something like the fact that being hit generally is not in one's interest or the fact that the choice whether or not to be hit should rest with the person who might be hit. It is a concern for Vinita that justifies Jeffery's obligation. Given plausible substantive views, argument B is sound and argument A is not. From a conceptual perspective, there is nothing wrong with argument A. But it is substantively preposterous. If one holds the substantive view that it is the harm to Vinita that does the justificatory work, then the feature of Brian noted in argument A is a redundant feature. Argument A would not be sound if pedophiles did not harm children. If pedophiles were harmless, then premise 2 of argument A would be false. It is the harm to Vinita that does the justificatory work, so it is Vinita who has the right that Jeffery not leave her alone with Brian.

Note that on this matter, all justification theories of rights are on a par. There is no problem unique to the justified-constraint theory. Both the justification version of the choice theory and the justification version of the interest theory need to note the distinction between conceptual and substantive issues and the distinction between redundant and non-redundant features. Failure to do so will cause the theory to misunderstand the nature of the justification of rights and so be open to counterexamples such as the pedophile case. Raz's theory is a good illustration of this point. He holds that a person has a right if one of that person's interests is a sufficient reason for holding some other person to be under an obligation. Brian has a (sick) interest in sexually molesting children. On Raz's conception of rights, there is no conceptual barrier to holding that this sick interest is a sufficient reason for holding others to be under an obligation. On Raz's theory, it is conceptually possible for a state to pass a law that grants pedophiles a right to $1,000 per month. That is the correct view. Such a law is conceptually possible. However, it is substantively preposterous to hold that the interests that pedophiles have in performing pedophallic acts are sufficient reason for holding others to be under obligations. It is for this reason that both Raz's theory and the justified-constraint theory include the non-redundancy qualifier.

The justified-constraint theory allows us to see the partial truth in the justification versions of the interest, choice, and will theories. According to each, an obligation is relational when a feature of an individual grounds the obligation. On both views, the answers to the questions: "What sort of individual feature grounds relational obligations according to the correct moral theory?" and "What is it for an obligation to be relational?" are both conceptual. On the justified-constraint view, the first question is a substantive question and the second is a conceptual question. On the justified-constraint view, as far as the concept of rights is concerned, any sort of individual feature is the correct sort of feature to ground rights. The justified-constraint theory of the relational nature of rights is neutral on the substantive question. On the justified-constraint conception, the analysis of the concept of a right does not tell us what feature of individuals in fact grounds obligations. The two implicit theories of the relational nature of rights found in the choice and interest theories disagree on the substantive question of what feature of individuals actually grounds obligations. Their substantive suggestions—interests and choices—are both features of individuals. In this way, both theories confirm the justified-constraint analysis of the relational nature of rights.

Another way to make the same point would be to say that interest and choice theorists have drawn the line between conceptual and substantive matters in the wrong place. The conceptual/substantive distinction is theory dependent. The line between conceptual and substantive matters will be drawn differently by different theories of rights. Interest theorists think that a reference to the interests of the right-holder is part of the concept of rights. Choice theorists think that protection of choice is part of the concept of rights. The justified-constraint theory disagrees with both interest and choice theorists. It holds that the conceptual/substantive line should be drawn "further back" than they do.

With the distinction between conceptual and substantive views on the table, we are now in position to fully respond to Hart's disadvantageous immunities objection to the justified-constraint theory. Because it matches Hart's usage, let us temporarily return to discussing matters in Hohfeldian terms. According to Hart,

> even in the loosest usage, the expression "a right" is not used to refer to the fact that a man is . . . immune from *advantageous* change; the fact that . . . my neighbor has no power to exempt me from my duty to pay my income tax, do[es] not constitute any legal right . . . for me. An individual's immunity from legal change at the hands of others is spoken and thought of as a right only when the change in question is *adverse*, that is, would deprive him of legal rights of other kinds . . . or benefits secured to him by law (1982, 191).

In Chapter 2, we saw that this is an initially plausible objection to the justified-constraint view and that four responses diminish much, but not all, of its force. Let us call my neighbor "Donna" and assume that the taxes in question are U.S. income taxes. We noted that it would be better if one could show that the justified-constraint theory does not imply that my immunity to Donna's removing my duty to pay my income taxes is one of my rights.

It is clear that Donna lacks the ability to remove my duty. I have some sort of immunity to her removing my duty. However, one must not forget that duties and disabilities can be regarding a person without being with respect to that person. Who is the object of Donna's disability to remove my duty? On the justified-constraint view, we answer this question by considering the justification of her disability. Why does Donna have this disability? The answer is that the revenues of the U.S. government would drop drastically if individuals generally possessed the power to relieve their neighbors of their duties to pay their income taxes. If individuals possessed this power, they would certainly enter into mutually advantageous agreements to relieve each other of their duties to pay their taxes. The justification for Donna's disability does not refer to a feature of me. It refers to a feature of the U.S. government. Unless one inserts a redundant feature, there is no sound argument of the form:

1. George is F.
2. If George is F, then Donna has an S disability to remove George's duty to pay his income taxes.
3. Therefore, Donna has an S disability to remove George's duty to pay his income taxes.

I am not the object of Donna's disability. The U.S. government is. The justified-constraint theory implies that *if* Donna's disability were justified by a feature of me, then I would be the object of that disability and I would have a right. It also implies that, as far as the concept of rights in concerned, it is possible for my immunity to be a right. One could adopt substantially odd views that would imply that the instance of the key argument form above is sound. But this disability is not, as a substantive matter, justified in this way. It is the interests of the U.S. government that provide the justification for my immunity. When combined with plausible substantive views about the justification of Donna's disability, the justified-constraint theory of rights implies that her disability is regarding but not with respect to me and therefore that my immunity is not one of my rights.

One might wonder if the U.S. government has a right that Donna not extinguish my duty to pay my taxes. Obviously, if governments cannot have rights then the answer is "no." We will examine the question of whether states can have rights in Chapter 7. For the sake of argument, let us assume that they can. If governments can have rights, the justified-constraint theory implies that the U.S. government has a right that Donna not extinguish my duty. It is a feature of the U.S. government, its need for revenue, that provides the justification for Donna's disability. Consider the full form of the Hohfeldian situation.

The U.S. government has an immunity against Donna that Donna
not change
    George has a duty to the U.S. government that George pay his income taxes
into
    George has a liberty against the U.S. government that George not pay his income taxes
by saying "George, you don't have to pay your income taxes."

Donna's disability is with respect to the U.S. government because it is a feature of the government that grounds, justifies, is the reason for, her disability. Her disability is with respect to the U.S. government and regarding me. Recall the case of Evelyn, Joshua, and Steve from Chapter 1. Evelyn has both a claim against Joshua that Joshua not drive Evelyn's car and an immunity against Steve that Steve not change Joshua's duty not to drive Evelyn's car into a liberty to drive her car. In Chapter 1, Evelyn's case was used to show that, in second-order relations, the object of primary relation can be a different person from the subject of both the original and resulting relations. Steve is the object of Evelyn's immunity, but Joshua is the subject of the original and resulting relations. The case of my immunity to Donna's removing my duty to pay my income taxes is another case that follows this pattern. Steve/Donna has a disability with respect to Evelyn/the U.S. government to remove Joshua's/my duty. The best theory of the relational nature of rights indicates that the obligations and impossibilities correlative to rights are to the right-holder because it is a feature of the right-holder that justifies those obligations and impossibilities. It may be that the person who is the source of an impossibility is not the same as the person whose relations may not be changed. A feature of X may be the reason that Y does not have the possibility to change Z's relations. In that case, it will be X who has a right that Y not change Z's relations, and the right will merely be regarding Z.

The justified-constraint theory does not imply that my immunity to Donna's removing my duty to pay my income taxes is one of my rights. If one is using "my" to indicate the subject of the immunity, then it is not my immunity at all. It is the U.S. government's. In this case, the "my" in "my immunity" is misleading. When "my" is found in front of the name of a Hohfeldian relation, it usually refers to the subject of the relation. But in this odd case it only indicates that the disability correlative to the immunity is regarding me. I am not the subject of the immunity or the object of the disability. Like the pedophile objection, Hart's objection relies on a misplaced line between conceptual and substantive matters. It also relies on the tempting but incorrect views about the conceptual restrictions on the object and subject of second-order Hohfeldian relations we noted in Chapter 1. Once that distinction and those restrictions are correctly noted, the objection has no remaining force. In fact, the justified-constraint theory provides a clear account of why my immunity to Donna's removing my duty to pay my income taxes is not one of my rights. The relational feature of rights is missing. I cannot think of a disadvantageous immunity that does not follow a similar pattern. In general, it is possible that any disadvantageous immunity is a right. But, when one adopts plausible substantive views, it turns out that they are not actually rights.

2. SIMPLE AND COMPLEX JUSTIFICATION

There are two ways in which rights can be justified.[2] The first and most obvious pattern of justification occurs when some feature of a person is a sufficient justifica-

---

[2] My thanks to William Nelson for bringing this point to my attention and for useful discussions of it.

tion of another's obligation. The right not to be assaulted is justified by something like the fact that being hit generally is not in one's interest or the fact that the choice as to whether or not to be hit should rest with the person who might be hit. In this case, it seems that the feature of the individual is a sufficient reason for the obligation. The justificatory work is done by the feature of the individual. If one asks, "Why shouldn't I assault Tim?" a plausible answer is, "It hurts him." Let us refer to cases like this as cases of simple justification. There are many cases of simple justification. In addition to the right not to be assaulted, the right to private property, the right to travel, and the right to marry are cases of simple justification. In Chapter 6, we will see that simple justification is not as simple as indicated here. The problem of rights conflict will require an explication of the sense in which a feature of a person is a *sufficient* justification of another's obligation. Let us set that problem aside until Chapter 6.

There are cases that do not fit the simple justification pattern. Recall that, according to Raz,

> the rights of journalists . . . to protect their sources are normally justified by the interest of journalists in being able to collect information. But that interest is deemed to be worth protecting because it serves the public. That is, the journalists' interest is valued because of its usefulness to members of the public at large (1986, 179).

As noted in Chapter 4, it does not seem plausible to hold that, in the absence of the general public's interest, a journalist's interest is sufficient to justify the journalist's right to protect her sources. Imagine that it was not in the public interest for journalists to keep their sources confidential. In that case, one would not set up a legal system that made it in a journalist's interest to protect her sources. In this case there is a complex, two-step, pattern of justification. If one asks, "Why does this particular person not have to tell us where she got her information (when others do)?" then the answer is, "Because she is a journalist." The first step in the justification of the rights of journalists merely refers to the feature of being a journalist. Note that, at this stage, the answer, "Because it benefits the public interest" may not be true. In many cases, that a particular journalist withholds information about her sources will have no effect on the public interest, and in some cases it will be contrary to the public interest. Yet we still want to protect that journalist's right to protect her sources. Assuming that there is no doubt that the individual in question is a journalist, the next natural question is, "Why don't journalists have to tell us where they get their information?" Here we have moved to the next step in the justification of the journalist's right. The answer to this second question is, "Because the practice of allowing journalists to protect their sources is in the public interest." There are many cases of complex justification. A judge's right to impose sentence is a case of complex justification, and many feel that the right to free speech is another. It seems that the rights of public officials typically have a complex justification. The two patterns of justification

129

are not mutually exclusive. It is at least arguable that the right to free speech is a case of both simple and complex justification. Free speech is something that many individuals find valuable for themselves, and it is plausible to think that a practice of protecting speech is in the public interest. The distinction between simple and complex justification is not novel. The classic statement of this distinction is Rawls' "Two Concepts of Rules." As Rawls put it, one must note "the distinction between justifying a practice and justifying a particular action falling under it" (1999, 20). Simple justification of a right does not refer to a practice. Complex justification of a right does.

Overlooking the distinction between simple and complex justification can lead one to an objection to the justified-constraint theory of rights. One might hold that journalists have a right to protect their sources but that there is no feature of journalists that justifies this right because it is the interest of the public that does the justificatory work. On this view, a journalist's interest in protecting her sources is a redundant feature because the real justificatory work is being done, not by a feature of an individual, but by the general public interest. So, the objection continues, the justified-constraint view implausibly implies that journalists do not have a right to protect their sources but the general public has a right that journalists not reveal their sources.

This objection falls prey to the tendency (so ably noted by Rawls) to confuse the justification of a rule system with justification of a person's rights within a system. The system of giving journalists the right to protect their sources is justified by the public interest. The rights of a particular journalist are justified by the rules of the system. The question about who has a right is a question about a particular action under a practice, not about a practice. To use Rawls' metaphor (1999, 31), the question of to whom, if anyone, an obligation is owed is a question within a game. The question of who, if anyone, is the object of an obligation is a question of the entailments of the system of rules, not of the justification of the system of rules itself. When we seek the justification of an obligation to determine whether or not it is relational (and if so to whom) we seek the feature that does the work in the system as it is. We are not seeking the justification for the inclusion of this feature in the rule system.

In the journalist case, the end of justification at the individual level is the fact that an individual is a journalist. Any further requests for justification (unless there are doubts as to whether the person in question really is a journalist) move to the practice level, to the level of questioning the rules of the system. We can be more precise. The right to protect one's sources is a liberty right, and the main point at issue is the Hohfeldian liberty not to tell others where one received certain information. The journalist holds that she has a liberty not to tell others where she received certain information and claims that protect this liberty. These claims include the claim not to be placed in jail for refusing to tell others where she received the information. Simplifying a bit to make the case easier to present, the key argument would be something like:

1. Virginia is a journalist.
2. If Virginia is a journalist, then James (a judge) has an obligation not to put Virginia in jail for failure to reveal her sources.
3. Therefore, James has an obligation not to put Virginia in jail for failure to reveal her sources.

This is a sound instance of the key argument form, so Virginia has a right that James not put her in jail. At the individual level, this is the end of justification, and the fact that Virginia is a journalist is the feature that does the justificatory work. It is not redundant. One can ask for further justification at the practice level, but that is not the level at which the justification of rights operates.

3. Non-relational Obligations

Any theory of relational obligations necessarily implies at least a partial theory of non-relational obligations. Relational obligations are not the whole of normative life. There are non-relational obligations as well. The obligation to give to charity is the standard example of a non-relational obligation. Let us simplify matters and assume that a rule system, P, contains the following statement:

> If X is a person who has an income over $100,000 per year and Y1, Y2, Y3, etc. are people who have incomes less than $1,000 per year, then X has a P obligation to give some money to Y1 or Y2 or Y3, etc.

Notice the nature of the "or" in this statement. A crucial feature of the obligation to give to charity is that X has latitude as to whom to give his charitable dollars. If I have an obligation to give to charity, I can meet this obligation by giving to the Red Cross, Habitat for Humanity, Oxfam, or any number of other organizations. X may meet the obligation to give to charity by giving to Y1 or by giving to Y2 or by giving to Y2 and Y3, etc. The "or" in the case of the obligation to give to charity indicates that the giver has an obligation with latitude. The giver may choose from a group of qualified recipients. (There are interesting questions about the nature of latitude in obligations and how this relates to the distinction between perfect and imperfect obligations. See Rainbolt (2000).)

Let us assume that there is a group of people who have an income less than $1,000 and that Tabitha has an income over $100,000. Tabitha has an obligation to give some money to some of those whose income is less than $1,000. There is no feature of any one person that is essential to a sound argument leading to the conclusion that Tabitha has this obligation with its latitude as to whom to give. Suppose that there are precisely three people who have incomes of less than $1,000 per year—Howard, Kate and George. The following argument is not sound:

1. Tabitha is a person who has an income over $100,000 per year and Howard has an income of less than $1,000 per year.

2. If Tabitha is a person who has an income over $100,000 per year and Howard has an income of less than $1,000 per year, then Tabitha has a P obligation to give some money to Howard or Kate or George.
3. Therefore, Tabitha has a P obligation to give some money to Howard or Kate or George.

The second premise of this argument is false because the mere fact that Howard has an income of less than $1,000 does not imply that Tabitha has an obligation to give some money to Howard or Kate or George. The latitude of Tabitha's obligation, that she may choose to give to Howard or Kate or George, is not correctly represented in the above argument. There is no feature of Howard or Kate or George which is a reason for Tabitha's obligation with its latitude to give some of her money to Howard or Kate or George. The justified-constraint analysis implies, as it should, that her obligation is non-relational. Tabitha's obligation is not *to* anyone. It is a non-relation obligation, and no one has a right to some of Tabitha's money.

Compare Tabitha's obligation to another one much like it. Suppose that there were a rule system, Q, that contained the following statement:

If X is a person who has an income over $100,000 per year and if Y is a person who has an income less than $1,000 per year, then X has a Q obligation to give Y some of his money.

Such a statement implies that, if Nikki has an income over $100,000 and Howard has an income less than $1,000, then Howard has a right to some of Nikki's money. A sound argument leading to the conclusion that Nikki has an obligation would look like this:

1. Nikki is a person who has an income over $100,000 per year and Howard is a person who has an income less than $1,000 per year.
2. If Nikki is a person who has an income over $100,000 per year and Howard is a person who has an income less than $1,000 per year, then Nikki has a Q obligation to give Howard some of her money.
3. Therefore, Nikki has a Q obligation to give Howard some of her money.

The obligation referred to in the conclusion of this argument is an obligation *to* Howard because the argument leading to this conclusion contains a statement that Howard has some feature—being a person who has an income less than $1,000.

Why does Howard have a right to some of Nikki's money while neither Howard nor Kate nor George has a right to Tabitha's? The answer can be found by comparing premise two of the two arguments above. The difference between the two premises is subtle but important. Rule system Q implies that each and every individual with an income over $100,00 has an obligation to give some money to each and every individual with an income less than $1,000. Rule system P does not have this implication. It gives those with incomes over $100,000 the latitude to give to some but not to others. Therefore, no individual has a right correlative to Tabitha's obligation. Whether or not an obligation is relational depends on the rule system in which the obligation appears. In one rule system, the obligation to give the poor some money could be relational while in another rule system it might not be.

One might think that the difference between relational and non-relational obligations is that the justification for relational obligations is found in the features of individuals while the justification for non-relational obligations is found in the features of groups. This might lead one to think that the group Howard, Kate, and George has a right that Tabitha gives some money to some of them. This view will be considered in Chapter 7.

Using the example of Tabitha and Howard above, one who overlooked the redundancy qualifier in the justified-constraint theory might assert that there is a feature of Howard that is part of a sound instance of the key argument form. The second premise of an instance of the key argument feature using such a property might be something like this:

> If Howard is one of three people, Howard, Kate, and George, with incomes under $1,000 per year and Tabitha is a person who has an income over $100,000 per year, then Tabitha has a P obligation to give some money to Howard or Kate or George.

This refers to Howard's redundant feature of being part of the group Howard, Kate, and George. This feature is redundant in just the same way that Mabel's being Fred's grandmother is redundant.

Another class of non-relational obligations are those whose justification rests on something other than the features of persons. Many people think that there are sound instances of arguments of the following form:

1. A is F.
2. If A is F, then X has an obligation to do A.
3. Therefore, X has an obligation to do A.

In other words, many people think that features of *acts* justify obligations. One might hold that one has an obligation to do an act if that act maximizes utility. If one held this belief, then one would be holding that there are some non-relational obligations. One might hold that one has an obligation to do an act if *and only if* that act maximizes utility. If one held this belief, then one would be holding that there are only non-relational obligations, that there are no moral rights. This view merits its own section.

4. CONSEQUENTIALISM

There has been a great deal of discussion concerning the conceptual space, if any, that consequentialism allows for rights. At least as far back as Mill, consequentialists have been worried that their view cannot provide a plausible account of rights. Mill held that rights were the basis of the distinction between justice and other parts of morality. He then noted that

> In all ages of speculation one of the strongest obstacles to the reception of the doctrine that utility or happiness as the criterion of right and wrong has been drawn from the idea of justice (1979, 41).

Hart held that

> there may be codes of conduct quite properly termed moral codes ... which do not employ the notion of *a* right, and there is nothing contradictory or otherwise absurd in a code or morality consisting wholly of prescriptions or in a code which prescribed only what should be done for the realization of happiness or some ideal of personal perfection. Human actions in such systems would be evaluated or criticised as compliances with prescriptions or as *good* or *bad*, *right* or *wrong*, *wise* or *foolish*, *fitting* or *unfitting*, but no one in such a system would have, exercise, or claim rights, or violate or infringe them (1979, 15).

The justified-constraint theory follows Hart (among many) and implies that act consequentialism does not leave conceptual space for rights. It is easy to get an intuitive grasp of why act consequentialists are committed to the view that there are no rights. Rights are obligations justified by the features of the right-holder. One who thinks that there are rights is necessarily committed to the view that individuals are a source of obligations. Act consequentialists think that features of acts, not individuals, justify all obligations. They are committed to the view that individuals are never the source of obligations.

This intuitive presentation is insufficiently precise. Exactly what is it about act consequentialism that makes it incompatible with rights? Consequentialist theories hold that morality is only a matter of determining an act's effect on the amount of G (the good). One kind of consequentialism is act consequentialism. According to act consequentialism, the moral rule system has the following form:

> A is obligatory if and only if A maximizes the amount of G in the world. Other-wise A is forbidden.

(Let us ignore ties.) G can be anything at all.[3] One common view is that G is happiness, preference satisfaction, or some similar mental state. If one holds this view, then one is an act utilitarian.

---

[3] This is not strictly true. I have assumed that we are discussing only the universalistic form of act consequentialism. Some things put in for G will turn act consequentialism into another theory. For example, if one puts in "the amount of G for X," then act consequentialism will become a version of egoistic act consequentialism.

Does act consequentialism leave conceptual space for rights? Consider premise two of the key argument form. If a moral rule system is to generate rights, it must assert that there are some occasions when statements of the form:

If X is F, then Y has a moral obligation to do A.

are true. However, according to act consequentialism, there are no occasions when statements of this form are true. There are no such occasions because, if act consequentialism is true, all arguments for moral obligations rest on statements of the form:

If A is F, then Y has a moral obligation to do A.

According to act consequentialism, the F in question is maximizing utility. Defenders of act consequentialism do not see individuals as the source of moral obligations. Instead, they see acts as the source of moral obligation. The argument just offered applies with equal force to moral and legal rights. Act consequentialism implies that there are neither legal nor moral rights. (Lyons (1994, 147–175) reaches the same conclusion by another route.) To modify Rawls' famous phrase, the problem with act consequentialism is that it does not take seriously the fact that individuals are the source of moral obligations (1971, 27).

The justified-constraint theory relies on an intuitive distinction between features of acts (a subclass of events) and features of persons. Consider such features as being a woman, being six feet tall and having red hair. These are features that are necessarily features of individuals. An act cannot be six feet tall. Other features, such as being performed by John, or maximizing utility, are necessarily features of acts. Although a person can do an act which maximizes utility, only an act can maximize utility. There are some features, such as spacial location, that both individuals and acts can have. As I write this, I have the feature of being in Atlanta, Georgia and my act of typing is occurring in Atlanta, Georgia. Matters can get a bit complex. Suppose that Tynisha hits Alex. Tynisha has the feature of being a person who hit Alex, Alex has the feature of being a person who was hit by Tynisha and the act that Tynisha performed has the feature of being an act of hitting someone. There is obviously much more that could be said here. But this is a work in rights theory, not action theory. For this book, it is sufficient to note that maximizing utility can only be a feature of an act. A person can do an act that maximizes utility, and thus we would understand it if someone said, "Tynisha maximized utility." But this statement is insufficiently precise. Strictly speaking, neither Tynisha nor any other person can maximize utility. All that a person can do is perform an act that maximizes utility.

Redundant features might be used by a defender of act consequentialism who wished to object to my claim that act consequentialism implies that there are no moral rights. Holly Smith has suggested that there is an instance of the key argument form that is sound even if act consequentialism is true.[4] Suppose that Jane is considering whether or not to hit Bob. Let us focus on the hedonist version of act consequentialism. On this view, maximizing utility consists in maximizing the amount of pleasure in the world. The defender of hedonistic act consequentialism holds that Jane has an obligation not to hit Bob if and only if the pain produced (in Bob and all others) by hitting Bob is greater than the pleasure produced (in Bob and all others) by hitting Bob. If hitting Bob causes a net increase in pleasure, then Jane has an obligation to hit Bob and if hitting him causes a net decrease in pleasure, then Jane has an obligation not to hit Bob. Let us assume that, in Jane's particular situation, not hitting Bob maximizes pleasure. In that case, according to hedonist act consequentialism, Jane has an obligation not to hit Bob. The justified-constraint theory holds that, if act consequentialism is true, this obligation is not to Bob and that Bob has no right that Jane not hit him. It seems that it is a feature of the *act* of not hitting Bob (that not hitting Bob maximizes pleasure), not a feature of *Bob*, that justifies Jane's obligation.

Smith points out that a clever defender of act consequentialism who wished to claim that her preferred moral theory leaves conceptual space for rights might point to the following feature of Bob as the feature that justifies Jane's obligation:

A. Bob is a person such that the pain produced in Bob by Jane's hitting Bob is greater than the pleasure produced in others by Jane's hitting Bob.

The defender of act consequentialism might claim that the following instance of the key argument form is sound and that the justified-constraint theory of relational obligation and act consequentialism imply that Bob has a right that Jane not hit him:

1. Bob is a person such that the pain produced in Bob by Jane's hitting Bob is greater than the pleasure produced in others by Jane's hitting Bob.
2. If Bob is a person such that the pain produced in Bob by Jane's hitting Bob is greater than the pleasure produced in others by Jane's hitting Bob, then Jane has a moral obligation not to hit Bob.
3. Therefore, Jane has a moral obligation not to hit Bob.

This argument is sound. It may seem that act consequentialism does leave conceptual space for rights. However, this would be incorrect. If the defender of act consequentialism were to use Smith's argument, she would be committed to the view that everyone in the world has a right that Jane not hit Bob. To see this, let us assume that there are only three people in the world—Jane, Bob, and Gareth. Then consider the following features of Jane and Gareth.

B. Gareth is a person such that the pleasure produced in Gareth and Jane by Jane's hitting Bob is less than the pain produced in Bob by Jane's hitting Bob.

---

[4] In conversation.

C. Jane is a person such that the pleasure produced in Jane and Gareth by Jane's hitting Bob is less than the pain produced in Bob by Jane's hitting Bob.

One could set out an instance of the key argument form for each of these two features. It would be just as sound as the one offered above that focused on the unusual feature of Bob. Smith's argument implies that Bob, Jane, and Gareth each has a right that Jane not hit Bob. It implies that all humans have a right that all humans maximize utility. This is a counterintuitive implication of Smith's argument.

Smith's argument relies on a redundant feature. The features of Bob to which Smith has pointed are redundant in just the same way that Mabel's feature of being Fred's grandmother was. Let us put these three slightly odd features side-by-side.

A. Bob is a person such that the pain produced in Bob *by Jane's hitting Bob* is greater than the pleasure produced in others *by Jane's hitting Bob*.
B. Gareth is a person such that the pleasure produced in Gareth and Jane *by Jane's hitting Bob* is less than the pain produced in Bob *by Jane's hitting Bob*.
C. Jane is a person such that the pleasure produced in Jane and Gareth *by Jane's hitting Bob* is less than the pain produced in Bob *by Jane's hitting Bob*.

In each case it is the feature of the act in question, the act of hitting Bob, that does the justificatory work. That Bob, Gareth, and Jane are persons does no justificatory work. All that matters, from the point of view of act consequentialism, is the effect the act has on the amount of pleasure and pain in the world. If act consequentialism is true, what counts morally, what does the justificatory work, is the features of acts, not the features of persons. Features of Bob, such as the fact that he was hit by Jane, do not count.

Someone might press this objection in another way. Even if one can get rid of Gareth, Bob and Jane are still in any relevant description of the grounding feature. Is there really a distinction here between features of acts and features of individuals? There is. Compare two different assertions.

1. If Bob was hit by Jane, then Jane ought to do A.
2. If Jane's hitting Bob maximizes utility, then Jane ought to hit Bob.

According to act consequentialism, the first assertion will not always be true. Whether 1 is true or not will depend on whether Jane's hitting Bob maximizes utility. But, if act consequentialism is true, the second assertion will always be true. This illustrates that, in act consequentialism, it is consequence C (the maximization of utility) that does the justificatory work.

The justified-constraint theory of rights allows one to see connections between debates on rights theory, act consequentialism, and agent-centered prerogatives/restrictions. There is a very large literature on agent-centered prerogatives and agent-centered restrictions. To offer a complete discussion of that literature would

137

take us far from rights theory. An incomplete (and in some respects over-simplified) discussion is worthwhile as a gesture toward directions further research might take. Let us focus on the *locus classicus* on agent-centered prerogative and agent-centered restrictions, Samuel Scheffler's *The Rejection of Consequentialism* (1994).

A person has an agent-centered prerogative when that person has "a permission to do what one wants to do even if that will not produce the best results overall" (Scheffler, 1994, 155). Suppose that Zac is trying to decide whether to buy a stereo system. It costs $400. Zac could send that $400 to organizations that are feeding starving people in Africa. Of course, if he did that he would lose the happiness that the stereo would have given him. But $400 could save a thousand lives in Africa. Assume that the "best results overall" would occur if Zac sent his $400 to help those in Africa. Zac has an agent-centered prerogative if he has permission to buy the stereo even though this action "will not produce the best results overall." Agent-centered prerogatives are defined in terms of permission. They are clearly related to liberty rights. Scheffler did not consider an Hohfeldian analysis, but it seems clear from context that when he is discussing agent-centered prerogatives, he is not using the "thin" notion of permission that is equivalent to an Hohfeldian liberty. Rather, he is using the "thick" notion of permission, the "thick" notion of liberty. An agent-centered prerogative is not a bare permission. It is a permission in a package that includes some claims against interference with the action in question. If Zac has an agent-centered prerogative to buy the stereo, not only does he have an Hohfeldian liberty but he also has claims that protect his liberty against some forms of interference. He has a right. (Agent-centered prerogatives may also come into play in case of permissible rights transgression. See Chapter 6.)

Agent-centered restrictions are

> restrictions on action which have the effect of denying that there is any non-agent-relative principle for ranking overall states of affairs from best to worst such that it is always permissible to produce the best available state of affairs (1994, 2–3).

We can use Scheffler's example.

> Suppose that if agent A_1 fails to violate a restriction R by harming some unde-serving person P_1, then five other agents, $A_2 \ldots A_6$, will each violate restriction R by identically harming five other persons, $P_2 \ldots P_6$, who are just as undeserving as $P_1 \ldots$ (1994, 84).

If you do not cut off innocent Emily's hand, then five members of a gang will each cut off the hand of someone as innocent as Emily. You have an agent-centered restriction if it would be wrong for you to cut off her hand. The relationship between agent-centered restrictions and rights is clear. It would be natural to say that Emily has a claim right that you not cut off her hand. (Those as innocent as Emily have rights as well. So this is a case of rights conflict. Let us set this issue aside until Chapter 6.)

Some, including Scheffler, think that there are agent-centered prerogatives but no agent-centered restrictions. Others think that there are both. Still others think that there are neither. We will not enter into this debate here. Some think that the existence of agent-centered prerogatives and/or agent-centered restrictions is incompatible with act consequentialism. Others deny this claim. The justified-constraint theory of rights provides a plausible analysis of agent-centered prerogatives and agent-centered restrictions. It also shows that they are incompatible with act consequentialism. Rights are obligations justified by the features of the right-holder. One who thinks that there are rights is necessarily committed to the view that individuals are a source of obligations. Thus the arguments that justify the obligations that are rights are ideally suited to justify agent-centered prerogatives and agent-centered restrictions. While there might be other ways to justify these prerogatives and restrictions, one natural way to do so would be to hold that there is some feature of Zac that justifies his permission to buy the stereo and that there is some feature of Emily that justifies her claim that you not cut off her hand. In this way, the justified-constraint theory allows one to see how rights fit into the debate over agent-centered prerogatives and agent-centered restrictions.

Another form of consequentialism is rule consequentialism. Rule consequentialism is the normative view that

A is obligatory if and only if the moral rule system which would, if adopted, maximize the amount of G in the world implies that A is obligatory.

(There are other sorts of rule consequentialism. For example, another sort of rule consequentialism might refer to rules actually in place rather than to hypothetical rules.) What counts as adoption of a moral rule system is a difficult problem that we will ignore. Very roughly, a moral rule system is adopted if most people act in accord with it. Some hold that rule consequentialism collapses into and is therefore not distinct from act consequentialism. If this is true, then rule consequentialism implies that there are no moral rights. Let us set this objection to rule consequentialism aside and assume that it is a distinct theory that does not collapse into act consequentialism. In that case, the justified-constraint view of relational obligation implies that rule consequentialism leaves conceptual space for rights.

Let us continue to focus on the case of Jane hitting Bob and consider hedonistic rule consequentialism. On this view, A is obligatory if and only if the moral rule system which would, if adopted, maximize the amount of pleasure in the world implies that A is obligatory. Let us assume that the following statement is part of the moral rule system that would, if adopted, maximize the amount of pleasure in the world:

Do not hit people.

Therefore, Jane has an obligation not to hit Bob. The following instance of the key argument form is sound:

1. Bob is a person.
2. If Bob is a person, then Jane has a moral obligation not to hit Bob.
3. Therefore, Jane has a moral obligation not to hit Bob.

Therefore, Jane's obligation not to hit Bob is to Bob, and Bob has a right that Jane not hit him.

Rule consequentialism allows for individuals to be a source of moral obligations. The reason it does so is that, according to versions of rule consequentialism that imply that there are moral rights, treating individuals as a source of moral obligations maximizes utility. The justified-constraint theory of relational obligation confirms the intuitive view that rule consequentialism has a combination of consequentialist and deontological features. According to rule consequentialism, the justification of all moral claims is complex. There is no simple justification. On rule consequentialism, general rules are justified by consequentialist considerations, but particular actions are justified by reference to the general rules—not consequentialist considerations. Because rule consequentialism holds that particular actions are justified by reference to general rules, it allows conceptual space for rights.

This is not the place for another discussion of the merits and demerits of the various versions of consequentialism. It would be tedious to spin out the implications of the justified-constraint theory for the myriad other forms of consequentialism. Nevertheless, the justified-constraint theory of relational obligation gains plausibility because it provides an enlightening account of the relationship between consequentialism and moral rights. It explains why many have thought that moral rights do not fit into a consequentialist framework. It explains why many have thought that rule consequentialism is more plausible than act consequentialism.

5. THE INDIVIDUATION OF RIGHTS

Lurking in the background of the discussion to this point is the issue of the individuation of rights. What is *a* right? What distinguishes a single right from a set or package of rights? As I sit here at my desk, I have the legal right to free speech. Is this one right or a package of rights? That the English language uses the definite article to refer to this right is some small reason to think that it is one right. However, no theorist accepts the individuation of rights in the English language at face value. It is common to refer to "the" right to free speech in the singular but my legal right to free speech is a package, a set, of rights. For example, it includes both my right to picket in front of a government building and my right to publish a newsletter.

Following Hohfeld, the justified-constraint theory individuates rights very finely. On this theory, if one wishes to speak strictly, each relational obligation is a right. Any difference in the subject, object, content, or rule system of an obligation means that it is a distinct obligation. Hassan's legal claim that Bill not interfere with his saying that Richard Nixon was a crook is a distinct right from his legal claim that Jeannie not interfere with his saying that Richard Nixon was a crook. The only difference between these two rights is that the object of them is different. Other than a single relational obligation or a single relational impossibility, all things that are referred to as "rights" are packages of rights (that is, claims and immunities) and other relations.

To avoid begging the question, the obligation referred to in the second premise of the key argument form is individuated without reference to an object. It is no objection to the justified-constraint theory that, once we have determined whether the obligation is relational or not, a difference in object implies a different obligation. If Tracy promises two people that she will vote in the next election, then she has two distinct obligations whose subject and content are the same but whose objects are different. One can have two distinct obligations with the same content. I have promised both my mother and my grandmother that I will come to Indiana this Christmas. I have two distinct obligations to go to Indiana. One is to my mother and the other is to my grandmother.

Raz does not individuate rights as finely as the justified-constraint theory does.

There is no closed list of duties which correspond to [a] right. The existence of a right often leads to holding another to have a duty because of the existence of certain facts peculiar to the parties or general to society in which they live. A change of circumstances may lead to the creation of new duties based on an old right. The right to political participation is not new, but only in modern states with their enormously complex bureaucracies does this right justify . . . a duty on the government to make public its plans and proposals before a decision is reached . . . (1986, 170).

(Jeremy Waldron (1993a) agrees with Raz.) On the justified-constraint view, a change of circumstance never leads, strictly speaking, to the creation of new duties based on an old right. Changes in circumstances of the kind Raz has in mind lead to the creation of new rights and the new duties (and disabilities) correlative to them. The right to political participation is not *a* right. It is a rights package. The package contains different rights under different circumstances. Only in modern states does this rights package include the right to public notice of plans or proposals. On the justified-constraint view, the right to public notice of plans or proposals is a rights package. For each person who has such a right, for each person who has a duty or disability correlative to such a right and for each plan or proposal, there is, strictly speaking, a distinct right to public notice. For convenience, we refer to this complex package as "the" right to public notice.

Wellman does not individuate rights as Raz does but, like Raz, he does not individuate them as finely as justified-constraint theory does. He claims that "a . . . right can result in a variable set of Hohfeldian positions depending on the circumstances" (1997, 7). Thus the justified-constraint theory differs from Wellman on this issue in the same way that it differs with Raz.

How should one individuate rights? One might object to the justified-constraint theory on the grounds that it implies an undue proliferation of rights. Many authors have recently commented that rights are proliferating and held that this proliferation is problematic. Sumner holds that "Like the arms race the escalation of rights rhetoric is out of control" (1987, 1) and Steiner notes that

> it has now become the standard practice for philosophical works on the nature of rights to begin their discussion . . . by complaining of the vast proliferation of (often opposing) moral and political demands that come wrapped in the garb of rights (Kramer et al., 1998, 233).

Because the justified-constraint theory individuates rights very finely, it implies that the number of rights is larger than that contemplated by Raz or Wellman. But whatever the merits of Sumner and Steiner's claim that rights proliferation is problematic, the justified-constraint theory of the individuation of rights does not cause the sort of proliferation that worries those who worry about rights proliferation. The worry is not that analysis will reveal that a more fine-grained individuation of rights will cause there to be numerically more rights. The worry is that people are asserting that they have rights to do things that they did not previously assert. Some worry that people are asserting rights to receive things when previously they were only asserting rights to do actions. Sumner (1987, 1–8) provides a long list of rights to things (e.g., an education, health care, employment, housing, clean water, etc.) that he claims were not previously thought of as matters of rights. The proliferation of rights seems to be seen as evidence that the new rights assertions are false. Whatever one's views on the proliferation of rights, they are no objection to the justified-constraint theory of the individuation rights. One who adopts this view could with perfect consistency hold that there are no rights in the domains Sumner lists. (One could adopt the justified-constraint theory of rights and hold that there are no rights at all.)

One might think that how one individuates rights has merely semantic implications, or one might follow Kramer (2001, 85–88) and hold that there is no one correct way to individuate rights. This would not be accurate. An incorrect individuation of rights leads one into theoretical muddles. In the next chapter, we will see that a correct individuation of rights does much to clarify the nature of rights conflict. Moreover, a coarse-grained individuation misleadingly takes one's mind off the fact that, in most cases, what we refer to as *a* right is a complex thing, not a simple one. It also leads one to seek answers to problems that do not exist. Since Wellman conceives of a right as a set of relations, he must ask, "how can an aggregate or collection of [relations], each of which is logically distinct and legally separable from all the rest, constitute *a* right?" (1985, 81). The idea of a core of a right with associated elements is an answer to this question. Since Wellman acknowledges that, in some cases, what we refer to as "a" right is a rights package, a set of rights, he must provide a theory that picks out a set of relations as a right. He must, on the one hand, distinguish a right from a single relation and, on the

142

other hand, distinguish a right from a rights package. As we saw above, Wellman's discussion of the core of a right is unclear at several points. Although it is hard to determine why this is so, one possibility is a failure to correctly individuate rights.

Some puzzles about rights are entirely resolved if one adopts the justified-constraint theory of individuation. MacCormick (1977) is led to into puzzling about the relationship between rights and duties because of an incorrect individuation. According to the Scottish legal rule system, if someone with an only child dies intestate (i.e., without a will), then the child has a right to the whole of the intestate estate. When someone with a child dies intestate, the child does not at the moment of death gain a right to the intestate estate. According to MacCormick, at the moment of death the child gains a right to "receive in due course ... the assets remaining in the executor's hands after satisfaction of prior claims [e.g., inheritance taxes]" (1977, 200). MacCormick thinks that this right does not imply a duty or disability because, until the court appoints an executor, there is no one who has the duty implied by this right. "Whereas the right vests at the moment of the intestate's death, there is not at that moment an executor to bear the correlative duty" (1977, 200). This leads MacCormick to conclude that some rights do not imply duties. (He would presumably also conclude from this case that some rights imply no duty or disability).

MacCormick's error becomes apparent if one considers what a child of someone who died intestate would do if the court did not appoint an executor. The child would assert that he has a right that the courts appoint an executor. Moreover, the Scottish legal rule system does imply this right. MacCormick was wrong to say that at the moment of death the child gained a right to "receive in due course ... the assets remaining in the executor's hands after satisfaction of prior claims." Rather, at the moment of death the child gains a right that the courts appoint an executor in a timely fashion. Only when the executor is appointed does the child gain the right to "receive in due course ... the assets remaining in the executor's hands after satisfaction of prior claims." And only after the "satisfaction of prior claims" does the child gain the right to the intestate estate. Thus, the right to "receive in due course ... the assets remaining in the executor's hands after satisfaction of prior claims" is a rights package, and each right in the package implies a duty. MacCormick is led astray because he does not individuate rights as finely as they need to be individuated.

Another puzzle that is at least much clarified by the correct individuation of rights can be found in a debate between Heidi Hurd (1999) and Leo Katz. In her illuminating book *Moral Combat*, Hurd defends what she calls "the correspondence thesis." As applied to rights, the correspondence thesis is the view that "if one has a right to do an act, then others have a duty not to interfere with one's performance of that act" (1999, 280). Hurd's first example of the thesis concerns a person, Smith, who is attacked by a hoodlum while she is walking her dog. Smith's life is in danger, so she has a right to kill the hoodlum. Jones happens to be jogging by at the time of the attack. The correspondence thesis implies that if Smith has a right to

143

kill the hoodlum, then Jones has an obligation not to interfere with Smith's killing the hoodlum. (There are some purely terminological differences between us. To simplify matters, her view is stated with the terms used in the rest of this work.) In a subsequent article, Katz points to what appears to be a counterexample to the correspondence thesis (2001, 351). A hunter is in hot pursuit of a fox. At the last moment, just as the hunter is about to catch the fox, another hunter appears from nowhere and kills the fox. At least on the surface, it seems that each hunter has a right to kill the fox, and, contra the correspondence thesis, neither hunter has a duty not to interfere with the other hunter's killing the fox.

Katz's example is wonderfully vivid but it might lead one to overlook the fact that cases such as this occur every day in the world of commerce. My son likes to get a lollipop when we go to a baseball game. Only one concession stand in the ballpark sells lollipops. At one game last season, we went to get a lollipop. As we approached the stand, we noticed that there was a long line and only one lollipop remaining. We got in line but a woman in front of us bought the lollipop. As we walked to the stand, if you had asked me, "Do you have a right to buy a lollipop at the stand?" I would have replied, "Of course." Yet it seems that the woman in front of us in line did not have a duty not to interfere with my buying the lollipop. It seems that the correspondence thesis is false.

Hurd considers a number of objections to her view but never precisely this one. She does consider Hohfeldian liberties as a counterexample to her view. Hurd notes that if one has a liberty to do A, then it is merely the case that others do not have a claim that one not do A. A liberty does not imply claims against non-interference with attempts to do A. Hurd then asserts that liberties "define arenas of amoral action" and that "actors within such arenas are not bound by any maxims of action" (1999, 281). They are, on her view, "untouched by deontological norms" and "are of no normative importance" (1999, 281). She thinks that they are actions in a moral state of nature. The correspondence thesis is a thesis "about the conditions of moral action" and therefore the correspondence thesis "does not apply" (1999, 281). It is hard to interpret these claims. The lollipop was certainly of great importance to my son, and we were certainly not operating in anything like a moral state of nature. The purchase of lollipops is governed by complex laws, and even the rules of standing in line are governed by complex social normative rules. The notion of an amoral action is never made clear in Hurd's work. In any case, liberties are not amoral positions. They are not "anormative" positions. They are normative positions just as claims, duties, etc. are. Hurd's description of liberties is not accurate.

Hurd has been led astray because she does not individuate rights finely enough. The antecedent of the conditional that is the correspondence thesis (one has a right to do an act) is not sufficiently analyzed. What precisely is *the* right to do an act? On the justified-constraint view, an active right is either a liberty right, a power right, a duty right, or a liability right. Hurd does not analyze the matter precisely, but all of her examples are liberty rights so let us focus on them. The discussion will apply, *mutatis mutandis*, to the other active rights. On the justified-constraint view,

144

a liberty right is a liberty to do A, a liberty not to do A, and at least one claim that protects the liberties. We can now see what is true in the correspondence thesis. If X has a liberty right to do A, then there must be at least one person, Y, against whom X has a claim that protects X's liberty to do A. The correspondence theory contains some truth because a liberty right to do an act necessarily implies another's duty either to refrain from interfering with the liberties or to aid the subject of the liberty in doing the act in question. What of my right to buy a lollipop? I have a liberty right to buy the lollipop. My liberty right to buy a lollipop includes some claims against interference (such as claims against others hitting me or cutting in line to get the lollipop first). Unfortunately for me and my son, it does not include claims against all forms of interference. It does not include a claim against the woman ahead of us in line that she refrain from buying the lollipop.

Hurd's statement of the thesis, "if one has a right to do an act, then others have a duty not to interfere with one's performance of that act," is unclear. The problem is the phrase "a duty." Does "a duty" mean to refer to a package of duties not to do any of the many things that would interfere with the performance of the act one has a right to do? If so, then the fox hunt and lollipop examples show that the correspondence thesis is false. On the other hand, should "a duty" be taken in the fine-grain justified-constraint sense and so mean that there is at least one other person who has at least one duty not to interfere in some specific way with the right-holder's liberty right? If so, and if one includes positive actions to help the right-holder do what he has a liberty to do under the rubric of "duty not to interfere," then the correspondence thesis is true. Hurd uses the correspondence thesis to draw conclusions about the nature of the law and morality. This is not the place to go into such details. But Hurd's work would be clearer and more precise if she individuated rights correctly.

Why do Raz and Wellman individuate rights as they do? In part, Raz (1980, 225–226) was led astray by MacCormick's example of a child who dies intestate. Raz took this example to show that rights could not be "reduced" to obligations (Raz 1980, 226). Above we saw that MacCormick was not correct. But this is not the whole story. Raz (1980, 225–227) and Wellman (1995, 227–229) provide two other arguments for their view.

The first argument begins by noting that the law is text-based. Legislatures write the law as text and judges interpret these texts. It continues by noting that the text of any law can never be fully complete and precise. Because texts must be written in a language and because languages are, to use Hart's (1994) phrase, open-textured, it is never the case that a law can avoid the need to be interpreted. For this reason, according to Raz and Wellman, judges are always revising the law. Thus, it is argued, when a law confers a right, there is no single and unchanging set of obligations implied by that right. Over time judges will interpret the texts which granted the right and thus change the obligations the right implies.

The second argument begins with the claim that judges are authorized to hold that a law which confers a right implies whatever obligations are necessary to see that the purpose of the conferral of the right is met. The world is an ever-changing place so a single legal right might imply obligations A, B, and C today and obligations X, Y, and Z tomorrow. As Wellman (1995, 9) put it:

> a legal right consists of whatever legal positions are validly recognized in the light of the relevant legal norms and the facts of the variable situations to which they must be applied, not merely of that set of Hohfeldian positions that happen to have received legal recognition to date (1995, 9).

There are three problems with these arguments. First, they seem to apply only to legal rights and other rights based on texts and changed by authorized officials. It is not at all clear that the arguments can be adapted to the case of moral rights. Some hold that moral rules, unlike legal rules, are not text-based and that there are no moral judges who are authorized to change moral obligations as the world changes. Unless they thought that moral rights are not individuated as legal rights are, those who hold these views about moral rules would not be convinced by Raz and Wellman's arguments. Second, the two arguments clearly rest on several controversial views about the nature of law, legal interpretation, and legal indeterminacy. Raz clearly has complex arguments for his views on these matters, but some do not find those arguments convincing. It would be better if a theory of the individuation of rights did not depend on controversial views which do not seem to be part of a theory of rights. The justified-constraint view avoids these two problems. Third, Raz and Wellman's theory of individuation will be more complex than the Hohfeldian account because, unless they wish to deny that there are rights packages, they will need to provide a theory of the difference between a legal right and a package of legal rights which we refer to as a single right. Raz did not attempt this task and we have seen that Wellman's attempt is flawed.

Raz and Wellman would argue that the justified-constraint individuation of rights has a serious flaw. It cannot account for what Raz (1984, 15) calls the "dynamic aspect" legal rights. Raz and Wellman would argue that any view which holds that, for example, the legal right to free speech, is logically equivalent to some fixed set of Hohfeldian legal relations cannot account for the fact (assuming that it is a fact) that in 1780 this right did not include the right to publish a web-log and now it does. This is not correct. Adopting the justified-constraint individuation of rights is no barrier to account for the dynamic aspect of legal rights.

For the sake of argument, let us assume that Raz and Wellman's views about the nature of law, legal interpretation, and legal indeterminacy are correct. Raz and Wellman hold that one right, R, can justify different obligations at different times. On the justified-constraint theory of the individuation of rights, one feature, F, can justify different rights at different times. So we both agree that there is a changing set of Hohfeldian legal relations over time. The law is dynamic. For example, Raz and Wellman see my right to drive my pickup truck as a right which remains the same right over the years I own the truck. The Hohfeldian sees some feature (or features) of me which remains the same feature over time but justifies different rights at different times. One reason in support of Raz's view is that the Courts often refer to "my right to drive my pickup truck" in the singular and thus seems to assume that it is a single right. But above we noted that no one (not even the Courts) takes this sort of individuation at face value. Everyone recognizes that some things which courts refer to as a single right are packages of rights. No one thinks that "the" right to free speech is a single right. The question is not whether to reject the face value individuation of the courts but how to do so.

Any feature F may (almost certainly will) justify different rights, different claims, and immunities, over time. Assuming that the importance of my choices about my pickup justify the rights package that we call my "right" (singular) to drive the truck, these choices will justify some rights now and different ones later. The feature F will stay constant over time but the rights it justifies will not. In many cases, what the law refers to as "a" rights is really a rights package, the contents of which change over time. We sometimes identify a rights package by the unchanging feature which justifies the obligations in the package.

I am not suggesting that courts, scholars, or ordinary folks should speak only with proper Hohfeldian individuation in mind. A theory of the individuation of rights is not a theory which seeks to legislate the usage of language. It is an attempt to understand what is underneath the usage of language. Neither Raz, nor Wellman, nor I deny that claims such as "my right to free speech implies . . . " are true on the grounds that the presupposed individuation is incorrect. Raz, Wellman, and I are offering an analysis of such assertions.

6. SOME IMPLICATIONS OF THE JUSTIFIED-CONSTRAINT THEORY

One judges a theory, in part, by its implications. Therefore, it is worth noting some of the implications of the justified-constraint theory.

What does the justified-constraint theory imply about Wellman's theory of relational obligation? Wellman refers to relational obligations as "relative duties."

A relative duty is a duty to the party with the moral power of claiming performance of that duty (1999, 218).

What is it to claim performance of a duty? Following Feinberg, Wellman holds that the power to claim performance

is exercised when the party to whom the duty is owed requests or demands performance of the duty and presents title to the duty-bearer (1999, 218).

Presenting title occurs when

one refers to or otherwise indicates the basis of one's moral claim in one's act of claiming (1999, 218).

Consider Wellman's example of his promise to help a colleague move some books next Saturday. On Friday, he informs her that he will not help her move the books

147

because he has decided to go play golf. If his colleague says, "I insist that you help me tomorrow as you promised," then she has presented title and exercised her power to claim performance of his duty to help her move the books. She has reminded him of the promise that is the basis of her moral claim. This account of relational obligation is a natural one for Wellman to adopt. It follows straightforwardly from his account of rights and inherits from that theory the problems noted in the previous chapter.

In one crucial respect, Wellman's account of relational obligation parallels the justified-constraint theory account. What Wellman calls "the basis" of an obligation is what the justified-constraint theory refers to as the "feature F" in the key argument form. The justified-constraint account of the relational nature of rights draws out and makes more precise Wellman's "basis of one's moral claim[s]," Ross' "grounded on facts relating to them," and Raz's "sound argument of which the conclusion is that a certain right exists and among its non-redundant premises is a statement of some interest of the right-holder."

The justified-constraint analysis of relational obligation differs from Wellman's in two ways. First, it does not analyze a relational obligation in terms of a power. As argued above when discussing a woman's right not to be raped under the criminal law, a power is not a necessary part of a right. The power to claim performance of a duty is a power right distinct from the claim right correlative to a duty. Second, the justified-constraint theory of relational obligation, unlike Wellman's, does not require that the object of a relational obligation be the sort of being which can have a power. Wellman's theory of relational obligation implies that only agents can be the object of an obligation. ("Object" is used in the technical way presented in Chapter 1.) On his view, one never has obligations to human infants, animals, or any other being that is not an agent.

It is interesting to examine the implications of the justified-constraint theory when it comes to the function of rights. It is natural to see the protection versions of the interest, choice, and will theories as theories of the function of rights. On the protection version of the interest theory, the function of rights is the protection of interests. On the protection version of the choice theory, the function of rights is the protection of choices. On the protection version of the will theory, the function of rights is to advantage wills. The justified-constraint analysis of relational obligation allows us to see why it is plausible to suppose that the function of rights is the protection of interests, the protection of choices, or the advantaging of wills.

Let us say that an analysis is *functional* if it has the following form: Xs are things that do task T. All other sorts of analyses are *structural*. "A pen is an object that writes" is a functional analysis. "A nappe is a sheet of water" is a structural analysis. The protection versions of the interest, choice, and will theories are functional analyses of rights. All of them analyze rights as things that perform a task. The justified-constraint theory of rights is structural. It does not analyze rights as things that do a certain task.

Good structural analyses explain why objects perform some functions well and others poorly. Suppose we analyze a pickup truck as a vehicle with a bed in back and a heavy-duty suspension. This is a structural analysis. This analysis explains why pickups perform some functions well (e.g., hauling large objects) and other functions poorly (e.g., rounding curves quickly). Pickups are good at hauling large objects because they have a bed in back. Pickups are not good at rounding curves quickly because they have a heavy-duty suspension.

The justified-constraint theory of rights is structural, but it explains why rights perform the task of protecting interests, protecting choices, and advantaging wills. Rights are normative constraints grounded by individual features. Rights perform the task of protecting individual features well. If one combines the justified-constraint analysis of relational normative constraints with the substantive view that interests, choices, and/or wills are the individual features that ground normative constraints, then one can easily explain why these obligations typically protect interests, choices, or wills. In this way, the justified-constraint theory of rights explains why these other theories are initially plausible even though they are incorrect.

Many have thought that there is something individualistic about rights. What does the justified-constraint theory imply about this issue? It easily explains why many have thought that there is something individualistic about rights. Rights are obligations justified by the features of the right-holder. Whether the justification of a right is simple or complex, the justification of the obligation correlative to a right must pass through, must refer to, a feature of an individual. At least some and perhaps all right-holders are individuals. One who thinks that there are rights is therefore committed to the view that individuals are a source of obligations. (The claim that only individuals can have rights is evaluated in Chapter 7.)

If one asks, "Why shouldn't I assault Tim?" the most plausible answer is, "It hurts him." In this case of simple justification the individualistic nature of rights is easy to see. The justification of the obligation not to assault Tim refers to a feature of an individual, Tim. In the journalist case, if one asks, "Why does this particular person not have to tell us where she got her information?" then the answer is, "Because she is a journalist." The first step in the justification of the rights of journalists refers to the feature of an individual, the feature of being a journalist.

This individualistic feature of rights allows us to explain the connection between rights and respect for individuals. Feinberg suggests that "respect for persons . . . may simply be respect for their rights" (1980, 151). The precise nature of the relationship between rights and respect has never been made clear. The justified-constraint analysis of relational obligation clarifies this relationship. To accord me my rights is to display a kind of respect for me because according me my rights acknowledges that one of my features justifies normative constraints. Rights are relational normative constraints. A relational normative constraint is a normative constraint justified by the feature of an individual. When I accord you your rights, I acknowledge that you are the source of normative constraints, of obligations. In this important sense, I respect you. When I fail to accord you your rights, I implicitly assert that you are not a ground of normative constraints. In this important sense, I fail to respect you.

The justified-constraint theory allows us to provide a plausible account of why the vast majority of people think that infants have rights. Consider the following argument from McCormick

> [T]here is a significant difference between asserting that every child ought to be cared for, nurtured, and, if possible loved, and asserting that every child has a right to care, nurture, and love. One way of showing the difference is to show that there are statements which could intelligibly be advanced as justifications for the former position but which could not be intelligibly be advanced in jus-tification of the latter. For example, along the lines of Swift's *Modest Proposal*, one could suggest as a reason why children ought to be cared for, nurtured and loved, that that would be the best way of getting them to grow into plump and contented creatures fit to enhance the national diet. Or again, one could argue that a healthy society requires healthy and well-nurtured children who will grow up into contented and well-adjusted adults who will contribute to the GNP and not be a charge on the welfare facilities or the prison service.
>
> Of course only one of these is a moral, or indeed a serious, argument. But neither is an argument which could be used directly to justify the proposition that children have a right to care, nurture, and love. Why not? Because both advance reasons for giving children care, nurture, and love solely on the ground that their well-being is a fit means to an ulterior end. I do not say that there can be no moral argument that certain beings ought to be treated in a certain way in order to achieve some end other than their well-being. I do say that such arguments are necessarily inept in justifying the ascription to them a right to that treatment (1982, 159).

McCormick was right to see that rights have an individualistic justification. One who denies that infants have rights denies that infants are a ground of obligations and impossibilities. In an important sense, they show a lack of respect for infants. They implicitly assert that infants are lesser beings than right-holders. The reason that the vast majority of people reject the view that infants do not have rights is that they implicitly see these links between rights, individualism, and respect and they do not think that infants are lesser beings than typical adults.

One of the most important implications of the justified-constraint theory is that those who have claimed that rights exist only when important normative matters are at stake are wrong. Richard Primus holds that

> Calling something a right endows it with a sacred status, deeming it important and worthy of special protection (1999, 36).

Sumner holds that "the normative function of the language of rights is to formulate one kind of urgent or insistent demand" (1987, 15). Many others have made similar assertions. Scholars who make this claim have focused too much of their attention on famous declarations of rights, such as the U.S. Bill of Rights or the Universal Declaration of Human Rights. They have a philosopher's perspective. A lawyer, on the other hand, is unlikely to agree with Primus and Sumner. The law contains many examples of trivial rights. Two or three days dealing with standard contract law makes it clear that calling something a right does not endow it with "sacred status." Suppose that you have a popcorn stand and put up a sign reading "Popcorn, five cents." I give you five cents and say, "I would like some popcorn." I then have a legal and a moral right to some popcorn. This is a trivial right. On the justified-constraint theory, rights are analyzed in terms of obligations *tout court*, not in terms of *important* obligations. This is an extremely important and possibly surprising point. As Raz notes, "it is not part of the very notion of right that rights have great weight or importance" (1986, 186). Trivial rights will not be mentioned in public manifestos. They do not merit the effort. Given how much it costs to take a matter to court, trivial rights will rarely find their way into court. It would be a waste of money for me to take you to court to get my bag of popcorn. Trivial rights are common and banal. Indeed, the fact that they are so common and banal is part of the reason that philosophers have overlooked them. It is crucial to the correct understanding of rights that scholars come to see the trivial rights all around them. (For more on this issue, see the discussion of Ronald Dworkin's view in Chapter 6.)

There is a closely related tendency to think that if someone has a right, then some sort of relatively heavy-handed enforcement is justified. Since only the mildest sorts of enforcement are appropriate if you refuse to give me a bag of popcorn, there is a tendency to think that no rights are involved. Trivial rights will not justify heavy-handed enforcement. Almost no sort of enforcement is justified if a popcorn vender refuses to hand over a bag of popcorn every now and then. Indeed, as noted in the previous chapter, enforcement is not necessary for a right to exist. A right that X do A is distinct from a right that another person force X to do A.

The tendency to link rights and enforcement is perhaps part of the tendency to think that rights are non-existent or irrelevant in relationships between friends and family members. As Neera Badhwar (1985) has noted, this tendency should be resisted. Actions that would otherwise be supererogatory can be matters of rights between friends and family members. I believe that I have a moral obligation to help my wife maintain our home. She has a right that I help with the many tasks required to keep one's house and home running somewhat smoothly. Because she is my wife and because of the many promises (both explicit and implicit) we have made to each other, if I were to refuse to do any cooking, cleaning, yard work, and house repair, I would be failing to live up to my obligations and violating her rights. Yesterday I saw my neighbor struggling to get some heavy containers of trash down to the curb for pickup. I put on my shoes and helped him get them to the curb. I did not have an obligation to do this. It was supererogatory. As I have argued elsewhere, some of our most important relational obligations are our obligations to family and friends (Rainbolt, 2000).

151

What does the justified-constraint theory of relational obligation imply about obligations to oneself? Whether one can have moral obligations to oneself is a matter of dispute. This case is too controversial for a theory of relational obligation to stand or fall with it, but it is interesting to note the implications of a theory of relational obligation regarding obligations to oneself.

Raz's theory implies that obligations to oneself are conceptually possible. According to the implicit theory of relational obligation found in Raz, an obligation is *to* someone if and only if that person's well-being is the sufficient reason for the obligation. If one holds, as a matter of substantive moral theory, that a person's well-being can be the sufficient reason for their own obligation, then one would hold that one can have obligations to oneself. So, according to Raz, obligations to oneself are conceptually coherent, although it would be perfectly consistent for Raz to hold that as a matter of substantive morality no such obligations exist.

According to Hart's theory, an obligation is to someone if and only if that person's choices are protected by the obligation. This view, like Raz's, implies that obligations to oneself are conceptually coherent. If John had an obligation that protected John's choices, then John would have an obligation to himself. Like Raz, Hart would be perfectly consistent if he held that, although obligations to oneself are conceptually coherent, as a matter of substantive morality, no such obligations exist.

On Wellman's view, obligations to oneself are a conceptual impossibility. According to Wellman's implicit theory of relational obligation, X's obligation is to Y if and only if X's obligation advantages Y's will. Furthermore, for Wellman an obligation advantages someone's will when it favors the one person's will "vis-à-vis the opposing will of any second party" (1985, 91–92). According to Wellman, obligations are necessarily to another person.

The justified-constraint view of relational obligation sides with Raz and Hart against Wellman. On the justified-constraint view, X's obligation is to Y if and only if a feature of Y is a reason X has an obligation. There is no conceptual reason that prevents X and Y from being the same person. It is possible that a feature of X could be a reason for X to have an obligation. As a matter of substantive moral theory, I lean toward the view that we have no obligations to ourselves. But the justified-constraint theory of relational obligation does not rule out this possibility.

What does the justified-constraint analysis imply about third-party beneficiaries? These cases have divided choice and interest theorists, and the justified-constraint theory reveals why this is so. Suppose that Sangita promises Fred Junior that she will pay his father, Fred Senior, $100. Sangita has an obligation to pay Fred Senior $100. It is not clear who the object of the obligation is and therefore who has the right that Sangita pay Fred Senior $100. A classic interest theorist would hold that the obligation is to Fred Senior because he is the beneficiary of the obligation. Fulfillment of Sangita's obligation forwards Fred Senior's interest. A classic choice theorist would hold that the obligation is to Fred Junior because, roughly speaking, it is Fred Junior who controls the obligation. It is Fred Junior who can waive the obligation. Some have attempted to use third-party beneficiary cases to defend either the choice theory or the interest theory. But these cases are not well suited to this purpose. Unfortunately for the partisans on both sides of the choice–interest debate, in third-party beneficiary cases the ordinary language of rights does not come down firmly on either side. Some think that Fred Junior has the right that Sangita pay Fred Senior $100. Others think that Fred Senior has the right that Sangita pay Fred Senior $100. Still others think that both Fred Junior and Fred Senior have a right that Sangita pay Fred Senior $100.

The justified-constraint theory of relational obligation explains why this case is controversial. It reveals that the dispute over the third-party beneficiary case is another case of confusion caused by theories which do not correctly draw the line between conceptual and substantive matters. On the justified-constraint conception of rights, the debate over the third-party beneficiary case is a substantive dispute over which individual features justify obligations in the rule system in question. It is not a conceptual dispute over the nature of relational obligation. Which feature(s) of persons justify obligations in the rule system in question, interests, choices, or wills? Whether Fred Junior or Fred Senior or both have a right that Sangita give Fred Senior $100 turns on this substantive issue. The justified-constraint theory of relational obligation is neutral on the third-party beneficiary case. It is perfectly possible to write a legal rule system that implies that Fred Junior has the right, to write a legal rule system that implies that Fred Senior has the right, or to write a legal rule system that implies that both of them have the right.

The justified-constraint analysis implies that the second half of the correlativity thesis is false. The correlativity thesis holds that all rights imply duties and all duties imply rights. In Chapter 2, we saw that the first half of the correlativity thesis, that all rights imply duties, is false. It is false because there are immunity rights. With the analysis of relational obligation in place, we can see that, on most plausible substantive views, the second half of the thesis, that all duties imply rights, is also false. While all Hohfeldian duties, all relational obligations, imply rights, in some rule systems there are non-Hohfeldian duties, non-relational obligations.

The justified-constraint theory implies that charity is importantly different from cases of easy rescue. Suppose that you are lounging by a pool and you see a baby drowning. Suppose that it would be extremely easy for you to rescue the baby. If there is a moral rule system and it is as we pretheoretically think it is, then it implies that you have an obligation to perform this easy rescue. Is this a relational or a non-relational obligation? If it is a relational obligation, then there is a right to easy rescue. If it is not a relational obligation, then there is not a right to easy rescue. Is the obligation to rescue like Nikki's obligation or like Tabitha's? It is like Nikki's. The moral rule system requires that one perform each and every easy rescue. It does not require that one perform any difficult rescues. Difficult rescues are supererogatory. Among the arguments that justify one's obligation to perform a particular easy rescue there will be some that contain an essential reference to the plight of the person whom you can easily rescue.

Ronald Milo has suggested the following counterexample to the justified-constraint theory of relational obligation.[5] Suppose that you see a motorist stranded in the snow, walking toward a service station a mile away. You know that picking up the motorist poses no danger to you. Milo would argue that failing to pick up the motorist is immoral, it is forbidden by the moral rule system and that this obligation is *to* the motorist. It is a feature of the motorist, that he will be cold and wet, that grounds the obligation to pick him up. Milo also argues that the motorist does not have a right to be picked up. This appears to be a counterexample to the justified-constraint theory of relational obligation because it appears to be a case of a relational obligation that does not imply a right.

One can see the problem with Milo's alleged counterexample once one sees that Milo's case straddles two different sorts of situations. The first sort of situations are cases of supererogation. The justified-constraint theory of relational obligation has no trouble with cases of supererogation. Supererogatory acts are not obligatory, so one never has a right that another perform a supererogatory act. The second sort of situations are cases of easy rescue. There are cases where one does have an obligation to help those in great need. One has an obligation to save an (easily savable) drowning baby from a swimming pool. This obligation is to the baby, and the baby has a right to be rescued.

The stranded motorist case is under-described and so seems to fall in between cases of supererogation and cases of easy rescue. If the motorist's need is great and the rescue is easy, then he has a right to be picked up. How great and how easy is a question the justified-constraint theory cannot and need not answer. The answer will depend on the moral rule system. If, on the other hand, the motorist's need is not great, then it is a case of supererogation. In either case, it is not a counterexample to the justified-constraint analysis of relational obligations. Milo's example is not clear as to which sort of situation the motorist is in. That is why the view that the motorist has no right but that the obligation is *to* him is initially plausible.

The justified-constraint theory implies that many of the obligations we have as citizens of a country are non-relational obligations. In Chapter 2 we considered the right to vote in countries like Australia where it is illegal not to vote. In those countries, one has a duty right to vote. In considering this duty right, we wondered whether it was an Hohfeldian or a non-Hohfeldian duty right. We can now see that it is a non-Hohfeldian duty right. There is no sound argument for an Australian citizen's obligation to vote that makes essential reference to any particular individual. Roughly, one has an obligation to vote because it is good for the country. While the possible sound arguments for an Australian citizen's obligation to vote will mention the other citizens of Australia, no particular citizen is essential to the argument. A citizen would still have the obligation if any one of the other citizens died or renounced her Australian citizenship and moved to another country. The

---

[5]   In conversation.

same sort of argument applies to the obligation to pay one's taxes and the obligation to perform military service (if one has such an obligation). In these case, like the case of the obligation to vote, no particular individual is essential to any sound argument for the obligation. Compare the obligation to pay one's taxes and the obligation to perform military service to the typical obligations imposed by the criminal law, e.g., my obligation not to assault Tony. The argument that one has an obligation under the criminal law not to assault Tony will make essential reference to Tony. It must do so to explain why I have an obligation not to assault Tony, but I have no obligation not to assault Evander, with whom I have agreed to compete in a boxing match.

It is interesting to see what the justified-constraint view implies about Feinberg's (1980, 143–155) Nowheresville, a place where there are almost no rights. People who live in Nowheresville are significantly morally better than people are in our world. They display more benevolence, compassion, sympathy, etc. In addition, there are non-relational obligations in Nowheresville.

> Let us introduce duties into Nowheresville, but only in the sense of actions that are ... morally mandatory, but not in the older sense of actions that are due others and can be claimed by others as their right (1980, 144).

Nowheresville also contains personal deserts. A personal desert is "simply a kind of fittingness between one party's character or action and another party's favorable response" (1980, 145). If someone doing something for you (say mowing your lawn) does a wonderful job, going above and beyond what she was contractually obligated to do, then it seems appropriate (but not obligatory) for one to reward the person who has done a wonderful job. This person deserves a little something extra. Finally, Feinberg adds the notion of a sovereign monopoly of rights to Nowheresville. In Nowheresville, the obligations formed by social arrangements (contracts, the law, clubs, universities, businesses, etc.) are all owed to a Hobbesian sovereign. They are not owed to others. In Nowheresville, if X and Y sign a contract, they do so with the sovereign. X promises the sovereign that he will do A1 for Y, and Y promises the sovereign that she will do A2 for X. Thus, in Nowheresville, there is only one right-holder, the sovereign.

Feinberg then wonders "what precisely a world is missing when it does not contain rights and why that absence is morally important?" (1980, 148). What, on the justified-constraint view, is missing from Nowheresville? The missing element is that people in Nowheresville are not sources of obligations. In Nowheresville, only the sovereign is a source of obligation. In Nowheresville, features of the individuals other than the sovereign never justify the obligations of others.

As Hohfeld was at pains to point out, the use of the term "rights" is extremely variable and ambiguous. No theory will imply that every single use and non-use of the term is correct. The question at issue is which conception of rights best fits the pattern of use and non-use found in the ordinary language of rights (i.e., is

155

extensionally best) and which brings us the most understanding (i.e., is theoretically best). Hohfeld himself saw this.

> Recognizing, as we must, the very broad and indiscriminate use of the term "right," what clue do we find, in ordinary legal discourse, toward limiting the word in question to a definite and appropriate meaning? That clue lies in the correlative "duty," for it is certain that even those who use the word and the conception "right" in the broadest possible way are accustomed to thinking of "duty" as the invariable correlative (2001, 13).

Removing the tie to meaning that Hohfeld has put into this passage, we can restate his point as one of analysis. The use of the concept of a right is "very broad and indiscriminate," so, to clarify and deepen our understanding, we must first find the conception of right that best fits the pattern of the use and non-use of right in ordinary discourse. But the preferred conception will also limit the concept of rights with "a definite and appropriate" analysis. I am arguing that one particular analysis is "a definite" and the most "appropriate" understanding of rights. The justified-constraint analysis is the most appropriate in three senses. First and most importantly, it fits the pattern of use and non-use of the term "rights" better than any other theory of rights. Second, the justified-constraint theory brings us the most understanding in that it, better than any other theory of rights, both allows one to see connections between rights and other moral concepts and solves problems in rights theory that have puzzled philosophers. Third, as we will see in Chapters 6, 7, and 8, it allows us to solve important problems in the application of a theory of rights.

6. Rights Conflict

Much of the interest in a theory of rights comes from its application to various controversies. There are too many of these to consider all of them here. The remainder of this book will examine two of these controversies and argue that the justified-constraint theory of rights provides the most plausible analysis of them. This chapter considers rights conflict. Chapters 7 and 8 consider what sorts of things can have rights. We will continue to simplify matters by ignoring impossibilities. There are two kinds of rights conflict. First, internal rights conflict occurs when rights conflict with each other. In these cases, there is a conflict between relational obligations. Second, external rights conflict occurs when rights conflict with non-rights-based moral considerations. In these cases, there is a conflict between relational and non-relational obligations. (It may seem odd that this chapter does not discuss John's Rowan's *Conflicts of Rights* (1999). This interesting and useful work is a discussion of the application of rights to various moral controversies (e.g., redistributive taxation, abortion). It does not discuss the issue considered in this chapter.)

1. PERMISSIBLE AND UNAVOIDABLE RIGHTS TRANSGRESSION

There are two different kinds of internal rights conflict. Perhaps the most famous example of the first kind of internal rights conflict is Feinberg's.

> Suppose that you are on a backpacking trip in the high mountain country when an unanticipated blizzard strikes the area with such ferocity that your life is imperiled. Fortunately, you stumble onto an unoccupied cabin, locked and boarded up for the winter, clearly somebody else's private property. You smash in a window, enter and huddle in a corner for three days until the storm abates. During this period you help yourself to your unknown benefactor's food supply and burn his wooden furniture in the fireplace to keep warm. Surely you are justified in doing all these things and yet you have infringed the clear rights of another person (1980, 230).

Let us call this case "Backpacker." Reviewing it using Hohfeldian terminology and the deontic and alethic normative concepts discussed above will allow us to see the nature of the conflict more clearly. To simplify matters, let us focus on one particular object in the cabin—a wooden chair that you burn to keep warm. The owner of the chair seems to have a claim right that you not burn the chair. Correlative to the claim is your duty not to burn the chair. Therefore, the following sentence seems to be true:

1. You have an obligation to the owner that you not burn the chair.

On the other hand, because burning the chair is necessary to save your life, it seems that you have a liberty right to burn the chair. You have a liberty to burn the chair, a liberty not to burn the chair, and claims that protect these liberties. You have a claim that the owner not interfere with your burning of the chair. How could the owner interfere? Perhaps he cannot. He might be in some warm house miles away. But suppose that the owner has outfitted the cabin with a video monitor and a remotely operated hypodermic-needle gun system. This allows the owner to view the cabin while he is away and shoot those who attempt to destroy his property. Those shot fall asleep for three days so that they can be arrested. In that case, if the owner was watching his cabin, you would have a claim that he not shoot you. (The storm is such that if you fell asleep for three days, you would die.) The conflict occurs because part of your liberty right, your liberty to burn the chair, implies that you have a permission to burn the chair. Therefore it seems that the following sentence is true:

2. You do not have an obligation to the owner that you not burn the chair.

1 and 2 form a contradiction, and this is the conflict. (Backpacker shows that Waldron (1993a) was wrong to assert that "talking about conflicts of rights is a way of talking about the incompatibility of the duties that rights involve" (211). In Backpacker the conflict is not between duties but between a duty and a liberty. Although there are cases in which rights conflict is conflict between the duties correlative to claim rights, not all conflicts of rights are of this form.)

Let us refer to cases like Backpacker as cases of *permissible rights transgression*. One transgresses on a right when one does not meet the obligation that is implied by the right. It seems that it is permissible for you to transgress on the cabin owner's property rights. Note that you are permitted to wander off to die. In that case, no rights are transgressed. There are many other cases of permissible rights transgression. Suppose I promise to meet you for lunch. It would seem that you have a claim right that I meet you for lunch. But then I become so ill that going to lunch will cause me severe pain. In that case, it seems that I have a liberty right not to go to lunch. Your claim right that I meet you for lunch seems to conflict with my liberty right not to go to lunch. It seems that it is permissible for me to transgress on your claim right.

Perhaps the most well-known example of the second kind of internal rights conflict was first mentioned by Philippa Foot and made famous by Thomson—the trolley problem.

Edward is the driver of a trolley, whose brakes have just failed. On the track ahead of him are five people; the banks are so steep that they will not be able to get off the track in time. The track has a spur leading off to the right and Edward can turn the trolley onto it. Unfortunately, there is one person on the right-hand track. Edward can turn the trolley, killing the one; or he can refrain from turning the trolley, killing five (1986, 80–1).

For reasons that will be become apparent later, clarity of exposition will be improved by first considering some modified versions of the trolley problem and then considering Thomson's version. Let us begin with the following version. Assume that there is only one person on each track. Sue is in her car, stalled on the spur, and Jane is standing on the main line. If Edward does not divert the trolley, Jane, because she is standing at a place where the banks are steep, will be killed. If he does divert the trolley, Sue's car will be destroyed. However, Sue can easily leave her car before the trolley arrives, so, if Edward diverts the trolley, she will not die. Call this case "Jane-or-Car." Once again, it will be profitable to set this case out in Hohfeldian terminology and the deontic and alethic normative concepts developed above. It seems that Jane has a claim right that Edward divert the trolley. Correlative to this claim is Edward's duty to divert the trolley. So it seems that

1. Edward has an obligation to Jane that Edward divert the trolley.

It also seems that Sue has a claim right that Edward not divert the trolley. Correlative to this claim is Edward's duty not to divert the trolley. So it seems that

2. Edward has an obligation to Sue that Edward not divert the trolley.

We do not have a contradiction. Unlike 1 and 2 in Backpacker, the obligations generated by the rights in question are not, in and of themselves, contradictory. (Waldron (1993a) has noticed this point.) However, while there is no contradiction, there is a conflict. As the case is described, Edward must either divert or not divert the trolley. He cannot stop it or take any other actions. Therefore, it is not physically possible for Edward to meet both of his obligations. Let us refer to cases such as Jane-or-Car as *unavoidable rights transgression*. These cases are different from cases of permissible rights transgression. In Backpacker, if the backpacker decides not to break into the cabin and wanders off to die, no rights are transgressed. It is physically possible for the backpacker to avoid transgressing a right. But in Jane-or-Car, it is physically impossible for Edward to avoid transgressing either Sue's right to use her car or Jane's right to live. There are many other cases of unavoidable rights transgression. Suppose that Jim has an obligation to Susan that Jim go to the airport on Tuesday. He promised to pick her up. Suppose also that Jim also has an obligation to Jessica that Jim not go to the airport. Jessica is worried about airport bombings and, to reassure her, Jim promised never to enter an airport.

I have divided rights conflicts in a novel way. It is more usual to divide cases of rights conflict using the active/passive and positive/negative distinctions noted in Chapter 1. Because these distinctions are orthogonal, there are four possible kinds of rights (active positive, active negative, passive positive and passive negative) and therefore ten different conflict possibilities (active passive vs. active passive, active passive vs. active negative, active passive vs. passive positive, active passive vs. passive negative, active negative vs. active negative, etc.) There is nothing wrong with this sort of classification. When it comes to substantive matters, it may well be more useful than the classification offered here. But as far as the conceptual nature

159

of rights conflict is concerned, the active/passive and positive/negative distinctions are not relevant. The structure of rights conflict does not vary along lines that follow these distinctions. Backpacker is a case of a conflict between an active positive right (your right to burn the chair) and a passive negative right (the owner's right that you not burn the chair). Jane-or-Car is a conflict between a passive positive right (Jane's right that Edward divert the trolley) and a passive negative right (Sue's right that Edward not divert the trolley). It is easy to construct cases of permissible rights transgression and cases of unavoidable rights transgression that fit any of the ten different categories of rights conflict generated from the active/passive and positive/negative distinctions. Two examples will be sufficient. Suppose that when you enter the cabin in Backpacker the heat is on and that you have promised the owner of the cabin that you will turn it off. But if you turn it off, you will die of cold. In that case, there is a case of permissible rights transgression in a conflict between an active negative right (your right not to turn off the heat) and a passive positive right (the owner's right that you turn off the heat). Suppose that there is only one trolley line. The run-away trolley is on the line, Sue is in her car at one point on the line, and Jane is farther down the line between steep embankments. If Sue doesn't move her car, she will die, but her car will stop the trolley and Jane will live. If Sue moves her car, then she will live and Jane will die. This is a case of unavoidable rights transgression in a conflict between an active positive right (Sue's right to drive herself off the tracks) and a passive negative right (Jane's right that Sue not drive off the tracks).

2. PRIMA FACIE AND SPECIFICATION

There are two frequently discussed views of internal conflicts between rights—the prima facie view and the specification view. (The formulations of the specification and prima facie views in this section owe much to Christopher Heath Wellman (1995). His defense of specification is illuminating. However, for the reasons noted below, it is not fully adequate.)

There are two key facets of the prima facie view. The first is the claim that there are some rights that are *not* absolute. An *absolute* right is a right that implies an absolute obligation. An absolute obligation is an "unconditionally incumbent" obligation (Feinberg 1973, 80). Absolute obligations might be, indeed will be, narrowly defined obligations. Suppose that a legal rule system implies that Hassan has an absolute legal liberty right to say that Richard Nixon was a crook. The legal rule system might imply that he has this absolute right only if he is in a certain place (e.g., Hyde Park). In this sense, the right is narrowly defined. If the right is absolute and he is in the specified place, then it is permissible for him to say that Richard Nixon was a crook. Even if his saying this would cost millions of lives, he is still permitted to do so.

The second key facet of the prima facie view is the concept of weighing. A *prima facie* right is a right that implies a prima facie (relational) obligation. A prima facie (relational or non-relational) obligation is an obligation that can be outweighed by other (relational or non-relational) obligations. An *actual* right is a prima facie right that *can be* but, in a particular situation, *is not* outweighed by any other (relational or non-relational) obligations. An absolute right is a prima facie right that *cannot* be outweighed in any possible situation. When there is a conflict between prima facie rights, one must weigh the conflicting prima facie rights to determine which right is over-ridden. The notion of weighing a right is metaphorical. One cannot literally weigh a right in the way that one can weigh a rock or a truck. In non-metaphorical terms, to weigh one right against another is to examine the arguments for the view for and against particular assertions of actual rights. In Backpacker, talk of weighing your right to burn a chair against the cabin's owner's right that you not burn the chair is a metaphor for examining the arguments to determine whether or not "You have an actual obligation to the owner that you not burn the chair" is true. The sorts of arguments one uses to make this determination are the familiar ones used in all philosophical discussions—real and hypothetical cases, moral principles, counterexamples, etc. Talk of weighing rights is a metaphor for the examination of arguments for and against the view that one right is more important than another. (Pietroski (1993) notes that "it is tempting to give 'prima facie' notions an epistemological gloss" (p. 491). Montague (2001) gives into that temptation. I find Pietroski's arguments against the epistemic understanding of "prima facie" completely convincing. As I have nothing to add to his arguments, I will not review them here.)

On the prima facie view, the owner of the cabin in Backpacker has a prima facie claim right that his chair not be burned. This right implies the backpacker's prima facie obligation not to burn the chair. The backpacker's prima facie liberty right implies that he does not have a prima facie obligation not to burn the chair. On the prima facie view, the conflict between the cabin owner's claim right and the backpacker's liberty right is resolved by asserting that the backpacker's prima facie liberty right outweighs the cabin owner's prima facie claim right. In non-metaphorical terms, it seems to most people that the arguments for the view that the backpacker has an actual liberty right to burn the chair are better than the arguments for the view that the cabin owner has an actual claim right that the backpacker not burn the chair. In this way the prima facie view attempts to resolve the problem of permissible rights transgression.

The prima facie view also attempts to provide a solution to the problem of unavoidable rights transgression. In Jane-or-Car, Jane has a prima facie claim right that Edward divert the trolley. This right implies Edward's prima facie obligation to divert the trolley. Sue has a prima facie claim right that Edward not divert the trolley. This right implies Edward's prima facie obligation not to divert the trolley. The conflict is resolved by asserting that Jane's prima facie claim right outweighs Sue's. Most people think that Jane's right that Edward divert the trolley outweighs Sue's right that he not divert the trolley. Jane's life is morally more important than Sue's car. In non-metaphorical terms, it seems that the arguments for the view that Sue has an actual claim right that Edward not divert the trolley are not as good as the arguments for the view that Jane has an actual claim right that Edward divert the trolley.

There are at least three possible objections to the prima facie view. First, one might hold that the view is inadequate because it implies that we frequently do not know whether or not one of our rights is actual. We do not have this information because it is possible that, unbeknownst to us, one of our prima facie rights has been outweighed by another prima facie right. The cabin owner might be unaware of the storm and so be unaware that his previously actual right that the backpacker not burn his chair has been outweighed. This assertion is true but no objection to the prima facie view. All of us have many rights of which we are not aware. The complexity of many rule systems (e.g., U.S. tax law) implies that many of us do not know the full extent and status of our rights. The prima facie view merely adds another way in which our knowledge of our own rights is limited. Rather than being an objection to the prima facie view, the claim that we do not know our actual rights is merely an instance of the general fact that we are beings with limited knowledge.

Second, some claim that the prima facie view lacks explanatory power. The problem is that the prima facie view is a view about the structure of rights conflict. It takes us to the point where the prima facie rights must be weighed against each other and then tells us nothing. This assertion is true. Beyond saying that we must examine the arguments to see which prima facie right is an actual right, the prima facie view does not tell us how to determine which right is the actual right. However, this assertion is no objection to the prima facie view. The prima facie view claims to be no more than a view about the structure of rights conflict. It is no objection to it that it does not provide a detailed method for resolving rights conflict.

Third, some might argue that the prima facie view is inadequate because it implies that statements of rights are not the end of moral discussion. Again, this assertion is true. The prima facie view implies that there are prima facie rights and prima facie rights are not actual rights. Actual rights are the end of moral discussion. As with the previous objection, this one correctly points to an implication of the prima facie view. However, as with the previous objection, this implication is no objection to the view. It is nothing more than a restatement of the view. To the objection that the prima facie view implies that statements of rights are not the end of moral discussion, defenders of the prima facie view need only reply, "Yes, that is an implication of the view and no objection to it."

On the specification view, most, perhaps all, statements of rights implicitly contain clauses that specify the situation in which one has the right. The crucial metaphor used in this view is that of a limit. According to this view, the cabin owner in Backpacker does not have a right against the backpacker that the backpacker not burn the chair. Rather, the owner has a more limited right such as the right against the backpacker that the backpacker not burn the chair unless it is necessary to save the backpacker's life or ... In this way, cases of permissible rights transgression are resolved. No rights transgression occurs because it merely seemed that the backpacker was transgressing on the cabin owner's rights. Once the correct limits of the right are determined, we see that the backpacker's burning the chair does not transgress on the cabin owner's right. Similarly, in Jane-or-Car, Sue does not have a right against Edward that Edward not divert the trolley. Rather, she has the more limited right that Edward not divert the trolley unless not diverting it would cause someone's else's death or ... In this way the conflict in unavoidable rights transgression cases is resolved. Obviously, on the specification view, rights statements contain long strings of disjunctively joined conditions after an "unless." It is conceptually possible for anything to appear in an unless clause. A right could have the following form: X has a right against Y to do A unless doing A would cause the loss of X or more units of utility or ... On this view, a landlord does not have a right to $750 from her tenant. Rather, she has a right to $750 from the tenant unless the tenant needs that money to prevent worldwide famine, or she fails to keep the building properly maintained, or the building burns down, or ... On the specification view, there is never any real rights conflict. There is only apparent rights conflict. The appearance of conflict disappears when the rights in question are fully specified. The specification view implies that all rights are absolute. On the specification view, rights conflict is resolved by considering arguments for and against different views about the limits of a right, by considering arguments for and against the existence of particular unless clauses.

The idea of limiting rights is a metaphor. The metaphor being used is the metaphor of a bounded physical space. Literally, a limit is the boundary surrounding a specific physical area. Rights are not physical things that have literal limits in the way that a baseball field does. In non-metaphorical terms, to limit a right is to specify its unless clauses. To discuss the limits of a right is to discuss the arguments for and against the existence and nature of the possible unless clauses contained in the right.

There are four possible objections to the specification view. First, some hold that the specification view cannot be true because it implies that no one knows her fully specified rights. The view does have this implication. The unless clauses of rights in any moderately complex rule system are bound to be such that many people will not know their full extent. Even if one did know the fully specified statement of a particular right, it is quite possible that one would not know whether a certain unless clause was fulfilled. The cabin owner in Backpacker, even if he knew that his right that the chair not be burned had an unless clause covering the case in which burning the chair was necessary to save a life, might not know whether, at a particular time, burning the chair was in fact necessary to save a life. However, this is no objection to the specification view. As with the similar objection to prima facie view, this argument merely points to an instance of the general fact that we are beings with limited knowledge.

Second, some claim that the specification view lacks explanatory power. The specification view is a view about the structure of rights conflict. Beyond saying that we must examine the arguments to see which unless clauses exist, the specification view itself does not tell us how to determine whether a particular unless clause exists. This assertion is no objection to the specification view. The specification view claims to be no more than a view about the structure of rights conflict. It is no objection to it that it does not provide a method for resolving rights conflict.

Third, some claim that the specification view is unable to account for the obligation to compensate for the transgression of rights. In Backpacker, if the backpacker burns the chair, it seems that the cabin owner has a right to compensation. Thomson thinks that the specification view cannot explain why you have a right to compensation. She regards this as a decisive objection to the view (1986, 41). Thomson thinks that only the fact that the backpacker transgressed one of the cabin owner's rights can explain why the backpacker owes compensation. According to the specification view, the backpacker has not transgressed on any of the cabin owner's rights because the full specification of the cabin owner's right that the chair not be burned contains an unless clause stating that the backpacker has no obligation to refrain from burning the chair if it is necessary to save the backpacker's life.

This objection is unconvincing. First, the objection is weakened once one notices that rights transgression and compensation are not well correlated. That X owes Y compensation does not imply that X transgressed one of Y's rights. My paycheck from Georgia State University reports my "total compensation" even though I have not violated any of Georgia State's rights. To make her objection go through, Thomson must at least distinguish two different forms of compensation and point to one that poses a problem for the specification view. She needs to distinguish the perfectly normal use of "compensation" to refer to payment made for goods or services and the use of the same term to refer to something given to requite for a person's losses. It is only compensation in the second sense that might imply that rights transgression has occurred.

That X has transgressed one of Y's rights does not imply that X owes Y compensation. Suppose that I kill you. This transgresses on your rights. It does not seem that I owe you compensation. At the very least, whether compensation makes sense and/or is appropriate in the case of murder is a complex issue. I will touch on it further in Chapter 8. However one resolves the murder case, it seems that Thomson herself provides a case of rights transgression in which no compensation is owed. In Jane-or-Car, Edward should divert the trolley and thus transgress on Sue's rights. But, assuming that the brake failure was in no way caused by Edward, he does not owe Sue any compensation for the destruction of her car. He does not even owe her an apology. He has a duty to provide her with an explanation of the incident, but if he has done nothing wrong then he has nothing for which to apologize. Neither an apology (if he owed one) nor an explanation would be a form of compensation. In light of this lack of implications between rights and compensation, Thomson needs to say more about why the fact that one violates another's rights explains the duty to compensate.

Second, rule systems can imply rights to be given money and other goods in all sorts of different situations. It is conceptually possible for the rule system to imply

164

that one has a right to a sum of money upon turning 18 or when one grows a beard. There is no conceptual barrier to the rule system implying that one has a right to the value of objects taken without one's consent from the person who takes the object. Thus the defender of the specification view can explain why the backpacker owes the cabin owner a certain sum of money for the chair without any reference to rights transgression simply by asserting that the rule system implies that when certain unless clauses apply, the backpacker owes the cabin owner the relevant sum of money. The rule system might contain statements with the following form:

1. X has a right against Y that Y do A1 unless conditions C1 or C2 or . . . Cn are true.
2. If C1 or C5 or C8 . . . are true, then Y has an obligation to X that Y do A2.

A fourth objection to the specification view is that it fails to "sufficiently bring out that we have interfered where justice says we should not" (Morris 1968, 499). This point seems intuitively plausible, but it is hard to tease an argument out of it. In the first place it is odd to say that in cases of permissible rights transgression we have "interfered where justice says we should not." The act is, by hypothesis, permissible. Perhaps one who makes this objection is suggesting that the specification view will tend to lead us to transgress on fully specified rights. One might hold that if we are used to thinking that rights have long unless clauses, then we are more likely to be tempted to assume the existence of one when we are tempted to transgress on a right. So the specification view would have immoral consequences. This argument is weak. The amount of rights transgression is not sensitive to the philosophical analysis of rights. Even if it were, this would only be an argument for not publicizing the specification view, not an argument for thinking that it is false.

There is a kernel of truth in the above point, a kernel that is important but no objection to the specification view. Rights are justified by the features of people. Rights are justified by features such as: certain acts cause people pain, certain acts take objects that people have worked for, certain acts fail to fulfill the expectations that people have, certain acts meet important human needs, etc. The kernel of truth in the fourth objection is that these features do not in any sense disappear when an unless clause is fulfilled. Suppose that one of the features that grounds the moral right not to be pinched unless . . . is that being pinched tends to cause pain. If one of the circumstances in the unless clause arises (e.g., thousands of lives will be saved), this does not mean that the pinching causes less pain. It is important to remember this fact, and this may well be the source of the initial plausibility of the fourth objection. The specification view does not imply that the pinching causes less pain when one of the circumstances in the unless clause occurs, so this is no objection to the view.

It is interesting to note that these two views seem more natural with respect to different rule systems. When it comes to non-moral rights conflict, the specification view seems more natural. When it comes to moral rights conflict, the prima facie view seems more natural. Consider a relatively simple non-moral rule system—the

165

baseball rule system. According to this rule system, a batter who gets three strikes is out. It seems that a batter who gets three strikes has a baseball obligation to leave the field and the opposing team has a baseball right that she leave the field. Another rule of baseball states that a batter may steal first. A batter steals first if he gets three strikes, the pitch is dropped by the catcher, he reaches first base before the ball, and he is not touched by the ball held by a member of the opposing team before reaching first. It seems that a batter who steals first has a baseball right to stay at first.

Imagine that a new catcher has just come up from the minor leagues. He is not quite up on the rules of baseball. After a batter steals first he turns to the umpire and says, "Wait a minute, he has three strikes. He's out. I have a baseball right that he leave the field." If the umpire were a kindly soul, she would carefully explain to the catcher that the rule that three strikes implies that a batter is out has an exception for those batters who steal first. She would explain that, strictly speaking, the team does not have the baseball right that a batter with three strikes leave the field. Rather they have the baseball right that a batter with three strikes leave the field unless he steals first or . . . The ellipses include such things as catcher interference or a balk. In this case, it would be (relatively) easy to state the fully specified baseball right concerning opposing batters leaving the field when they have three strikes.

The prima facie view seems unnatural in this case. It is would be odd to assert that the team has a prima facie baseball right that the batter leave the field that is over-ridden by the batter's prima facie baseball right to remain at first given that she has stolen it. Given that the batter stole first, it seems that the team has no sort of baseball right that he leave the field. If one knows the full specification of the baseball rights (as many baseball fans do), there is never even the appearance of a conflict.

Conflict in legal rule systems is similar to conflict in the baseball rule system in that it is usually thought of in specificationist terms. I own a pickup truck and I am married. In a hasty moment, someone might assert that part of my ownership of my pickup as defined by the legal rule system is the legal right that no one use my pickup. Of course, given the legal rule system in the United States, I do not have this legal right. My wife violates no laws if she uses my pickup. Stating the fully specified legal right concerning car ownership would be much more difficult than stating the fully specified baseball right discussed above. It would sound odd to assert that I have a prima facie legal right that my wife not drive my pickup that is over-ridden by her prima facie legal right to drive it. It is most natural to say that I have no sort of legal right that my wife not drive my pickup.

However, when it comes to Backpacker and Jane-or-Car, the specification view seems odd and forced. The notion of moral unless clauses seems odd. A reason for this may be that, in the case of moral rule systems, there is no hope of reaching a final and definitive statement of the unless clauses of any right. New technologies and the great complexity of human life will inevitably create cases of rights conflict that no one has ever considered before. This cannot be the end of the explanation for the difference because the same technology changes and complexities of human life will also lead common law judges to decide novel cases. Another reason that the specification view is more natural when it comes to non-moral rights conflict and the prima facie view is more natural when it comes to moral rights conflict is that non-moral rule systems are typically written down while the moral rule system is not. The mere fact that a rule system is written down makes it is easier for us to imagine the full specification of a right even if, as is generally the case, most do not know the fully specified right. Another reason for the naturalness of the specification view with respect to non-moral rights conflict may be that in non-moral rules systems there are usually parties who make definitive decisions about conflicts. There are no moral courts and no moral sheriffs, but there are legal judges and baseball umpires.

3. THE IDENTITY OF PRIMA FACIE AND SPECIFICATION

Despite initial appearances, there is no non-semantic difference between the prima facie view and the specification view. They are merely two different ways of saying the same thing. There are four reasons for thinking that the prima facie and specification views of internal rights conflict are not different views.

First, there is no case of right conflict in which the prima facie view and the specification view imply different answers about the resolution of the conflict. There is no case in which one of the views implies that a person ought to do A1 but the other view implies that the person ought to do A2. Backpacker and Jane-or-Car are perfectly typical in this respect. It is not true that the prima facie view implies that the backpacker ought not burn the chair but the specification view implies that the backpacker may burn the chair. Similarly, it is not true that the prima facie view implies that Edward ought not divert the trolley but the specification view implies that Edward ought to divert the trolley. The difference between the prima facie and specification views is not like the difference between the justified-constraint theory of rights and the theories of rights offered by Martin, Feinberg, Hart, Raz, and Wellman. Each of these theories of rights implies different things about different cases. Feinberg's view implies that there are no immunity rights while the other views do not have this implication. Wellman's and Hart's views imply that infants do not have rights while the justified-constraint view does not have this implication. This is not true of the prima facie and specification views. If there is a difference between these two views, it is not a difference that makes a difference when it comes to the moral evaluation of action.

Second, as noted above when considering objections to the prima facie and specification views, they have the same implications regarding our knowledge of rights and the explanatory power of rights. Both imply that our knowledge of our rights is imperfect, and neither provides a method for resolving rights conflict.

Third, both the prima facie view and the specification view rely on the examination of arguments. On the prima facie view, how does one determine which of two conflicting rights is the actual right? One examines the arguments for and against the view that each of the two conflict rights is an actual right. On the specification view, how does one determine whether a particular unless clause exists? One examines the arguments for and against the view that the unless clause in question exists. Here is the only difference between the two views. The prima facie view and the specification view differ only as to *when* one must examine the arguments to resolve the conflict. On the specification view, one examines the arguments *before* determining the complete specification of a right. On the prima facie view, one examines the arguments *after* determining the complete specification of a right. This difference as to the timing of the consideration of arguments is merely a semantic difference. It is a difference as to the way one wishes to speak of rights conflict, not a difference as to the nature of rights conflict.

The point made in the previous paragraph is confirmed when one looks at the arguments offered in a particular case by those who defend the prima facie view and those who defend the specification view. Consider Backpacker. It seems to most people that the backpacker may burn the chair. What sort of argument would a defender of the prima facie view provide to support the view that the backpacker's liberty right to burn the chair outweighs the cabin owner's right that the backpacker not burn the chair? The key points in such an argument would be that the backpacker must burn the chair or die and that the backpacker's life is morally more important that the cabin owner's interest in his chair. What sort of argument would a defender of the specification view provide to support the view that the cabin owner's right that the backpacker not burn the chair contains an unless clause something like "unless burning the chair is necessary to save a person's life"? The key points in such an argument would surely be that the backpacker must burn the chair or die and that the backpacker's life is morally more important than the cabin owner's interest in his chair. The arguments offered are the same. The only difference between the prima facie view and the specification view is the metaphor one uses to present the arguments.

At this point, one might object that the analysis to this point has misunderstood the nature of the difference between the prima facie view and the specification view. One might hold that it misunderstands the nature of rights principles. The second premise of the key argument form,

If X is F, then Y has an S obligation to do A,

is a rights principle. Assume that the features, F, in question are rather simple features such as "acting in ways necessary to save one's life" or "acting to prevent the destruction of one's property." Some sample rights-principles would be:

If X is acting in ways necessary to save her life, then Y has an S obligation to refrain from interfering with X's actions.

If X is acting to prevent the destruction of his property, then Y has an S obligation to refrain from interfering with X's actions.

In cases such as Backpacker, these principles, if they were both true, would lead to a conflict. The objector to the view that there is no non-semantic difference between the prima facie and specification views holds that the key feature of the prima facie view is that it rejects the claim that rights-principles take the form:

If X is F, then Y has an S obligation to do A.

Rather, on the prima facie view, rights-principles take the form:

If X is F, then Y has a prima facie S obligation to do A.

The objector holds that the key feature of the specification view is that, although it accepts that the rights principles have the form found in the second premise of the key argument form, it rejects the claim that the features, F, in question are rather simple features. Instead, on the specification view, the features F must be understood as complex features such as "acting to prevent the destruction of one's property without interfering with actions of another person that are necessary for that person to save her life." According to this objection, the distinctive feature of the prima facie view, is that it is not possible to deduce conclusions about actual rights merely from (a) rights principles and (b) facts about the features that various individuals have. On the prima facie view, one can only reach conclusions about actual rights when one combines (a) and (b) with (c), assertions of the weight of various prima facie rights. According to this objection, the distinctive feature of the specification view is that it is possible to deduce conclusions about actual rights merely from (a) rights principles and (b) facts about the features that various individuals have. According to the objection we are considering, there is a crucial difference between the prima facie view and the specification view when it comes to the structure of rights conflict. The prima facie view claims that we must consider assertions about the weight of various prima facie rights while the specification view rejects this claim.

This is an accurate way of presenting the prima facie and specification views. Indeed, it is enlightening to point out that the second premise of the key argument form is what some have called a rights principle. There is a difference between the prima facie view and the specification view over whether one must consider assertions about the weight of various prima facie rights to reach conclusions about actual rights. However, this difference is merely semantic. It is true that to reach conclusions about actual rights, a defender of the prima facie view will consider (a), (b), and (c) while a defender of the specification view considers only (a) and (b). But this way of presenting the situation masks the fact that a defender of the specification view must provide (d) a justification of the complex features, F, that must figure in rights principles. The arguments for these complex features will replicate the arguments that a defender of the prima facie view must make to justify (c) assertions of the weight of various prima facie rights. This objection does not provide any reason to reject the view that the difference between the specification and prima facie views is merely semantic.

The fourth reason to think that there is no non-semantic difference between the prima facie and specification views is that it is easy to transform any theory of rights from a prima facie view into a specification view or vice versa. One need do no more than change the place at which the consideration of arguments occurs. This transformation can be done with the views of Feinberg, Hart, Raz, and Wellman.

In Chapter 3 we saw that Feinberg thinks that rights are valid (non-Hohfeldian) claims. He thinks that one has a claim when one is in a position to make a claim to or to claim that. To have a claim, one must have at least a case meriting consideration. He holds that many individuals might have a claim to something. According to Feinberg, the only person who has a right to it is the person who has the best or strongest case. If one has a valid claim, a right, then one has the claim for which the best or strongest case can be provided. This is clearly a specificationist view. The weighing of arguments/claims occurs and then one discovers who has the best case, the valid claim, the right. In Backpacker, both the cabin owner and the backpacker have claims, but only the backpacker has a valid claim. Only the backpacker has a right. It is extremely easy to transform Feinberg's version of specification view into a version of the prima facie view. One merely asserts that prima facie rights are Feinbergian claims and that actual rights are valid Feinbergian claims.

According to Hart, rights are protected choices. He thinks every right contains two liberties and claims that protect these liberties. Hart's view is easily stated in either prima facie or specification form. If Hart favored the prima facie view, he need only hold that the liberties and claims are prima facie liberties and claims that must be weighed against conflicting liberties and claims to determine if they are actual liberties and claims. If, on the other hand, Hart favored the specification view, he need only hold that the liberties and claims in rights are specified so that they do not conflict.

Raz holds that

> X has a right if and only if other things being equal, an aspect of X's well-being (his interest) is a sufficient reason for holding some other person to be under an obligation.

This is also a version of the specification view. The effect of the words "sufficient reason" in the analysis is that if X's well-being is not morally important enough to generate an actual obligation, then X does not have a right. It is easy to transform it into a version of the prima facie view. First, one adds the terms "prima facie" as follows:

> X has a *prima facie* right if and only if other things being equal, an aspect of X's well-being (his interest) is a *prima facie* reason for holding some other person to be under a *prima facie* obligation.

Then one provides an analysis of actual rights as follows:

X has an *actual* right if and only if other things being equal, an aspect of X's well-being (his interest) is a *sufficient* reason for holding some other person to be under an *actual* obligation.

Of the authors discussed in this chapter, Wellman has the longest explicit discussion of rights conflict. It takes up Chapters 7 and 8 of *Real Rights* (1995). Before critically evaluating his view of rights conflict, we must examine it in some detail. As noted in Chapter 4, according to Wellman,

a ... right ... is a complex ... advantage to which the right-holder can appeal in the event of some possible confrontation with one or more second parties (1985, 91–92).

This analysis is nicely ambiguous in the sense that it does not commit Wellman to either the prima facie view or the specification view. If he wanted to hold the prima facie view for all rights conflict (which he does not) he could hold that

a *prima facie* right is a complex *prima facie* advantage to which the right-holder can appeal in the event of some possible confrontation with one or more second parties and an *actual* right is a complex *actual* advantage to which the right-holder can appeal in the event of some possible confrontation with one or more second parties.

On the other hand, if Wellman wanted to hold the specification view for all rights conflict (which he does not) he could hold that

a right is a complex *actual* advantage to which the right-holder can appeal in the event of some possible confrontation with one or more second parties.

Because his analysis of rights is nicely ambiguous, Wellman is free to hold (as he does) that some rights conflicts are resolved according to the prima facie view and others are resolved according to the specification view. Wellman holds that there are three possible resolutions to a case of rights conflict. First, in some cases "one of the alleged rights is unreal" and there is no real conflict of rights (1995, 242). Second, in some cases "although both rights are real, one or both are limited so that they do not conflict" (1995, 242). Third, in some cases "both rights are real and they really do conflict" (1995, 242.). Wellman calls cases of the first sort "not even apparent rights conflict," cases of the second sort "apparent rights conflict" and cases of the third sort "real rights conflict" (1995, 204). He holds that the distinction between not even apparent rights conflict on the one hand and apparent/real rights conflict on the other "is based on the vague but important difference between a clear case and a hard case" (1995, 204). Cases of not even apparent rights conflict are clear cases while cases of apparent rights conflict and cases of real rights conflict are hard cases.

There are, according to Wellman, at least five ways in which not even apparent rights conflict occurs. First, one can hold that one of the alleged right holders lacks

171

the qualifications necessary to have the relevant right. Wellman's example is *Roe v. Wade* (410 U.S. 113, 1973). In this case, the Court held that human fetuses do not have a constitutional right to life because fetuses are not persons as the term "person" is used in the U.S. Constitution. There can be no conflict between the legal rights of a woman and a fetus she carries because fetuses have no rights.

Second, one can hold that the alleged right does not exist because its implications are false. Wellman's example of this form of not even apparent rights conflict is Thomson's (1986) famous-violinist argument against the view that one has a moral right to use another's body if use of another's body is necessary for one to remain alive. Thomson asks us to imagine the following case. You are knocked unconscious, kidnaped, and attached to the circulatory system of a famous violinist. The violinist has a rare and fatal kidney disease. You are the only person in the world whose blood type matches his. If you remain hooked to the violinist for nine months, he will be cured. If you unplug yourself, he will die. Thomson holds that the view that one has a moral right to use another's body if use of another's body is necessary for one to remain alive has the false implication that it would be wrong for you to unplug yourself. In the abortion debate, some hold that there is a conflict between the fetus' right to use the woman's body if use of the woman's body is necessary for the fetus to remain alive and the woman's right to control her body. Wellman thinks that, if Thomson is correct, there is not even an apparent rights conflict in this case because Thomson has shown that there is no moral right to use another's body if use of another's body is necessary to remain alive.

Third, one can hold that a right does not exist because "it has no ground" (1995, 243). There is no good reason to think that the right exists. Wellman's example is *In re Barrie Estate* (35 N.W. 2nd 658, 1949). Mary Barrie, a resident of Illinois, willed the proceeds of the sale of some real property located in Iowa to the First Presbyterian Church, a church located in Illinois. Under the laws of Illinois, the will was invalid because someone had written the word "void" in at least five places in the will. Under the laws of Iowa, the will was valid. Under Iowa law, the mere appearance of "void" written over the will does not make the will void, but under Illinois law it does. If the will was void, the property in Iowa would pass to Ms. Barrie's heirs. Ms. Barrie's heirs therefore sued to have the will declared void. If the will was valid, the property would be sold and the proceeds would be given to the First Presbyterian Church. The Court held that the law of the state in which the real property was located controlled and so the will was valid. Therefore, the church received the proceeds of the sale of the property. The alleged right of Ms. Barrie's heirs to the Iowa property was found to be unreal because its alleged grounding in Illinois law was found to be irrelevant to the case at hand. The alleged right had no real ground, and therefore the alleged right did not exist.

Fourth, Wellman holds that an alleged specific right may be unreal because the more general right on which it is grounded, although real, is limited so that it does not imply the alleged specific right. Wellman's example is *McCulloch v. State of Maryland* (17 U.S. 316, 1819). The U.S. Congress created a Bank of the United States, and that bank opened a branch in Maryland. The state of Maryland then passed a law imposing a tax on all banks that had branches in Maryland but were not chartered by the state of Maryland. McCulloch, the cashier of the Maryland branch of Bank of the United States, refused to pay the tax. The U.S. Supreme Court held that the state of Maryland's real and general right to tax businesses within its borders is limited so that it does not imply a specific right to tax the federal government even though the federal government had offices, including a bank, in Maryland (1995, 243). With this talk of limiting rights so that they do not conflict, this is a clear case of the specification view.

Fifth and finally, according to Wellman, one can argue that a "concrete right is unreal because the more abstract right on which it is grounded is *outweighed* by one or more conflicting abstract rights" (1995, 243, emphasis added). In *Marsh v. Alabama* (326 U.S. 501, 1945), the U.S. Supreme Court held that a company did not have the specific right to prohibit the distribution of religious literature in the company town because the abstract right to religious freedom outweighs the company's property rights. (A company twon is a town in which a company owns all the land in the town.) With this talk of weighing rights, this is a clear case of the prima facie view. In addition to these five types of not even apparent rights conflict, Wellman thinks it "likely" that "there are others as well" (1995, 244).

Apparent rights conflict occurs when there are two rights that appear to conflict and "although both rights are real, one or both are limited so that they do not conflict." As an example of apparent rights conflict, he considers Backpacker and Feinberg's discussion of it.

> Whatever reasoning Joel Feinberg might accept to resolve the conflict of rights in this classic case, he clearly regards this as an example of real, not merely apparent, conflict of moral rights. This is shown by the fact that he definitely rejects any attempt to resolve this conflict by limiting the content of the owner's property rights to exclude "emergency circumstances such as the ones that obtained" here . . . Accordingly, Feinberg's way of resolving this conflict does recognize that it is real, not merely apparent, conflicts of rights (1995, 217).

In this discussion, the phrase "limiting the content of the owner's property rights to exclude 'emergency circumstances such as the ones that obtained' " indicates that what Wellman calls apparent rights conflict is what we have called specification.

According to Wellman, real rights conflict occurs when rights are weighed against each other. One of Wellman's examples is *Jefferson v. Griffin Spalding County Hospital Authority* (274 S.E. 2nd 457, 1981). Jefferson was pregnant and had a complete placenta privia. This condition occurs when the afterbirth is between the baby and the birth canal. If a woman with a complete placenta privia attempts to give birth vaginally, there is 99% chance that the baby will die and a 50% chance that the mother will die. If a woman with a complete placenta privia gives birth by caesarian section, there is a 99% chance that both the baby and the mother will live. Jefferson, due to her religious beliefs, refused a caesarian section. The hospital sued asking for the Court to order Jefferson to have a caesarian section. The trial court issued the order. The Georgia Supreme Court denied Jefferson's motion for a stay and commented as follows:

> In denying the stay of the trial court's order and thereby clearing the way for immediate . . . surgery, we weighed the right of the mother to practice her religion and to refuse surgery on herself, against her unborn child's right to live. We found in favor of her child's right to live (274 S.E. 2nd 457, 460, 1981).

Wellman then comments that

> Because the judicial reasoning rested entirely on the judgment that . . . the child's right to live outweighed the lesser conflicting rights of the pregnant woman *without* going on to interpret these rights of the defendant as limited so as to be inapplicable to this case, it recognized that under these special circumstances the right to life of the unborn child really did conflict with the mother's right to refuse surgery and to freedom of religion (1995, 212).

The defining feature of real rights conflict is weighing, the hallmark of the prima facie view. Wellman holds that some cases of rights conflict are resolved by specification and others are resolved according to the prima facie view. His nicely ambiguous analysis of rights leaves room for him to take this interesting position.

Wellman's view of rights conflict is interesting, subtle, and complex. It is also flawed. The first problem is that the concept of not even apparent rights conflict is not clear. An adequate theory of not even apparent rights conflict needs to provide a clear distinction between cases that are cases of not even apparent rights conflict and cases that are not cases of not even apparent rights conflict. As Wellman admits, his five cases are most likely not an exhaustive list of the different kinds of not even apparent rights conflict. So we cannot use these five cases to develop a clear distinction. He asserts that the distinction between not even apparent rights conflict and apparent/real rights conflict can be defined in terms of the distinction between an easy case and a hard case. But the distinction between easy and hard cases is, as Wellman admits, vague. It is too vague to be of use. Fetal rights, *In re Barrie Estate, McCulloch v. State of Maryland* and *Marsh v. Alabama* are not easy cases. Fetal rights have been the subject of years of controversy, and these three court cases are famous partially because they are difficult.

The second problem with Wellman's analysis of rights conflict is that, by his own admission, some cases of rights conflict can be seen as falling into two or even all three of his categories. He holds that *Marsh v. Alabama* can be seen as either a case of not even apparent rights conflict, a case of apparent rights conflict, or a case of real rights conflict.

> *Marsh* is an especially interesting case because the Supreme Court could have recognized a real conflict of rights and resolved it by balancing those rights against each other. Instead, it chose to carry its judicial reasoning one step further and use the relative weight of these rights as its reason for reinterpreting one of them as circumscribed in such a way as to render their conflict apparent rather than real (1995, 210).

As noted above, Wellman uses *Marsh* as an example of not even apparent rights conflict. Wellman also asserts that *McCulloch v. State of Maryland* can be classified as a case of not even apparent rights conflict or as a case of apparent rights conflict.

> Two readings [of this case] are possible, both correct depending on how the two conflicting rights are specified. If the conflict is seen as between the power-right of Congress to create . . . a Bank of the United States and the power-right of the state of Maryland to tax that bank, the Supreme Court declared the former real and the later unreal. Viewed in this way, the judicial reasoning in *McCulloch* is analogous to that in traditional conflict of laws cases, [which are cases of not even apparent rights conflict]. If the conflict is seen as between the right of Congress to create a bank and the right of Maryland to tax, the Court granted the reality of both rights but eliminated any possible conflict between them by defining the latter as limited by the former (1995, 207–208).

Wellman has correctly pointed out that, on some occasions, courts and people use the prima facie view to discuss rights conflict while on other occasions they use the specification view. Because there is no non-semantic difference between the prima facie view and the specification view, it is natural that many cases of rights conflict can be discussed using either or both views. Wellman has failed to show that there is more here than two different ways of speaking of rights conflict. Indeed, the fact that he admits that cases of rights conflict can be classified into more than one of his three categories lends support to the view that the prima facie view and the specification view are merely two different ways of saying the same thing. What he calls apparent rights conflict is conflict that is discussed using the specification view. What he calls real rights conflict is conflict that is discussed using the prima facie view. What he calls not even apparent rights conflict is a miscellaneous collection that includes the two rights conflict views and some examples of the kinds of substantive arguments one can give to resolve a case of rights conflict. In sum, Wellman's theory of rights conflict is not sufficiently illuminating. It conflates substantive and conceptual matters. We will now see that the justified-constraint theory provides a more illuminating account of rights conflict and of the examples cited by Wellman.

4. RIGHTS CONFLICT AND ARGUMENTS

Rights conflict occurs when there are plausible arguments both for and against the view that a particular obligation exists. There are plausible arguments for the view that the backpacker should not burn the chair and plausible arguments for the view that the backpacker may burn the chair. There are plausible arguments for the view that Edward should divert the trolley and plausible arguments for the view that Edward should not divert the trolley. It is the existence of plausible arguments on both sides of an issue that creates cases of rights conflict. To resolve a conflict of rights, one must determine which arguments are stronger. The way one decides to speak of rights conflict, prima facie or specification, does not help one make this determination. No view about the conceptual structure of rights conflict can relieve us of the need to do the hard substantive philosophical work needed to resolve a conflict of rights.

The justified-constraint theory of rights easily accounts for this picture of rights conflict. Rights are obligations justified in a particular way. Justification is to be understood in terms of arguments. Therefore, it makes sense that rights conflict is conflict between the arguments for the obligations implied by rights. Cases of permissible rights transgression arise when there are plausible arguments both for the view that X has an obligation to do A and for the view that X does not have an obligation to do A. Cases of unavoidable transgression arise when there are plausible arguments both for the view that X has an obligation to do both A1 and A2 and for the view that X does not have an obligation to do both A1 and A2. In both types of cases, there is a debate, proposals of alternative justifications of the relevant obligations.

On the justified-constraint theory, X has a right when a feature of X justifies an obligation. There are three different justificatory effects that a feature can have. A feature can be positively relevant, negatively relevant, or irrelevant. A particular rule system picks out a feature as *positively relevant* when it appears in the antecedent of the conditional premise in a sound instance of the key argument form. Barbara (a typical adult human) has a right that David not kill her. This is a claim right with a correlative duty not to kill. David has an obligation not to kill Barbara. What is the reason he has this obligation? Oversimplifying a great deal and assuming that the moral rule system is as most people think it is, the following argument is sound:

1. Barbara is a person.
2. If Barbara is a person, then David has a moral obligation not to kill Barbara.
3. Therefore, David has a moral obligation not to kill Barbara.

The conditional premise reveals that, according to the moral rule system, being a person is a positively relevant feature. To put it a bit imprecisely, a positively relevant feature is a *reason* that a person has an obligation.

In addition to positively relevant features, there are *negatively relevant* features. Consider a rock that Eddie found on a forest path. Pending the discussion in

Chapter 7, let us assume that this rock does not have a moral right that Eddie not destroy it and that the reason the rock does not have this right is that it is inanimate. On these assumptions, the following argument is sound.

1. The rock is inanimate.
2. If the rock is inanimate, then Eddie does not have a moral obligation not to destroy the rock.
3. Therefore, Eddie does not have a moral obligation not to destroy the rock.

It is close to being a sound instance of the key argument form. But there is a crucial difference. The conclusion of this argument is that an obligation does *not* exist while the conclusion of an instance of the key argument form is that an obligation does exist. A feature is negatively relevant if and only if there exists a sound argument of this second form. On the assumptions made above, "being inanimate" is a negatively relevant feature. The negatively relevant feature is the feature in the antecedent of the conditional premise of an argument that has this second form. A negatively relevant feature is a reason that a person does not have an obligation.

Unfortunately, the features thought to be negatively relevant need not be so banal. The Nazis had horrific views about the moral rule system. Many Nazis thought that the following argument was sound:

1. Eva is a Jew.
2. If Eva is a Jew, then Adolf does not have a moral obligation not to kill Eva.
3. Therefore, Adolf does not have a moral obligation not to kill Eva.

Many Nazis thought that being a Jew was a negatively relevant feature. It is an extraordinarily unfortunate fact about the world we live in that many people believe that some feature or features of other people are negatively relevant.

In addition to positively relevant features and negatively relevant features, there are irrelevant features. A feature is irrelevant if and only if it is neither positively nor negatively relevant. Consider the feature of having mass. Many things have mass: desks, people, computers. Most people think that having mass is an irrelevant feature. It justifies no obligations and it excludes no obligations. Most people think that there is no sound argument of the forms indicated above from the statement that something has mass to the statement that one has or does not have an obligation.

The above analysis focuses on the justificatory effect of one feature in isolation from all other features. In the real world things have many features. To understand the nature of rights conflict, the analysis of rights needs to be modified to pick out the justificatory effect of one feature in isolation.

X has an S right that Y do A if and only if
in the possible world identical to the actual world except that X has no features other than F and those logically and nomologically entailed by F,
there is a sound instance of the following argument form:

1. X is F.
2. If X is F, then Y has an S obligation to do A.
3. Therefore, Y has an S obligation to do A.

The addition in italics picks out the justificatory effect of one feature. This allows for a much better understanding of rights conflict.

Internal rights conflict occurs when both positively and negatively relevant features are present. Consider the possible world identical to the original world of Backpacker except that the cabin owner has no features other than that of being the owner of the chair and those features logically and nomologically entailed by this feature. In particular, in this possible world the cabin owner is not the owner of the chair *that must be burned for the backpacker to live.* In that case, the following argument is sound:

1. The cabin owner is a person who owns the chair.
2. If the cabin owner is a person who owns the chair, then the backpacker has a moral obligation not to burn the chair.
3. Therefore, the backpacker has a moral obligation not to burn the chair.

This implies that there is a positively relevant feature in Backpacker.

Consider the possible world identical to the original world of Backpacker except that the backpacker has no features other than that of being a person who will die if he does not burn the chair and those features logically and nomologically entailed by this feature. In particular, in this possible world the chair in the cabin is not owned by anyone. In that case, the following argument is sound:

1. The backpacker is a person who will die if he does not burn the chair.
2. If the backpacker is a person who will die if he does not burn the chair, then the backpacker does not have a moral obligation not to burn the chair.
3. Therefore, the backpacker does not have a moral obligation not to burn the chair.

This implies that there is a negatively relevant feature in Backpacker.

These examples pick out the features that do the justificatory work. The fact that the chair is blue is not morally relevant. If the backpacker came across an abandoned chair in a cave, burning it to stay warm would not cause any conflict. It is the fact that someone owns the chair that causes the conflict. Set out in this way, the question that needs to be answered to resolve the conflict is clear: Does the backpacker have an obligation not to burn the chair when the chair is the cabin owner's property *and* burning the chair is necessary to save the backpackers life? To resolve the conflict we must consider whether the following argument is sound:

1. The cabin owner is a person who owns the chair and the backpacker is a person who will die if he does not burn the chair.
2. If the cabin owner is a person who owns the chair and the backpacker is a person who will die if he does not burn the chair, then the backpacker *has* a moral obligation not to burn the chair.
3. Therefore, the backpacker *has* a moral obligation not to burn the chair.

or whether the following argument is sound:

1. The cabin owner is a person who owns the chair and the backpacker is a person who will die if he does not burn the chair.
2. If the cabin owner is a person who owns the chair and the backpacker is a person who will die if he does not burn the chair, then the backpacker *does not have* a moral obligation not to burn the chair.
3. Therefore, the backpacker *does not have* a moral obligation not to burn the chair.

Substantively, it seems clear that the second argument is sound and the first is not. *Rights conflict is resolved by looking at what obligations are justified by the union of all relevant features.* In typical cases of a backpacker coming across a boarded up cabin on a pleasantly sunny day, the cabin owner's ownership of the chair is the only positively relevant feature present and no negatively relevant features are present. So the backpacker has an obligation not to burn the chair. In Backpacker the judgment of most people is that the negatively relevant feature outweighs or limits (depending on the metaphor one prefers) the positively relevant feature. Not all negatively relevant features need have this effect. Suppose that burning the chair was necessary to save the backpacker two hours sitting in an unpleasantly cool summer rain. This is a negatively relevant feature, but most people would not think it sufficiently important to outweigh/limit the cabin owner's positively relevant feature.

This analysis of the conceptual structure of rights conflict may seem so simple as to be simplistic. But this simplicity is a virtue. An analysis of the conceptual nature of rights conflict does not, and should not be expected to, remove the burden of doing the substantive philosophical work necessary to determine the relative importance of conflicting obligations. An analysis of the conceptual nature of rights conflict should clarify the structure of the conflict, remove conceptual muddles, and then stand aside while substantive debate takes place.

Having discussed Backpacker, let us examine Jane-or-Car. In cases of unavoidable rights transgression it is physically impossible to avoid transgressing on a right. In Jane-or-Car, Edward must trangress on Sue's right (by diverting the trolley and thus destroying her car) or Jane's right (by not diverting the trolley and thus killing her). There is a positively relevant feature because, in the possible world identical to the original world of Jane-or-Car except that Jane has no features other than that of being a person who will be killed if Edward does not divert the trolley and those features logically and nomologically entailed by this feature, the following argument is sound:

1. Jane is a person who will be killed if Edward does not divert the trolley.
2. If Jane is a person who will be killed if Edward does not divert the trolley, then Edward has a moral obligation to divert the trolley.
3. Therefore, Edward has a moral obligation to divert the trolley.

There is another positively relevant feature because, in the possible world identical to the original world of Jane-or-Car except that Sue has no other features other than that of being a person whose car will be destroyed if Edward does divert the trolley and those features logically and nomologically entailed by this feature, the following argument is sound:

1. Sue is a person who owns a car that will be destroyed if Edward diverts the trolley.
2. If Sue is a person who owns a car that will be destroyed if Edward diverts the trolley, then Edward has a moral obligation not to divert the trolley.
3. Therefore, Edward has a moral obligation not to divert the trolley.

The claims numbered 3 in the arguments above imply that

4. Edward has both a moral obligation to divert the trolley and a moral obligation not to divert the trolley.

However, there is a negatively relevant feature as well.

1. Edward is a person who must either divert the trolley or not divert the trolley.
2. If Edward is a person who must either divert the trolley or not divert the trolley, then Edward does not have both a moral obligation to divert the trolley and a moral obligation not to divert the trolley.
3. Therefore, Edward does not have both a moral obligation to divert the trolley and a moral obligation not to divert the trolley.

Jane-or-Car is more complex than Backpacker because instead of having one positively relevant feature and one negatively relevant feature, we have two positively relevant features and one negatively relevant feature. But the resolution proceeds in the same way. We need to consider what obligations Edward has when both positively relevant features and the negatively relevant feature are present. As in Backpacker, we must consider what obligations are justified by the union of all relevant features. We need to ask if the following argument is sound:

1. Jane is a person who will be killed if Edward does not divert the trolley and Sue is a person who owns a car that will be destroyed if Edward diverts the trolley and Edward is a person who must either divert the trolley or not divert the trolley.
2. If Jane is a person who will be killed if Edward does not divert the trolley and Sue is a person who owns a car that will be destroyed if Edward diverts the trolley and Edward is a person who must either divert the trolley or not divert the trolley, then Edward has a moral obligation *to divert* the trolley.
3. Therefore, Edward has a moral obligation *to divert* the trolley.

or if the following argument is sound:

1. Jane is a person who will be killed if Edward does not divert the trolley and Sue is a person who owns a car that will be destroyed if Edward diverts the trolley

and Edward is a person who must either divert the trolley or not divert the trolley.

2. If Jane is a person who will be killed if Edward does not divert the trolley and Sue is a person who owns a car that will be destroyed if Edward diverts the trolley and Edward is a person who must either divert the trolley or not divert the trolley, then Edward has a moral obligation *not to divert* the trolley.

3. Therefore, Edward has a moral obligation *not to divert* the trolley.

Substantively, it seems that the first argument is sound and the second is not. If we look only at the feature that Sue is a person who owns a car on the line onto which Edward can divert the trolley, thus ignoring that Jane is on the other line, it is clear that this feature would justify Edward's obligation not to divert the trolley. If we look only at the feature that Jane is a person who will die if Edward does not divert the trolley, thus ignoring that Sue's car is on the other line, it is clear that this feature would justify Edward's obligation to divert the trolley. Suppose it were possible for Edward to do something other than divert or not divert the trolley. Suppose that he could stop the trolley by applying the brakes and thus save Jane's life and Sue's car. It is clear that Edward should stop the trolley.

Let us move toward the trolley problem as Thomson stated it. Consider the case in which one person will die whether Edward diverts the trolley or not. Jane is on one line and Sue is on the other. However, both are standing at a place where the banks are steep. So if Edward diverts the trolley, Sue will be killed, and if Edward does not divert the trolley, Jane will be killed. Call this case "Jane-or-Sue." It seems that

1. Edward has an obligation to Jane that Edward divert the trolley.

and that

2. Edward has an obligation to Sue that Edward not divert the trolley.

Edward must either divert or not divert the trolley. It is not physically possible for Edward to meet both of his obligations.

One reason that Jane-or-Sue is particularly puzzling is that, unlike Backpacker and Jane-or-Car, it is not at all obvious to most people how to resolve this conflict. While it is obvious to most people that the backpacker may burn the chair and that in Jane-or-Car Edward should divert the trolley, it is not at all obvious to most people what Edward should do in Jane-or-Sue. The reason for this is that, as the case is stated, it naturally leads one to assume that there is no morally relevant difference between Jane and Sue. In Jane-or-Car, there does seem to be a morally relevant difference between Jane and Sue's car and this makes the case an easy one to resolve.

It is worth noting that Jane-or-Sue is similar to two other famous cases of rights conflict. The first is Feinberg's pool lounger case.

Suppose that there are two drowning babies in [a] pool, one twenty meters to [a] lounger's right and the other twenty meters to his left and that the circumstances

> make it clear that the lounger, by taking a few steps in either direction, can easily scoop up one baby, but that there is insufficient time to rescue both (1984, 144).

Let us call this case "Pool Lounger." This is a case of easy rescue. Let us assume, as Feinberg does, that people have a claim right to be rescued if the rescue is an easy one. The only morally relevant difference between Pool Lounger and Jane-or-Sue is that it is physically possible for the pool lounger to allow both babies to die but Edward cannot do anything which would result in the death of both Jane and Sue. Pool Lounger, like Jane-or-Sue, naturally leads one to assume that there is no morally relevant difference between the two babies. The case is easily resolved if one baby, if not rescued, will spend a week in the hospital but recover while the other baby, if not rescued, will die. We can imagine many other sorts of morally relevant differences between the two individuals whose lives are at risk in these cases. Assume that Sue hates Jane, intentionally damaged the trolley's brakes so that it could not be stopped, and is standing on the track to which Edward can divert the trolley so that she can watch Jane die. It seems clear in this case that Edward should divert the trolley because Jane is innocent and Sue is not.

The other famous case that is similar to Jane-or-Sue is nicely presented by Claire Oakes Finkelstein.

> Following a shipwreck, two men converge simultaneously on a plank in the sea. There is no other plank available and no immediate hope of rescue. Unfortunately, the plank can support only one; it sinks if two try to cling to it (2001, 279).

Call this case "Plank." Unlike Jane-or-Sue and Pool Lounger, Plank is a case of permissible rights transgression. If one of the two men decides to swim off to die, then no rights are transgressed. Plank is also different from Jane-or-Sue and Pool Lounger because its structure is not that of one person choosing between the rights of two other people. In this respect, Plank is like Backpacker. Plank is similar to Jane-or-Sue in that as the case is presented there is no morally relevant difference between the individuals involved. The case is easily resolved if one of the men is a terrorist who caused the shipwreck or if one of the men is such an excellent swimmer than he can, with some annoying effort, survive until rescued without the plank. Plank and Backpacker cease to be cases of permissible rights transgression and become cases of unavoidable rights transgression if one assumes that the parties involved have a right against themselves that they preserve their own lives. Suppose that you are the backpacker and that have a duty to yourself to stay alive. Correlative to this right is your obligation to yourself to stay alive. Above we assumed that if you decided not to break into the cabin and wandered off to die that no rights would be transgressed. But if, for example, one holds some religiously motivated moral view that one has a duty to oneself to stay alive then Backpacker becomes a case of unavoidable rights transgression. Jane-or-Sue, Pool Lounger, Plank and other cases like them are particularly puzzling because they involve at least two problems—the problem of rights conflict and the problem of no morally relevant difference.

A theory of rights cannot be faulted for its implications regarding cases of rights conflict with no morally relevant difference. These are not the sort of cases from which one begins in building a theory. Nor are they the sort of cases against which one can check a theory. They are too unusual and difficult for that. But it is interesting to see what a theory of rights conflict implies about such a case.

Some think that the pool lounger has an obligation to save one of the two babies and that he has latitude as to which baby to save. Let us call this view "the latitude view." Some think that the pool lounger could choose to save B1 because B1 happens to look like his own child while B2 does not. On one version of the latitude view, the pool lounger may use any criteria at all to choose which baby to save. On this version of this view, the pool lounger could choose to save B1 because B1 is white while B2 is black. On another version of the latitude view, the pool lounger has latitude as to which baby to save but certain sorts of features (e.g., race, sex, etc.) may not be used to make the decision as to which baby to save. A defender of this version might hold that the pool lounger may choose to decide which baby to save based on which one is screaming louder but not on the basis of race.

Others think that the pool lounger has an obligation to save one of the two babies and that he must use a random procedure to choose the baby to save. This view is generally expressed by saying that each baby has a right to equal consideration, so let us call it "the equal consideration view." Suppose that the pool lounger happens to be using a random number generator to choose the lottery numbers he will play later that day. On the equal consideration view, the pool lounger should label a baby as baby one, label the other baby as baby two, use the random number generator to generate the number one or the number two, and then save the indicated baby.

On the justified-constraint theory of rights, the latitude view implies that no rights are created in Jane-or-Sue and Pool Lounger. On the latitude view, Pool Lounger and Jane-or-Sue are parallel to Tabitha's obligation discussed in Chapter 5. Tabitha has a P obligation to give some money to Howard or Kate or George. She has the latitude to choose to whom to give. The latitude view holds that the pool lounger and Edward have the exact same sort of latitude that Tabitha has. The same arguments used to show that Tabitha's case generates no rights can be used to show that, if the latitude view is correct, no rights are created in Pool Lounger and Jane-or-Sue.

On the justified-constraint theory of rights, the equal consideration view implies that B1 has a right that the pool lounger choose which baby to save using a random procedure and that B2 has a right with the same content. Both babies have a right that the pool lounger choose which baby to save using a random procedure. The baby selected by the random procedure would then have a right to be saved. The arguments for this view are parallel to the arguments for relational obligations discussed in Chapter 5.

The analysis of rights conflict offered here cannot be used to argue that the justified-constraint theory of rights is superior to the justification versions of the interest theory, the choice theory, or the will theory. The analysis above could be adopted by any holder of a justification theory of rights. The difference between the analysis offered above and the one that could be offered by a defender of the justification version of the interest theory is that the defender of this version of the interest theory would have particular substantive views about which versions of the key argument form are sound. She would argue that the conflicts should be resolved by looking at which obligations are justified by the interests at stake in the conflict situations. A defender of the justification version of the choice theory would argue that the conflicts should be resolved by looking at which obligations are justified by the importance of the choices at stake in the conflict situations.

On the other hand, analysis of rights conflict offered here shows that there is an important respect in which any justification theory of rights is superior to any protection theory of rights. A protection theory of rights cannot analyze rights conflict in terms of the arguments for and against the existence of certain obligations. Of course, a protection theory of rights could hold that rights conflict is conflict between arguments for and against protecting a particular feature. But that move turns a protection theory of rights into a justification theory of rights.

The relationship between rights and latitude is worth a brief digression. John Stuart Mill held that

> No one has a moral right to our generosity or benevolence, because we are not morally bound to practice these virtues towards any given individual (1979, 49).

Mill was not quite right, but he was on the right track. The phrase "practice these virtues *towards* any given individual" is most naturally read as a statement about the subjects of the content of a right. It seems to say that the subject of the content of an obligation implied by a right must pick out one particular individual. But if one considers the charity case and the case of rights conflict with no morally relevant difference, it becomes clear that the "given individual" that must be one particular individual is the object of the obligation, not the subject of the content of the obligation. Rights are not obligations that we are morally bound to practice *towards* a given individual. Rights are obligations *owed to* and *justified by* the features of a particular individual.

This view is confirmed by the analysis of cases in which the object of a right (and therefore the subject of the obligation implied by the right) has some latitude as to how to fulfill the obligation. Consider again the case of Squam Lake from Chapter 2. Suppose that my fond memories are of two lakes, Squam Lake and Lake Winnipesaukee. I ask you to promise me that you will stick your feet in either Squam Lake or Lake Winnipesaukee. You make the promise so I have a right, and you have an obligation, that you stick your feet in either Squam Lake or Lake Winnipesaukee. Despite the fact that this obligation allows you to choose which of two lakes you may stick your feet into, your obligation is still to me and I still have a right. This shows that latitude in the fulfillment of an obligation is consistent with that obligation being an obligation that is correlative to a right.

184

But what if the latitude is precisely the latitude to which Mill points? In the case of your Squam Lake/Lake Winipeasukee promise to me, the content of the obligation does not give you the latitude to fulfill the obligation by treating two different *people* differently. To explore this case, let us consider a variation of the third-party beneficiary case discussed in Chapter 5. Suppose that Sangita promises Fred Junior that she will pay, at her discretion, $100 to Fred Senior or $100 to Fred Junior's mother, Fredericka. Sangita has an obligation to pay $100 to Fred Senior or to Fredericka. Let us first assume that the moral rule system is as classic choice theorists think it is and therefore that choice is the only feature of individuals that justifies obligations correlative to rights. In that case, Sangita's obligation is to Fred Junior and Fred Junior has a right that Sangita give $100 to Fred Senior or Fredericka. If classic choice theorists are correct, then this case is one in which a person has an obligation correlative to a right whose content allows the subject of the obligation to decide which of two people she may give money to in order to fulfill the obligation. If classic choice theorists are correct, then this case is a counterexample to Mill's claim that one does not have a right if one is not required to fulfill the obligation correlative to the right with actions *towards* a given individual. Now let us assume that the moral rule system is as classic interest theorists think it is and therefore interests are the only features of individuals that justify obligations correlative to rights. In that case and if there is no morally relevant difference between Fred Senior and Fredericka, then this is a case of rights conflict with no morally relevant difference and no one has a right that Sangita give $100 to Fred Senior or $100 to Fredericka.

Returning to the main line of argument, let us consider Thomson's trolley problem as originally proposed. Assume that Sue is by herself on the track onto which Edward can divert the trolley and Jane and four friends are on the track down which the trolley will go if he does not divert the trolley. Let us call this case "Five-or-Sue." To resolve this case, one must first answer a substantive moral question. Do numbers matter? Is the fact that five people will die if Edward does not divert the trolley but only one will die if Edward diverts the trolley a morally relevant difference? Some hold that numbers do not matter. The argument for this view is that most people think it would be wrong to kill one person in order to transplant her organs and thus save the lives of five people. If numbers do not matter, then Five-or-One is a case of rights conflict with no morally relevant difference. It is just like Jane-or-Sue and Pool Lounger. If numbers do not matter, then whether rights are present in Five-or-One depends on whether one adopts the latitude view or the equal consideration view. (Those who favor the equal consideration view must decide the interesting question of whether equal consideration requires choosing randomly between the six people or choosing randomly between the two tracks.)

But most people think that, in this case, numbers do matter. Most people think that, in Five-or-Sue, Edward should divert the trolley. On the assumption that numbers do matter, Five-or-Sue is an interesting and puzzling case distinct from Jane-or-Sue and Pool Lounger. If numbers do matter and if Edward has an obligation to divert the trolley, is his obligation correlative to anyone's right? If it is correlative to someone's right, whose right is the correlative of his obligation? Interestingly, the justified-constraint theory implies that his obligation is not correlative to any right. The reason for this implication is that no feature of any of the five people who will be killed if Edward does not divert the trolley is essential to the justification of his obligation to divert the trolley. This is clear once one realizes that Edward would still have the obligation to divert the trolley if any one of these five people were to be magically transported off the track to safety. Edward would still have the obligation to divert the trolley if there were only three friends with Jane. This reveals that the view that Edward has an obligation to divert the trolley has a consequentialist justification. It is parallel to the Australian citizen's obligation to vote.

This analysis of Five-or-Sue is natural and plausible. If I may be a bit imprecise, it has always seemed to me that the conflicting views people hold about Five-or-Sue and the case of killing one person to transplant their organs and save five others reveal the deep and conflicting pull of consequentialist and deontological moral views. Five-or-Sue brings out consequentialist intuitions. The transplant case brings out deontological intuitions. As noted above, consequentialist obligations are not correlative to any right. The obligations correlative to rights are deontological obligations. It would be well beyond the scope of this book to try to reconcile these two deeply opposed moral views. But it is a small point in favor of the justified-constraint theory of rights that it illuminates the nature of this long-standing debate.

Above we saw that the theories of rights provided by Feinberg, Hart, Raz, and Wellman can be transformed from a prima facie view into a specification view or vice versa. With the justified-constraint theory of rights conflict now on the table, it would be well to show that it can be transformed just as the others can be. Still ignoring impossibilities in order to simplify presentation, the justified-constraint theory of rights holds that

X has an S right that Y do A if and only if
in the possible world identical to the actual world except that X has no features other than F and those logically and nomologically entailed by F, there is a sound instance of the following argument form:
1. X is F.
2. If X is F, then Y has an S obligation to do A.
3. Therefore, Y has an S obligation to do A.

As it stands, this analysis is a version of the prima facie view. It is a version of the prima facie view because it holds that one has a right on the basis of looking at feature F in isolation. That X has a right that Y do A on the basis of F in isolation is compatible with X not having a right that Y do A when all morally relevant features are considered. One could make this explicit as follows:

186

X has a *prima facie* S right that Y do A if and only if
in the possible world identical to the actual world except that X has no features
other than F and those logically and nomologically entailed by F, there is a sound
instance of the following argument form:
1. X is F.
2. If X is F, then Y has an S obligation to do A.
3. Therefore, Y has an S obligation to do A.

X has an *actual* S right against Y that Y do A if and only if
there is a sound instance of the argument form in which F is the union of all morally
relevant features.

If one wished to hold the specification view, one need only hold that this analysis
of actual rights is the analysis of rights *tout court* and then choose some other word
(perhaps "entitlement," "title," or some invented term) and use that word in place
of "a prima facie S right" in the analysis above.

5. WELLMAN'S EXAMPLES

It is enlightening to apply the justified-constraint theory of rights conflict to some
examples. Let us reconsider some of examples offered by Wellman. In *Roe v.
Wade*, a central issue was whether fetuses are persons under the U.S. Constitution.
The justified-constraint analysis of this part of the case is simple. The conflict of
rights occurs because there are plausible arguments for and against the view that
fetuses are persons under the Constitution. Some of the arguments that convinced
the Court to rule that fetuses are not persons are of a standard textual variety.
The Court pointed to the fact that none of the uses of the term "person" in the
Constitution has a clear prenatal application and several clearly have only postnatal application. The persons who are to be electors of the President and Vice
President are clearly intended to be postnatal beings. Those who think that fetuses
are persons under the Constitution marshal many arguments. Among them are the
genetic similarities between pre and postnatal humans as well as the potential of
fetuses to become adult humans. In *Roe v. Wade*, we have a debate over whether
being a human fetus is a positively relevant feature.

With regard to the right to use of another's body if use of another's body is necessary for one to remain alive, Thomson has provided well-known counterexamples
to the view that this right exists. But part of the reason her counterexamples are so
well-known is that there are plausible arguments for the view that this right does
exist. Her examples are counterexamples to plausible views. After all, it seems
initially plausible to hold that a person's life is morally more important than being
confined with another person for 9 months. Thus it is not absurd to hold that the
kidnaped person's right to freedom of movement is less morally important than the
famous violinist's right to life. These two rights conflict because there are initially
plausible arguments for both of them.

In re Barrie Estate is a case in which there are plausible arguments for the view that Ms. Barrie's will is legally void and plausible arguments for the view that her will is legally valid. The facts that the word "void" was written on the will, that Ms. Barrie lived in Illinois and that, according to the laws of Illinois, a will with the word "void" on it was void provide an argument (with a complex negatively relevant feature) for the view that Ms. Barrie's will justified no obligations. The facts that the property was in Iowa and that, according to the laws of Iowa, the will is valid in spite of the word "void" being written in it provide an argument (with a complex positively relevant feature) for the view that Ms. Barrie's will justified obligations. The existence of plausible arguments on both sides of the issue created the conflict of rights. The Court resolved the case by looking at both arguments and deciding that the second was superior to the first, that the union of the negatively and positively relevant features created a sound argument for the view that the will justified obligations.

In re Barrie Estate is a convenient case with which to consider the issues of rights conflicts between different rule systems. In this case, the legal rule system of Illinois conflicts with the legal rule system of Iowa. In the law, cases such as these are called conflict of laws cases. But these cases are not unique to the law. Many think that legal rule systems can and do conflict with the moral rule system. So there are cases of conflict of rule systems. One virtue of the justified-constraint theory of rights conflict is that conflict of rule systems cases pose no special problem. As *In re Barrie Estate* shows, cases of rights conflict generated by a conflict of rule systems, like cases of rights conflict within one rule system, are resolved by evaluating arguments. In conflict of rule systems cases, these arguments are often presented as arguments for and against the view that one of the conflicting rule systems is more important than the other. Should the baseball rule system conflict with the legal rule system, one might hold that the legal rule system is always more important.

While I will not argue the point here, it seems unlikely that one will be able to defend the view that some rule systems have this sort of lexical priority over other rule systems. It seems more likely that the sound arguments will establish priority at the level of particular statements, not at the level of entire rule systems. It seems possible that an obligation of the baseball rule system could be more important than some of the very trivial obligations of the legal or moral rule system.

In *McCulloch v. State of Maryland*, the U.S. Supreme Court held that the state of Maryland's right to tax businesses within its borders is limited so it does not imply a specific right to tax the federal government (even though the federal government has offices, including a bank, in Maryland). The rights conflict occurs because there are plausible arguments on both sides of this issue. The arguments for McCulloch's position are based on Article 6, Section 2 of the U.S. Constitution.

This Constitution and the Laws of the United States which shall be made in Pursuance thereof; and all Treaties made or which shall be made, under the Authority of the United States, shall be the supreme Law of the Land; and the

Judges in every State shall be bound thereby, any Thing in the Constitution or Laws of any state to the Contrary notwithstanding.

This is the basis for the argument that the states may not tax or otherwise regulate the institutions of the federal government. The arguments for the state of Maryland's point of view are equally clear. States generally have the power to tax businesses located within their territory and the Bank of the United States had opened a branch in Maryland. The Supreme Court decided that the first argument was better than the second.

At issue in *Marsh v. Alabama* was the right to distribute religious literature in a company town. The U.S. Supreme Court held that the company did not have the right to prohibit the distribution of religious literature in the town. Once again this case of rights conflict is a clear case of plausible arguments for opposing rights. The arguments for the company's view rest on their ownership of the town and the control of a piece of land that usually comes with ownership. The arguments for the residents' view rest on the importance of religious freedom and the fact that, unlike most towns, company towns contain no public space where the distribution of religious literature is allowed.

In *Jefferson v. Griffin Spalding County Hospital Authority*, the Georgia Supreme Court ordered Jefferson, a pregnant woman with a complete placenta privia, to give birth by caesarian section. Once again, this case is most clearly understood as a case of conflicting arguments. The arguments for Jefferson's position rest on views about the importance of freedom of religion. The arguments for the Court's view rest on views about the importance of preserving the life of Jefferson and her baby.

The analysis of these cases shows that the justified-constraint theory of rights conflict is simpler, clearer, and more systematic than Wellman's complex seven-fold classification. Wellman's view is not false. He has correctly pointed to the prima facie and specification views and some of the kinds of substantive arguments that appear when there is rights conflict. Unfortunately, his classification is not illuminating because it includes both conceptual views and substantive arguments without distinguishing them. The justified-constraint view is a better theory of the conceptual nature of rights conflict. It is neutral as to metaphor and substantive argument. Rights are obligations justified by a particular kind of argument—arguments grounded in the features of individuals. Rights conflict occurs when there are plausible arguments both for and against the view that a particular obligation exists. All rights conflict is resolved in the same way—by the examination of the plausible arguments to determine which are stronger.

6. DWORKIN: TRUMPS

We now turn to external rights conflict. Ronald Dworkin famously holds that "rights are best understood as trumps over some background justification for political decisions that states a goal for the community as a whole" (1984, 153). Dworkin's theory is most naturally considered in a discussion of external rights conflict because he defines rights as things that necessarily conflict with non-relational obligations. He claims that one prominent theory of the goals for the community as a whole is consequentialism. As we saw in the last chapter, obligations justified by consequentialist reasoning are non-relational obligations. Thus Dworkin makes conflict between relational obligations (a.k.a. rights) and non-relational obligations a necessary feature of rights.

Dworkin's analysis of rights is not as clear as one might wish. It will require some work to explicate it. It is best to start with his explicit analysis in his own words.

> I begin with the idea of a political aim as a generic political justification. A political theory takes a certain state of affairs as a political aim if, for that theory, it counts in favor of any political decision that the decision is likely to advance or to protect, that state of affairs and counts against the decision that it will retard or endanger it. A political right is an individuated political aim. An individual has a right to some opportunity or resource or liberty if it counts in favor of a political decision that the decision is likely to advance or protect the state of affairs in which he enjoys the right, even when no other political aim is served and some political aim is disserved thereby and counts against that decision that it will retard or endanger that state of affairs, even when some other political aim is thereby served. A goal is a nonindividuated political aim, that is, a state of affairs whose specification does not in this way call for any particular opportunity or resource or liberty for particular individuals (1978, 91).

A number of clarifications are necessary. First, although Dworkin does not say so explicitly, it seems clear from context that he is following a common practice and using "if" to mean "if and only if." Second, it is not clear whether Dworkin is offering a general theory of all rights or merely a theory of political rights. The quote at the beginning of this section seems to be an analysis of rights *tout court*, but the long paragraph just quoted seems to be an analysis of political rights. Dworkin does not explicate the distinction between political and non-political rights. This book is an analysis of rights *tout court*, so let us assume, at some risk of doing a disservice to Dworkin, that his analysis is intended as a general theory of all rights. Third, the explicit analysis of rights is circular because, in the fourth sentence quoted above, the term of "rights" is among the analysans. Thus the analysis of an individuated political aim is circular. There is a seemingly non-circular analysis of a non-individuated political aim. It is "a state of affairs whose specification does not in this way call for any particular opportunity or resource or liberty for particular individuals." Unfortunately, the phrase "in this way" refers back to the circular analysis in the fourth sentence.

In spite of these problems, it seems that the most natural way to read this passage is to take Dworkin to hold that an individuated aim, a right, is a state of affairs whose specification calls for some particular opportunity, resource, or liberty for some particular individuals. On the other hand, a non-individuated aim, a goal, is a state of affairs whose specification does not call for some particular opportunity, resource, or liberty for some particular individuals. We can be more precise.

An individual, X, has a right that some state of affairs, S, obtain if and only if
1. S is a state of affairs in which X has some opportunity or resource or liberty and
2. it is a good reason to take some political action, P, that it is likely to advance or protect S even when doing P would not advance or protect any other state of affairs whose the advancement or protection is a good reason for political action and even when doing P would retard or endanger some other state of affairs whose advancement or protection is a good reason for political action and
3. it is a good reason not to take some political action, P*, that it is likely to retard or endanger S even when doing P* would advance or protect some other state of affairs whose advancement or protection is a good reason for political action.

The phrase "political action" is preferable to Dworkin's "political decision" because not all decisions lead to action and that it is the action, not the decision itself, to which Dworkin intends to refer. The phrase "good reason" is preferable to Dworkin's "counts in favor of" because it brings out the fact that Dworkin holds a justification theory of rights. According to Dworkin, "a political aim [is] a generic political *justification.*" The "even when" clauses reflect the trumping metaphor for which Dworkin's view is famous. Although Dworkin did not present his view as clearly as one might wish, one can see why it has been influential. It is an interesting and very plausible theory of rights. The trumping metaphor has been particularly influential. The following quote from Lyons is typical of many works on rights. "Moral rights make a difference to evaluation of conduct by excluding a range of direct utilitarian arguments . . ." (1994, 150). Waldron makes the same point this way:

> Rights express limits on what can be done to individuals for the sake of the greater benefits of others; they impose limits on the sacrifices that can be demanded from them as a contribution to the general good (1993a, 209).

Dworkin's theory of rights contains important insights that must be incorporated into any plausible theory of rights. However, as a complete theory of the nature of rights, it is inadequate.

The first problem with Dworkin's view is that he has focused on cases in which the right-holder has a right that others provide the right-holder with an opportunity, resource, or liberty. His paradigm right is the right of speech. I have a right to free speech because others should provide me with this liberty. Dworkin has overlooked two sorts of cases. First, he has overlooked power rights. Power rights are fundamentally rights to *make* a state of affairs obtain, not merely rights that a state of affairs obtain. This problem is easily fixed by modifying the view to say that "S is a state of affairs in which X has some opportunity or resource or liberty *or power.*" Second and more importantly, he has overlooked cases in which one person has a right that another person do something that has nothing to do with the first person's opportunities, resources, or liberties. The Squam Lake example is a case in point. Because of your promise, I have a right that you stick your feet in Squam Lake. This claim does not increase or decrease my opportunities, resources, or liberties. It has nothing to do with my opportunities, resources, or liberties. My right decreases your liberties. It normatively constrains you.

The second problem for Dworkin is that the theory of the relational nature of rights implicit in his view is implausible. Althought Dworkin never explicitly considers the relational nature of rights, it seems that the most natural view for him to hold is that the obligations correlative to a right are to the person whose opportunity, resource, or liberty is brought about or protected. The Squam Lake example shows that this theory of relational obligation is not a good one. My right that you stick your feet in Squam Lake does not increase or decrease my opportunities, resources, or liberties. Dworkin's view implies that your obligation is not to me. But your obligation clearly is to me.

The third problem with Dworkin's view is that the metaphor of trumps is misleading. Consider how trumps work in bridge. If one suit is trump, then any card of that suit, even the lowest, takes the trick when played against any card of any other suit, even the highest. If spades are trump, then the two of spades takes the trick even when played against the king of hearts. Only a higher spade can take a trick if the two of spades is played. Thus Dworkin's trump metaphor naturally leads one to think that he holds that even the least important right outweighs the most important goal. It naturally leads one to think that the only thing that can be more important than a right is another right. But this claim is false. Suppose that, because of a promise you made to me, I have a right that you give me a five-cent bag of popcorn. Through some bizarre set of circumstances, if you bring me the bag of popcorn, the economic efficiency of the world will be dramatically reduced for generations to come. If you bring me the bag of popcorn, millions will be much poorer than they would be if you did not bring me the bag of popcorn. My right to the bag of popcorn is not as important as the loss of economic efficiency. Rights are not trumps. Dworkin himself recognizes that rights are not trumps.

> Arguments of principle are arguments intended to establish an individual right; arguments of policy are arguments intended to establish a collective goal. [. . .] Rights may . . . be less than absolute; one principle might have to yield to another or even to an urgent policy with which it conflicts (1978, 90 and 92).

To continue with the bridge metaphor, it is clear that the king of hearts can take a trick against the two of spades even if spades are trump. In non-metaphorical terms, Dworkin does not hold that rights exclude consideration of goals. Rather, rights are an important and independent consideration that must be weighed against goals.

The justified-constraint theory of rights conflict allows one to see the important points that Dworkin's trump metaphor struggles to reveal. Rights are relational obligations. They are obligations justified by a particular kind of argument—arguments grounded in the features of individuals. With his theory of individuated and non-individuated aims Dworkin is attempting to pull out the same feature of rights highlighted by the justified-constraint theory of relational and non-relational obligations. Relational obligations are obligations justified by the features of individuals, while non-relational consequentialist obligations are obligations that are justified by the features of acts. The crucial difference between the justified-constraint view and Dworkin's is that, on the justified-constraint view, it is not the right-holder's opportunities, resources, and liberties that define the relational nature of rights but the fact that a feature of the right-holder justifies the obligation correlative to the right.

Dworkin's trump metaphor may be the result of the impression, noted and refuted in Chapter Five, that rights imply especially important obligations. Dworkin may be led to this error by focusing too much on constitutional rights. Rights do not *exclude* consideration of "direct utilitarian arguments." Rights do not *trump* goals. The metaphor that best describes external rights conflict is a simple imaginary card game with no trump suits. Imagine a game in which each card has its point value. Suppose that jacks are worth eleven points, queens twelve, kings thirteen and aces fourteen. Each person plays four cards from their hand. One adds the points from each person's four cards and the person whose cards total to the most points wins the trick. If there is a tie, no one takes the trick and another is played. The winner of the next non-tied trick takes all the tied tricks as well. If one uses a metaphor in which the red suits stand for rights and the black suits stand for non-relational obligations, then the conflict between rights (a.k.a. relational obligations) and non-relational obligations is like the conflict between the various four-card sets played. Four low-value red cards (rights) can be outweighed by one high-value black card (a non-relational obligation). Four low-value black cards can be outweighed by one high-value red card. A four-card set played by a player may include both red cards and black cards. In non-metaphorical terms, obligations can be justified by relational or non-relational arguments and whether the obligations are relational or non-relational has nothing to do with the importance of those obligations. Obligations justified by relational arguments do not exclude or trump obligations justified by non-relational arguments.

The justified-constraint theory of rights follows Lyons in holding that rights provide an argumentative threshold.

> If I have a right to do something, this provides an argumentative threshold against objections to my doing it as well as a presumption against others' interference. Considerations that might otherwise be sufficient against my so acting, in the absence of my having the right . . . are ineffective in its presence.
>
> Consider, for example, my right to life. This entails that I may act as to save it and that others may not interfere, even if these acts or the results would otherwise be subject to sound criticism. I need not show that my life is valuable or useful,

and the fact that my defending it would have bad overall consequences . . . does not show that my defending it is wrong . . .

This point is sometimes distorted by exaggeration. Note, however, that my right to life does not automatically justify any course of action whatsoever that may be needed to save it . . .

I may defend my life even at *some* cost to overall welfare, and others may not interfere *just* because it would promote overall welfare to *some* degree if they did. In this way, the arguments that flow from moral rights appear to diverge from those predicated on the service of welfare. If one accepts moral rights, one cannot accept absolute guidance by welfare arguments (1994, 152–153).

Lyons has seen something deep and important about rights. Dworkin has seen it too but, with the metaphor of trumps, he has "distorted by exaggeration." The justified-constraint theory provides a conceptual underpinning for Lyons' insight. Rights are constraints on the actions of others justified by features of the right-holder. A crucial feature of rights is that they use a particular argumentative, a particular justificatory, strategy. One who holds that I have a right to life is committed to the soundness of a particular kind of argument, one that focuses on features of me. This kind of argument is a natural basis upon which to rest the view that "I may defend my life even at *some* cost to overall welfare." (Raz has seen this point as well in a slightly different way. See his analysis of duties as exclusionary reasons (1986, 195 and 1977). Lyons presentation of this point is clearer because Raz's term "exclusionary" reasons makes it sound as if rights exclude consideration of all other reasons. However, Raz, does not mean for the term to have this implication.)

There is an important insight in Dworkin's theory of rights. An important feature of rights is that they protect individuals from those who would focus exclusively on maximizing utility. The trumping metaphor incorrectly suggests that the protection rights provide is complete. The justified-constraint theory of rights can explain how rights protect individuals while avoiding the misleading trumping metaphor. Obligations justified by relational arguments are importantly different from obligations justified by non-relational arguments. Both kinds of obligations must be considered in the moral evaluation of an action. The two kinds of obligations can conflict. In particular cases, obligations justified by relational arguments may carry the day. In all cases, that one is the object of a relational obligation is a measure of protection from those would hold that all obligations are non-relational. This protection is not complete. Its strength depends on the strength of the arguments for the asserted relational obligation and on the moral importance of that obligation.

7. Right Holders: Present

To this point, we set aside the question of what sorts of things can have rights. It is now time to argue that the justified-constraint theory implies that many things besides typical adult humans can have rights. This point is important for at least two reasons. First, Hart's and Wellman's theories of rights are seriously flawed because they imply that human infants cannot have rights. This is only a relative advantage for the justified-constraint theory of rights if it does not have this implication. Second and more importantly, a great many practical debates over rights involve, to a greater or lesser extent, the issue of what sorts of things can have rights. Does abortion violate the rights of human fetuses? Do the dead have a right that their wills be respected? Do future generations have a right that we leave them an environment of as good a quality as we have now? Do groups, such as minorities who have been the victims of discrimination, have rights? Do animals have a right that we not kill them for food? One could add many other such questions.

Rights have been ascribed to at least the following sorts of entities: typical adult humans, human children, human infants, humans with various levels of physical and mental defects (including human "vegetables," senile humans, and insane humans), human fetuses, dead humans, humans who will exist but do not exist at present, animals who are the subject-of-a-life, sentient animals, non-sentient animals, living things, structured nonliving things (including works of art, crystals, and rocks), groups of humans (including families, corporations, countries, and ethnic/cultural communities), groups of nonhuman things (including ecosystems and landscapes), and groups of human and nonhuman things (including the biosphere and cities). The issues surrounding the rights of things that do not presently exist (e.g., past and future generations of humans) are sufficiently complex as to require a chapter of their own. Therefore, this chapter considers the rights of presently existing things. Presently existing things can be usefully divided into two categories: presently existing individual things (e.g., human children, human infants, sentient animals, and structured nonliving things) and presently existing groups (e.g., groups of humans, groups of nonhuman things, and groups of human and nonhuman things).

The question that this chapter attempts to answer is, "Which presently existing things can have rights?" This question is easily confused with some distinct questions. First, this chapter focuses on what sorts of things can have rights. It is important to distinguish this issue from the issue of what sorts of things can have obligations and impossibilities. Although there is a great deal of debate about what sorts of things can have rights, there is more consensus concerning what sorts of things can have obligations and impossibilities. Very roughly, the standard view is that to be the subject of an obligation a thing must have the ability to consider moral principles to decide what should be done as well as the ability to freely choose to act (or not to act) as morality requires. These abilities are generally held to be necessary and sufficient to be the sort of thing that can be the subject of an obligation or an impossibility. Although there is much that might be said here, none of it is relevant to the issues discussed in this book. Therefore, we will set aside the debates over what sorts of things can be the subject of an obligation or impossibility.

Second, the "can" in "Which presently existing things can have rights?" is referring to the limits on what can be the object of an obligation or impossibility that are set by the concept of rights. This chapter considers the limits, if any, that the concept of rights places on the range of presently existing things that can have rights. It may be that other things (e.g., substantive moral views, the rules of certain rule systems, and other concepts) place restrictions on the range of presently existing things that can have rights. Such restrictions are not at issue in this chapter.

Third, one must be careful to distinguish the question of which presently existing individual things can have rights from the question of which presently existing things actually have rights. Some presently existing things can have rights but do not have them. I can have the right to live in my neighbor's house. The concept of rights places no barrier to my having the right to live in her house. But I do not now have the right to live in my neighbor's house. Suppose that in some (morally horrid) country there existed "a class of helots whom free citizens were allowed to treat as they wished or interfere with at will" (Hart 1982, 173). It is possible that the concept of rights places no barrier to the helots having legal rights, but (assuming that some version of legal positivism is true) the legal system of the country implies that they do not have any legal rights.

1. INDIVIDUALS, GROUPS, AND RELEVANT FEATURES

Let us begin by considering limits the concept of rights places on the rights of presently existing individual things. Hereafter, "present individuals" refers to presently existing individual things. We will then consider the rights of presently existing groups. For simplicity's sake, let us focus on obligations. On the justified-constraint view, whether a thing can have rights depends on whether it can be the object of an obligation. Whether a thing can be the object of an obligation depends on whether a particular rule system picks out a feature of that thing as a positively relevant feature. A particular rule system picks out a feature as positively relevant when it appears in the antecedent of the conditional premise of a sound instance of the key argument form. On the justified-constraint analysis, the concept of rights is extremely permissive when it comes to what sorts of present individuals can have rights. The analysis implies that the concept of rights itself places no restrictions on the sorts of present individuals that can have rights. The analysis implies that restrictions on what sorts of present individuals have rights are placed, not by the concept of rights, but by the substantive normative statements of the rule system.

Restrictions on what sorts of present individuals have rights are determined by the features of things that, in a particular rule system, justify obligations.

Let us consider a rock and a typical adult human, Barbara. As noted in Chapter 6, most people think that the following instance of the key argument form is sound:

1. Barbara is a person.
2. If Barbara is a person, then David has a moral obligation not to kill Barbara.
3. Therefore, David has a moral obligation not to kill Barbara.

But, as far as the concept of rights is concerned, there is no barrier to holding that the argument is not sound. The concept of rights is no barrier to the claim that the second premise of this argument is false.

As noted in Chapter 6, most people think that the following argument is sound:

1. The rock on the forest path is inanimate.
2. If the rock is inanimate, then Eddie does not have a moral obligation not to destroy the rock.
3. Therefore, Eddie does not have a moral obligation not to destroy the rock.

But the concept of rights is no barrier to holding that the following argument is sound:

1. The rock on the curb is inanimate.
2. If the rock is inanimate, then Eddie has a moral obligation not to destroy it.
3. Therefore, Eddie has a moral obligation not to destroy this rock.

The second premise of this argument is absurd, but the concept of rights does not show that it is absurd. Demonstrating its absurdity is a matter of substantive moral philosophy. (Although he has a distinct argument, a similar conclusion is reached by Kramer (2001).) As far as the concept of rights is concerned, the claim that rocks can have rights is coherent. It is only because it is plausible to hold that neither the moral rule system nor any other rule system implies that any feature of any rock is positively relevant and that being inanimate is negatively relevant that it is plausible to hold that rocks do not have rights. A person might disagree. One might claim that rocks in general or certain rock do have a positively relevant feature and that being inanimate is not a negatively relevant feature. One might hold some sort of religious view according to which it is morally wrong to destroy certain rocks (and not merely because their destruction would adversely affect some persons). This person would, on the justified-constraint theory, be committed to the view that rocks have moral rights. The claim that Jews cannot have rights is not barred by the concept of rights. One should attack Hitler's views, not on the grounds that they are based on a flawed conceptual analysis of rights, but on the grounds that they are substantively false. Being a Jew is not a negatively relevant feature. The answer to the question, "What sorts of present individuals can have rights?" is "Any sort of present individual." The justified-constraint theory of rights, unlike Hart's and Wellman's, implies that human infants can have rights.

Having considered the rights of individuals, let us turn to the rights of groups. The ontological nature of groups has raised many philosophical questions. Many have considered whether groups are merely collections of individuals or whether they are an entities in their own right. These questions will not be answered here.

There can be no doubt that it is common for people to speak of the rights of groups. One often hears statements such as "The Québécois have a right to speak French," and "Georgia State University has a right to $325 from Kyle." At least some of these statements appear to be true. If Kyle registers for a class at Georgia State University, then it seems that Georgia State has a right to $325 from Kyle. (Kyle has a scholarship which covers his tuition but not his fees, and the fees are $325.) In the above claims, groups are the subjects of rights. In other cases, people make claims in which groups are said to be the objects of rights. "Addurrahim has a right that the quartet play because he paid for a private performance." In cases like these, the group is said to have the duty correlative to the right. There are assertions in which groups are said to be both the subject and the object of a right. "The Hopi have a right that the U.S. meet its treaty obligations."

What does the justified-constraint theory of rights tell us about the rights of groups? On this theory, whether a thing can have rights depends on whether it can be the object of an obligation. Whether a thing can be the object of an obligation, in turn, depends on whether a particular rule system picks out a feature of that thing as a positively relevant feature. A particular rule system picks out a feature as positively relevant when it appears in the antecedent of the conditional premise of a sound instance of the key argument form.

The justified-constraint analysis implies that groups can have rights. The argument for this view is perfectly parallel to the argument that any present individual can have rights. Restrictions on group rights are determined by the features of things that are, in a particular rule system, positively relevant. Groups can have features. Therefore, on the justified-constraint theory, groups can have rights. Restrictions on group rights are placed, not by the concept of rights, but by the substantive normative statements of the rule system.

The fact that it is a neutral theory of rights is an important advantage of the justified-constraint theory of rights over the interest, choice, and will theories of rights. These theories assert that there is a conceptual connection between rights and some particular feature of presently existing things (i.e., interests, choices, or wills). On the justified-constraint theory, there is no such conceptual connection. Whether or not a particular presently existing thing has rights is a substantive matter. It depends on substantive matters. Thus, the justified-constraint theory of rights closes no conceptual doors. This is a crucial respect in which the theory is superior to others.

We can now return to the view that, in the case of the obligation to give to charity, the group of those who are the appropriate objects of charity has a right. Let us reconsider the case of Tabitha discussed in Chapter 5. The rule system P contains the following statement:

> If X is a person who has an income over $100,000 per year and Y1, Y2, Y3, etc. are people who have incomes less than $1,000 per year, then X has a P obligation to give some money to Y1 or Y2 or Y3, etc.

Assume that there is a group of people who have an income less than $1,000 and that Tabitha has an income over $100,000. Tabitha has an obligation to give some money to some of those whose income is less than $1,000. There is no feature of any one person that is essential to a sound argument leading to the conclusion that Tabitha has this obligation with its latitude as to whom to give. There are precisely three people who have incomes of less than $1,000 per year—Howard, Kate, and George. The following argument is not sound:

1. Tabitha is a person who has an income over $100,000 per year and Howard has an income of less than $1,000 per year.
2. If Tabitha is a person who has an income over $100,000 per year and Howard has an income of less than $1,000 per year, then Tabitha has a P obligation to give some money to Howard or Kate or George.
3. Therefore, Tabitha has a P obligation to give some money to Howard or Kate or George.

There is no feature of Howard or Kate or George that is a reason for Tabitha's obligation with its latitude to give some of her money to Howard or Kate or George. The justified-constraint analysis implies that her obligation is non-relational.

However, someone might claim that the group composed of Howard, Kate, and George has a right that Tabitha give some money to Howard or Kate or George. The justified-constraint analysis of rights allows for groups to have rights, so this position is compatible with this view. Of course, it is also compatible with the justified-constraint theory to hold that, for reasons other than the restrictions placed by the concept of rights, groups do not have rights and therefore that the group composed of Howard, Kate, and George does not have a right that Tabitha give some money to Howard or Kate or George.

Although this is not the place to fully resolve substantive debates about group rights, the justified-constraint theory has important implications concerning the nature of group rights. The systematic analysis of rights in terms of Hohfeldian and moral concepts provides a better understanding of the nature of group rights. The lack of a clear understanding of the nature of rights and the nature of the group rights debate has led to a great deal of confusion among those considering whether groups have rights. Much, but not all, of the plausibility of the view that there are some assertions of the rights of groups that cannot be analyzed as sets of assertions of the rights of individuals rests on this confusion. It will be profitable to remove it.

2. CLEARING SOME UNDERBRUSH

What are group rights?[1] In other words, what is the proper analysis of claims in which groups are said to be the subject and/or object of rights? Some, let us call them "analytic individualists," think that all group rights can be analyzed as complex sets of individual rights, rights in which only individuals are the subjects and the objects. Others, let us call them "analytic collectivists," think that some claims of group rights cannot be analyzed as complex sets of individual rights.

Analytic individualism and analytic collectivism must be distinguished from value individualism and value collectivism. Michael Hartney defines value individualism as the view that

> only the lives of individual human beings have ultimate value and collective entities derive their value from their contribution to the lives of individual human beings (1991, 297).

Value collectivism, on the other hand, is

> the view that a collective entity can have value independently of its contribution to the well-being of individual human beings (1991, 297).

Value individualism and value collectivism are views about what has ultimate value. Analytic individualism and analytic collectivism are views about the correct analysis of claims concerning group rights. One might argue that value individualism implies that groups cannot have rights. If value individualism implies that groups cannot have rights, then this would be a restriction on the scope of what can have rights that is placed by a substantive moral view. Hereafter, "individualism" refers to analytic individualism and "collectivism" refers to analytic collectivism.

Individualists and collectivists are defending a conceptual analysis. Conceptual analysis is the task of determining what a concept is. When one wonders what knowledge is, when one seeks to determine what it is to have a belief, one is doing conceptual analysis. Questions such as "What is law?" "What is knowledge?" and "What are group rights?" are typically requests for conceptual analysis. The central question of this book, "What is a right?" is a request for a conceptual analysis, and therefore this book is an extended conceptual analysis of rights. This book defends a conception of the concept of rights.

A successful conceptual analysis does *not* show that the concept being analyzed has no instantiation. Suppose it were shown that knowledge is justified true belief. This would not show that there is no knowledge. A correct conceptual analysis shows that X (the analysandum) is identical to Y (the analysan). So if Y exists, then X exists as well. Some, but not all, analyses are eliminative. An eliminative analysis makes two claims: that X is Y and that, since Y does not exist, neither does X. Dragons are large, flying, fire-breathing lizards and there are no such lizards,

---

[1]   This section and the next are drawn from Rainbolt (2001).

so there are no dragons. An individualist might defend an eliminative or a non-eliminative analysis of group rights. An eliminative individualist thinks that there are no group rights and therefore that all claims of group rights are false. A non-eliminative individualist thinks that there are group rights, that some claims of group rights are true, and that all group rights can be analyzed as sets of individual rights.

On the non-eliminative individualist's view, group rights are similar to Hassan's legal right to free speech. His legal right to free speech as currently interpreted by the U.S. Supreme Court is a bundle of a great many Hohfeldian relations among which are the following:

(1) A liberty to say that Richard Nixon was a crook.
(2) A liberty not to say that Richard Nixon was a crook.
(3) A claim that the police provide protection when he says that Richard Nixon was a crook.
(4) A large set of claims that others not interfere with his saying that Richard Nixon was a crook.
(5) A set of immunities to having the above relations extinguished.

The non-eliminative individualist thinks that, just as Hassan's legal right to free speech can be analyzed as a large and complex set of individual Hohfeldian relations, all group rights can be analyzed as large and complex sets of individual rights. Consider Georgia State University's legal right to $325 from Kyle. The non-eliminative individualist holds that Georgia State's right to $325 is identical to a large set of Hohfeldian relations of a large set of individuals. The relations in this set might include:

(1) The liberty right of certain employees in the registrar's office to send Kyle's file to the transcript office.
(2) The duty right of certain employees in the transcript office to refuse to give out Kyle's transcript.
(3) The liberty right of certain employees of Georgia State to send Kyle's file to an outside collection agency.
(4) The duty right of a judge to enter an order to garnish Kyle's wages.

Like the analysis of the right to free speech, this analysis is incomplete. The precise contents of the rights package that is Georgia State's legal right to $325 from Kyle is determined by the legal rule system.

The eliminative individualist holds that the correct analysis of group rights refers to at least one analysan that does not exist. Therefore, group rights do not exist. One might hold that the correct analysis of statements about group rights refers to a ghostly group substance, that there is no such substance, and therefore that there are no group rights.

The distinction between eliminative and non-eliminative individualism shows that one must distinguish conceptual analysis from questions about the truth conditions of claims. "When, if ever, are claims of group rights true?" is a question distinct from the question, "What are group rights?" Both non-eliminative individualists and collectivists can consistently assert that some claims of group rights are true. One reason we are interested in conceptual analysis is to help us determine the truth conditions of claims. A good conceptual analysis must preserve the truth conditions of clear uses of the concept being analyzed and give us plausible truth conditions in the unclear cases. This is the extensionally test of a conceptual analysis. A good conceptual analysis must also provide us with a fruitful understanding of the concept. This is the theoretical test of a conceptual analysis.

Eliminative individualism is false. It is difficult to defend the view that all claims concerning group rights are false. The examples given above stand as counterexamples to the eliminative individualist's view. "Georgia State University has a right to $325 from Kyle" and "The Hopi have a right that the U.S. meet its treaty obligations" certainly seem to be true statements. Apparently true statements of group rights can easily be found in the most superficial review of legal documents. In the face of this evidence, the eliminative individualist must provide strong arguments. However, no one provides any arguments in defense of eliminative individualism. Individualists have overlooked the distinction between eliminative and non-eliminative individualism and so do not make arguments to defend the second of these two views. The counterexamples just mentioned stand unrefuted, and therefore the most plausible of the two individualist views is non-eliminative individualism.

Many of those who write about group rights have failed to understand that a successful conceptual analysis does not show that the concept being analyzed is not instantiated. This fundamental confusion about the nature of conceptual analysis has greatly muddied the waters of the group rights debate. In discussing the rights of corporations, Wellman asks

> How, then, should one interpret a statement like "Gulf Oil Corporation has a moral right to join a uranium cartel" or "Gulf has a moral right to be paid for gas delivered to Ted's Filling Station"? (1995, 165).

He answers that

> the former amounts to the assertion that X, Y and Z each have a liberty-right *as* holders of offices A, B and C in the corporate group named the Gulf Oil Corporation to act in whatever manner the relevant rules recognize as voting to join the cartel. The latter means that whatever person or persons are authorized by the rules that constitute the Gulf Oil Corporation to claim payment for services rendered by its members has or have a moral right *as* holder(s) of the office of corporate claimant to be paid for gas delivered by its employees (1995, 165).

So far so good. Wellman seems to be a straightforward non-eliminative individualist. My only suggestion would be that Wellman's use of "interpret a statement," "amounts to the assertion," and "means" is slightly confusing. Rather than these three different expressions, it would serve clarity to explicitly refer to "the analysis" of the rights claims. But it is clear that, with these three expressions, Wellman is referring to what this work calls "an analysis."

However, Wellman goes on to assert that

> if my interpretation is accepted, corporate groups in and of themselves cannot be understood to be moral right-holders. (1995, 165)

It is clear from context that "interpretation" refers to the analysis in the previous quote. Wellman has therefore made the mistake of thinking that the analysis of group rights in terms of the rights of individuals implies that group rights do not exist.

The analysis of rights in terms of Hohfeldian relations and the deontic and alethic normative concepts reveals that individualism is a more flexible position than many have thought. Individualists are not necessarily committed to many of the views that have been ascribed to them. Here is a list of views to which the individualist is not committed.

Individualism does not imply a particular political view. It is possible for individualists to disagree among themselves about which statements of group rights are true. A more right-wing individualist might assert that some claims of corporate rights are true but all claims that ethnic groups have rights are false. A more left-wing individualist might defend the opposite view. (For the same reasons, collectivism is also politically neutral.)

The individualist need not deny that individuals can have rights because they are members of groups. Let us suppose that the American Philosophical Association (APA) contracts with a certain book supplier and, according to this contract, the book supplier agrees to give APA members 10% off its regular prices (perhaps in exchange for the use of the APA mailing list). In that case, I, because I am a member of the APA, have a right to buy books from this supplier at 10% off the regular price.

The individualist is not committed to the view that the subjects, objects, or contents of the individual rights that make up a group right must be the same as the subject, object, or content of the group right itself. Georgia State University has a right to $325 from Kyle. The individualist is not committed to the view that some individual in the employ of Georgia State has a right to $325 from Kyle. It may well be the case that the analysis of Georgia State's right will not include any right of any employee of Georgia State to $325 from Kyle. The list above does not include any claim right, held by an individual employee of Georgia State, to $325 from Kyle.

The individualist is not committed to the view that a group's rights must be analyzed only in terms of the rights of members of that group. Part of the analysis may refer to the rights of individuals not in the group. Larry May has claimed that corporate rights cannot be analyzed as the rights of stockholders and managers (1987, 125–134). The individualist might argue that corporate rights can be analyzed as the rights of stockholders, managers, *and other individuals*—such as employees and certain legal officials (e.g., judges). So the following two views are compatible:

203

individualism is true and there is no plausible analysis of corporate rights as the rights of stockholders and managers.

May also claims that one cannot analyze corporate rights as individual rights because no one stockholder owns or controls all of any corporate asset. This over-looks the point that the content of the individual rights into which a group right is analyzed can differ from the content of the group right. The individualist is not, therefore, committed to an analysis of classic corporate property rights as classic individual property rights of stockholders and managers. As May points out, classic property rights are complex bundles of rights, and different individuals have different sorts of property rights. Stockholders are often said to own corporations, but their property rights in the corporation are clearly lacking some of the elements that one finds in classic property rights, such as my property right to my pickup truck. In particular, in the typical case, no one stockholder controls any corporate asset in the way I control my truck. But this does not imply that the rights of corporations cannot be analyzed as complex sets of (limited) rights of managers, employees, stockholders, suppliers, judges, etc. The individualist might argue that corporate rights may be analyzed as a set of individual rights in which one individual has part of the classic property right bundle and another individual has another part.

Finally, May also argues that corporate rights cannot be analyzed as individual rights because the law limits corporate liability but does not limit personal liability. He thinks that this shows that corporate rights cannot be analyzed as individual rights. This does not follow. All that May has pointed out is that some of the individual rights in a plausible analysis of corporate rights will be rights of limited liability.

3. INDIVIDUALISM VERSUS COLLECTIVISM

Having cleared some conceptual underbrush of the debate between individualism and collectivism, we are in a better position to evaluate the arguments for and against each view.

There are some things that, as a matter of logic, only groups can do. Only a group can play a quartet, secede, have a philosophical discussion, or get married. A collectivist might be tempted by the following simple argument:

1. Only a group can marry.
2. X can have a right to do A only if X can do A.
3. Therefore, only a group can have a right to marry.

One could replace "marry" with "play a quartet," "secede," etc. Something seems amiss with this argument. It implies that neither you nor I have the right to marry. It seems that individuals do have the right to marry and yet, in some sense, only a group can marry. No one actually makes this simple argument, but it is useful to examine it in some detail because it throws light on more complex arguments similar to this simple one.

When Maiwan was single, it seems that he had a right to marry. He is now married. It seems that he no longer has a right to marry. Hohfeldian analysis allows us to give a much more precise analysis of this right. Let us follow through the legal steps that occurred when Maiwan married his wife. In typical legal rule systems, a marriage requires two individuals to be married by an appropriate official. Correlative to the officials' powers are the liabilities of two individuals to be married. In typical legal rule systems, one must have a license to marry. Before Maiwan obtained a license, he did not have a liability to be married. Each person who makes up the couple to be married must gain the approval of the other to obtain a license. So Maiwan's future wife had the power to give him the power to apply for a liability to have the liability to be married to her. He exercised this power when he signed and submitted the application for a marriage license. The exercise of his power only gives Maiwan a liability to have the liability to be married because the application for a license must be approved by certain individuals in the government of the county in which he was married. Because he met the qualifications necessary to have the liability to be married, those individuals had a duty right to grant him the liability to be married. His wife had similar powers and liabilities. In particular, Maiwan had the liability to be married to her and she had the liability to be married to him. The powers correlative to the liabilities that Maiwan and his wife had after they obtained the marriage license were held by those officials authorized by the government to marry people. The minister who performed the marriage was one such individual. In addition to the liabilities that Maiwan and his future wife had, each of them also had a liberty to exercised the powers noted above. Furthermore, the power and the liberty that each of them had were protected by claims. Others had a duty to refrain from kidnapping them while they were going to the church in which they were to be married.

With this analysis in front of us, it is easy to see the mistake in the simple argument presented above. It contains a confusion regarding the phrase "Only a group can marry." One might understand this phrase to say that it is not conceptually possible for individuals to marry. This would be incorrect. Once one examines the Hohfeldian situation, it is clear that "Only a group can marry" means that an individual, X, has a right to marry only if Y agrees to marry X. The fact that someone's agreeing to marry Maiwan is a necessary condition for Maiwan having a right to marry that person does not show that only the group Maiwan-and-future-wife-and-minister has a right to marry any more than the fact that the existence of Georgia State is a necessary condition for Mark having a right to attend Georgia State shows that only the group Georgia State-and-Mark has a right to attend Georgia State. The simple argument above is not valid.

Réaume (1988, 1994) and Waldron (1993b) have presented another argument for collectivism. They have argued that there is a certain subclass of the actions that only groups can perform that cannot be analyzed as sets of individual rights. They begin by noting that certain goods are participatory. The crucial feature of participatory goods is that, not only does one value them, but that one values

205

the fact that one is valuing them *with others*. I enjoy watching baseball games with my family (my mother and my sister). I enjoy watching a baseball game by myself as well, but not as much. The difference is that I enjoy the fact that, as a family, we are enjoying something together. My mother and my sister have similar feelings. This is, as Réaume and Waldron point out, an important feature of many activities. Attending movies with a friend is more fun than going alone. Many group rights seem to be rights to participatory goods. Consider the Hopi's right to engage in their religious rituals. Many Hopi not only want to practice their rituals but wish to do so with other Hopis. An individual Hopi would feel a genuine loss if she were the only person performing the ritual actions. On the other hand, the participatory rights argument does not seem to apply to some group rights, e.g., corporate rights. Perhaps some value being in a corporation with others, but most seem to be primarily motivated by individual monetary considerations.

The next step in Réaume and Waldron's argument is the assumption that Raz's theory of rights is correct.

> X has a right if and only if other things being equal, an aspect of X's well-being (his interest) is a sufficient reason for holding some other person to be under an obligation.

Réaume and Waldron think that no adequate account of the desirability of participatory goods can be pinned down to an individual. Therefore, no individual's interest in participatory goods can be a sufficient reason for others to have a duty. According to Réaume and Waldron, the duty to realize these goods is grounded, not in an individual's interest, but in the group's interest. On this view, an individual's interest in a participatory good cannot ground a right because we cannot say that it is for the individual's sake that the duty is imposed. As Waldron puts it:

> Since no adequate account of its [a participatory good's] desirability can be pinned down to either X or Y or Z, there can be no *point* in saying that it ought to be pursued as X's or Y's or Z's right. (1993b, 359)

This argument is not sound. First, the individualist is not committed to the view that group rights must be analyzed as disjunctions of individual rights ("X's or Y's *or* Z's right"). In most cases, group rights will be analyzed as conjunctions of individual rights. Second, it is true that my enjoyment of a baseball game is increased if my family members are enjoying it with me. It is also increased if I have a bratwurst. Individuals can value many things, including bratwursts and the fact that other individuals value something. The individualist has no more problem providing an analysis of rights to participatory goods than she does of providing an analysis of rights to bratwursts. I have a right to watch a baseball game while eating a bratwurst. This right is not plausibly analyzed as my right to watch a baseball game and my right to eat a bratwurst because eating a bratwurst while watching a baseball game is more fun than eating a bratwurst at home and then going to a baseball game. My family has a right to watch baseball games together. This right is not plausibly analyzed as my right to watch a game by myself and my mother's right to watch a game by herself and my sister's right to watch a game by herself. It is plausibly analyzed as my right to watch a game *with my family* and my mother's right to watch a game *with her family* and my sister's right to watch a game *with her family*.

Raz provides another argument for collectivism (1986, 193–216). He begins by noting that Yasser Arafat has an interest in Palestinian self-determination. Palestinian self-determination is one of his important long-term projects. Does Arafat have a right to Palestinian self-determination? According to Raz, Arafat's interest alone is not sufficient to justify the far-reaching duties of others that a right to Palestinian self-determination implies. If there is a right to Palestinian self-determination, then a large collection of individuals all over the world have a duty to help the Palestinians gain self-determination. Some would have negative duties not to interfere with Palestinian efforts to gain self-determination. Others would have positive duties to vacate land and give it to the Palestinians. According to Raz, Arafat's interest is not a sufficient reason for such a large set of others to have such extensive duties. His interest is not of sufficient moral importance to justify all these duties. So Raz's theory of rights implies that Arafat does not have this right. However, Arafat is not alone in having an interest in Palestinian self-determination. Many other Palestinians have a similar interest. If there is a right to Palestinian self-determination, it is only these interests, collectively, that are sufficient to justify the far-reaching duties that the right implies. According to Raz, the right to Palestinian self-determination cannot be analyzed as the rights of individuals because no single individual's interest, by itself, would justify the correlative duties, and an individual has a right only if that individual's interest is sufficient to justify correlative duties. Raz thinks that there are many rights that have the same structure as the Palestinians' right to self-determination. He thinks that there are rights to many public goods (e.g., clean air, a cultured society) and that they cannot be analyzed as sets of individuals' rights.

It has seemed to some that Raz's argument for group rights does not correctly draw the line between individual and group rights. Jones (1999) considers the case of the group formed by all those individuals in a city who would use a proposed bike path. Suppose that each of these individuals has an interest in the construction of the bike path. They would each use and enjoy the proposed path. However, they have no group identity. None of them even knows of the existence of any of the others. As far as Raz's argument goes, this lack of group identity is irrelevant to the issue of whether the group constituted by the cyclists has a right that the bike path be built. If the collection of all their interests in the building of the bike path is sufficient to justify a duty of some others to build it, then this group that lacks group identity has a right that the path be built. Some think this is a counterintuitive implication of Raz's view of group rights. Whatever one thinks of this objection to Raz, his argument for group rights is extremely interesting. It shows that if Raz's theory of rights is true, then individualism is false. Raz's theory of rights is committed to the view that groups have rights in the sense that the subject of some assertions of rights cannot be analyzed as complex sets of individual rights, rights in which only individuals are the subjects and the objects. Of course, we have seen that Raz's theory of rights is not correct.

Wellman provides an argument for individualism. He is committed to the view that groups cannot have rights. According to Wellman, being an agent is a necessary condition for having rights. He also holds that groups are not agents.

> I persist in my conclusion that there could be no irreducible moral group rights because no group *as such* possesses the agency required to be a moral right-holder (1995, 176).

Wellman holds the individualist view that all claims of group rights can be analyzed as sets of the rights of individuals. Given his views about the importance of agency, this is a natural view for him to take. However, we have seen that Wellman's theory of rights is not correct. (In the quote above, the qualifier "irreducible" indicates that perhaps Wellman is a non-eliminative individualist in spite of his many assertions that groups cannot have rights.)

The most common argument for individualism begins by comparing paradigm right-holders (e.g., typical adult humans) with paradigm non-right-holders (e.g., rocks) and asking, "What are the necessary conditions for having the ability to have rights?" Wellman argues that the ability to make choices is a necessary condition for having rights. Feinberg (1980, 159–184) argues that having a conative life, having the mental states needed for purposive behavior, is a necessary condition for having rights. Regan (1992) argues that sentience, the capacity to have sensations or feelings, is a necessary condition for having rights. Because sentience is a nomologically necessary condition for having a conative life or making choices, Wellman and Feinberg are committed to the view that sentience is a necessary condition for having rights. Let us assume that groups are not sentient. Groups are composed of sentient individuals, but they do not themselves feel anything. (This does not imply that claims that groups feel, suffer, etc. are false. Because conceptual analysis is distinct from questions of truth conditions, it only implies that claims about group interests, like claims about group rights, are analyzable as a set of individual interests.) If sentience is a necessary condition for rights and groups are not sentient, then either ascriptions of rights to groups can be analyzed into sets of the rights of sentient individuals or there are no group rights and all claims of group rights are false. Since some claims of group rights are true, the rights of groups must be analyzable as a set of individuals' rights.

This argument for non-eliminative individualism has a great deal of initial plausibility. This argument, like an argument for collectivism based on the truth of value collectivism, rests on substantive views (such as the view that rocks do not have rights) and so is beyond the scope of this book. It is interesting to note that the rights of past and future generations are hard cases for this view. If sentience is a necessary condition for having rights and if (as seems very plausible) only presently existing things are sentient, then it seems that only presently existing things can have rights. If a correct understanding of relational obligation removes this difficulty, then individualism will be that much more plausible. An implication of the argument to be found in the next chapter is that being sentient may be a necessary condition for having rights, but this does not imply that only presently existing things can have rights.

8. Right Holders: Past and Future

Having considered the rights of presently existing things, let us turn to the rights of past and future things. Let us refer to them as "past individuals" and "future individuals." We will continue to ignore impossibilities in order to simplify presentation. Let us assume that death is complete. In other words, assume that there is no prelife and no afterlife of any sort. If this assumption is not made, the question of the rights of past and future individuals does not arise. Instead, one would consider the rights of individuals who are presently existing in a form other than the form with which we are most familiar. Specifying the range of future individuals is somewhat complex. It clearly includes humans who do not presently exist but will exist at some time in the future. However, the line between those humans who will exist and those humans who presently exist is controversial. Some hold that beings do not become humans until birth. Others draw the line at conception. Still others draw this line somewhere between conception and birth. Fortunately, we need not resolve this issue. One is free to draw the line wherever one wishes. Where one draws this line will not affect the central conclusion of this chapter—that the justified-constraint theory of rights solves the problem of the subject of the rights of past and future individuals.

Past and future individuals raise a host of philosophical questions, and one cannot answer them all in one book. Some have asked, "Is death and/or prenatal nonexistence something we should fear?" "Is death bad for the one who dies?" or "If we fear death, why do we not fear prenatal nonexistence?" Others have asked "Can past or future persons be harmed?" These questions will not be answered here. This chapter considers the limits, if any, that the concept of rights, and the concept of rights alone, places on the range of past and future individuals that can have rights. There are other arguments for the view that past and future individuals, although they can have rights, in fact have no rights. More precisely, we will examine the limits that the conception of the concept of rights defended in this book places on the range of past and future individuals that can have rights.

For example, one might hold the substantive moral view that the only right any being has is the right not to be harmed. One might then go on to claim that past and future individuals cannot be harmed. From these premises it follows that past and future individuals cannot have rights. But this conclusion is not drawn from the concept of rights. The central points at issue in this argument would be the truth of the claim that past and future individuals cannot be harmed and the truth of the view that the only right any being has is the right not to be harmed.

1. THE PROBLEM OF THE SUBJECT

While they are living, people frequently enter into contracts that specify that others have obligations to do things after they have died. Life insurance contracts are the most obvious example. As for future individuals, most legal rule systems hold that actions that occur before one's birth can violate one's rights. A person who was a fetus when her father died can have a legal right to inherit her father's estate. It is common to talk of the rights of posterity.

On the other hand, there is an ancient, simple, and powerful argument against the view that past and future individuals can have rights. It is the problem of the subject and was first noted by Epicurus.

> Death, therefore—the most dreadful of evils—is nothing to us, since while we exist, death is not present and whenever death is present, we do not exist (1993, 63).

A right cannot exist unless there is a subject of the right (who would also be the object of the correlative obligation). The past and future individuals do not now exist and therefore they cannot now have rights. Here is a modern formulation offered by Richard DeGeorge.

> Future generations by definition do not now exist. They cannot now, therefore, be the present bearer or subject of anything, including rights (1981, 159).

As Feinberg notes when discussing harms to future generations,

> This powerful argument against [the view that past and future individuals can be harmed] is indeed a problem for the position on the other side.... Like a rock withstanding the lashings of a storm, it stands resistant to all counterarguments, maintaining and reiterating that there cannot be a harm without a subject to be harmed (1984, 80).

Note that the problem of the subject is neither the problem of showing that we have an obligation to do things that will benefit those who will exist nor the problem of showing that we have an obligation to fulfill the promises we made to the dead. One could consistently hold that we have these obligations but that they are not relational obligations. The question at issue is whether the obligations just noted have correlative rights. One could follow Partridge (1981) and hold that utilitarian considerations justify obligations concerning past and future individuals but that, because of the problem of the subject, these individuals have no rights.

As Feinberg notes, this view is open to a serious objection.

> It is absurd to think that once a promisee has died, the status of a broken promise made to him while he was alive suddenly ceases to be that of serious injustice to the victim and becomes instead a mere diffuse public harm (1984, 95).

Epicurus would surely reply that his view is less absurd than the view that people have rights when they do not exist. The problem of the subject must be solved if we are to move beyond this impasse. It is instructive to begin by examining two other enlightening, but ultimately inadequate, attempts to solve the problem—Feinberg's and Wellman's.

2. FEINBERG'S PROPOSED SOLUTION

Feinberg has provided an argument for the view that past individuals can have rights. His explicit focus is the question of whether past and future individuals can be harmed. But with the addition of the plausible substantive view that one has a right not to be harmed, the arguments can be transformed into arguments for the view that past and future individuals have rights. The argument begins with the claim that

> the sorts of beings who *can* have rights are precisely those who have (or can have) interests (1980, 167).

The second claim in the argument is that it is possible for a person's interests to survive after he has died.

> All interests are the interest of some persons or other and a person's surviving interests are simply the ones that we identify by naming *him*, the person whose interests they were. He is of course at this moment dead, but that does not prevent us from referring now, in the present tense, to his interests ... (1984, 83).

Therefore, past individuals have rights when they have interests that survive after they have died. On Feinberg's view, some interests cannot survive after one's death. Suppose that I have tickets to a baseball game tomorrow night. Suppose that I were to die tonight. I would lose my interest in attending the game. What I have an interest in is having certain (baseball) experiences and, after I am dead, I cannot have any experiences at all. Feinberg calls this a "self-regarding" interest (1984, 86). On the other hand, there are other interests that, according to Feinberg, can survive one's death. I have an interest in my son's future happiness. This is what Feinberg calls an "other-regarding" interest, and it is the reason that I have a life insurance policy that names him as the beneficiary (1984, 86). Feinberg holds that other-regarding interests can survive a person's death. If I were to die tonight, my interest in my son receiving the amount indicated in my life insurance policy would survive me and, on Feinberg's view, I would have a right that it be paid.

Feinberg then confronts the problem of the subject. Who is the subject of surviving interests? Feinberg borrows a distinction from Pitcher (1984). Pitcher notes that the subject of surviving interests could either be the antemortem person, the living person who no longer exists, or the postmortem person, the dead person as he is now—perhaps as ashes in an urn. Feinberg holds that the postmortem person does not have interests and therefore cannot have rights. The antemortem person

213

has interests, and it is this antemortem person who is the subject of the surviving interests and rights.

On Feinberg's view, if a past individual's right is violated, *when* was it violated? Feinberg argues that the past individual's right was violated when he first acquired it.

> Exactly when did the harmed state of the antemortem person, for which the posthumous event is "responsible," begin? I think the best answer is: "at the point, well before his death, when the person had invested so much in some postdated outcome that it became one of his interests (1984, 92).

Feinberg's argument for the view that future individuals can have rights is parallel to his arguments concerning past individuals. As before, he begins with the claim that the sorts of beings who can have rights are precisely those who have interests. He next claims that, just as there are surviving interests, there are potential interests. While surviving interests exist after their subject dies, potential interests are not-yet-existing interests. Actions at one time can have effects in the future that set back interests that come to exist after the action that causes them to be set back. Feinberg does not consider the question of when rights violations of future individuals occur.

Although Feinberg's theory asks many of the right questions, it is flawed. Feinberg's view concerning the time at which the violations of the rights of past individuals occur is at least slightly odd. Consider the following two cases. I take out two insurance policies. The first is a standard life insurance policy with my son as the beneficiary and in the amount of $25,000. The second insurance policy is with the same company but it is a disability policy according to which the beneficiary, my son, will receive $25,000 if and when I become disabled. Unfortunately for me, the policies are with a company that will not pay off. It is, unbeknownst to me, an unethical insurance company that is taking people's money but never paying any claims. In the case of the disability insurance it seems clear that no rights are violated until I become disabled and the company fails to give my son the $25,000. No matter how the company has been treating others, until I become disabled, I do not have the right that the company give my son $25,000. It would seem that the case of the life insurance company should be parallel. Until I die, I do not acquire the right and the company does not have the obligation to pay my son $25,000. However, on Feinberg's view, the two cases are not parallel. On his view, my life insurance policy right is violated at the point, before my death, when I have invested so much in the not-to-be-paid life insurance policy that it is one of my interests. The disability-policy right, on the other hand, is presumably violated at the time when the company refuses to pay. This is a counterintuitive implication of Feinberg's view.

Loren Lomasky rejects Feinberg's view concerning the time at which the violations of the rights of past individuals occur. He discusses the following quote from Feinberg:

214

An event occurs after Smith's death that causes something to happen at that time. So far, so good; no paradox. Now, in virtue of the thing that was caused to happen at that time it is true that Smith was in a harmed condition before he died. It does not suddenly "become true" that the antemortem Smith was harmed. Rather it becomes apparent to us for the first time that it was true all along—that from the time Smith invested enough in his cause to make it one of his interests, he was playing a losing game (1984, 91).

To this, Lomasky responds:

This does not have even the *feel* of a correct analysis. Suppose that the event that "causes something to happen" is a false and malicious defamatory utterance about Smith"s alleged secret life and that what happens is that Smith's reputation plummets. Feinberg would have it that the deliverance of the utterance is not what makes it become true then that the antemortem Smith was harmed; it rather enables us to know that "Smith was in a harmed condition all along." But that would render the significance of the utterance purely epistemic; it provides us knowledge of a circumstance that already was in effect. On what basis, then, could we possibly condemn the utterance? It has caused the scales to fall from our eyes, letting us in on the fact that poor Smith had lived out his life in a harmed condition of which he and we were altogether ignorant (1987, 220).

Lomasky's criticisms of Feinberg's position are sound. What is Lomasky's own view concerning the time at which the violations of the rights of past individuals occur?

Feinberg confuses timeless truth with "being true all along." It is not true all along, that is, from some stipulated beginning and at every subsequent moment up until the present, that 4 plus 7 is 11. It is timelessly true that the defamatory utterance constitutes a harm for Smith.... It can therefore be claimed, quite unparadoxically, that harms ... come to be when the harmful event does and that the occurrences of harmful events are not just the visible signs of previously existing harms but are rather the causally potent instruments through which harms are generated (1987, 220–221).

On Lomasky's view, when a past individual's rights are violated, it is "timelessly true" that they were violated. This view has problems of its own. The ordinary view of time and causation is that events change the truth value of statements at a particular time. An hour ago, I was in bed but now I am at my computer. The ordinary view is that "George is at his computer" was false an hour ago and that it became true at the moment that I sat down at my computer. Moreover, it will become false again when I get up. It seems to be that, unlike "George is at his computer," "4 plus 7 is 11" is true at all times. It was true a 1000 years ago, it is true now and it will be true in a 1000 years. Mathematical and logical statements may or may not be timelessly true, but statements about events are not timelessly true.

Suppose that defamatory utterances violate one's rights. Compare Jones with Feinberg's Smith. Suppose that the same defamatory utterances were said about Jones and Smith. Jones is alive at the time of utterances while Smith is not. Consider the claim that "Jones's rights have been violated." It seems that this claim becomes true at the time the utterance is made. It was false before that time. So this claim about Jones is not timelessly true. If that is the case, then there is no reason that Smith's rights should differ with regard to time of existence. Lomasky's view is not plausible.

Another problem with Feinberg's view is that, at least when it comes to the rights of past individuals, the problem of the subject remains unsolved. The notion of an interest that survives the interest-bearer does not withstand critical analysis. Feinberg holds that

> the interests harmed by events that occur at or after the moment a person's nonexistence commences are the interests of the living person who no longer is with us (1984, 89).

He claims that "the main obstacle" to holding this view "is its apparent implication that 'posthumous harms' are *retroactive*" (1984, 90). Feinberg responds that posthumous harms are not retroactive because it is true from the moment that the person has the interest-to-be-set-back that he is harmed. This is not the main obstacle to Feinberg's view. The main obstacle is the problem of the subject. After Smith's death, the question remains: How can it be true that the living Smith who is no longer with us has interests that survive? Feinberg does not think that potential interests are interests that exist before the interest-bearers. Because of the nature of time and causation, an event at one time can cause events to happen at a later time, so Feinberg does not need to hold that potential interests are interests that exist before the interest-bearers. But, in the case of past individuals, he is driven to the view that interests survive their bearers. Feinberg needs to point to the flaw in the following simple argument that would surely be pressed by Epicurus and his contemporary defenders:

1. The living Smith is no longer with us.
2. Those who are no longer with us have no interests.
3. Therefore, the living Smith (who is no longer with us) has no interests.

The rock has withstood the lashing from Feinberg's storm.

3. WELLMAN'S PROPOSED SOLUTION

Wellman takes another tack in attempting to solve the problem of the subject. Let us first consider his analysis of the rights of past individuals. Wellman begins by noting that, with regard to the rights of past individuals, what is most important, in theory as in practice, are posthumous duties such as that to keep a deathbed promise or not to damage the reputation of someone now dead (1995, 155).

He then asserts that

surviving duties are not general duties to the public; they are duties implied by the rights of individuals who have died. But this need not be to ascribe rights to the dead; it can and should be to assert that the rights of the living continue to impose duties even after the persons who possessed those rights have ceased to exist (1995, 156).

So Wellman holds that past individuals have no rights. All assertions of the form

Makeba has a right that . . .

become false at the moment that Makeba dies and remain false at every moment thereafter. However, some of Makeba's rights continue to impose duties on others even after Makeba is no more. Wellman calls rights that impose duties that exist in the future (when the right does not exist) proactive rights.

Wellman then asks the correct question.

If a person's rights perish with the right-holder, how can they continue to impose duties on those who survive? (1995, 156)

The key, on Wellman's view

is to recognize that much of our language of rights is highly metaphorical. We speak of rights as though they were objects, pieces of furniture in our world . . . . But rights and duties are really positions under norms and their existence consists in the existence of these norms . . . . What sounds like causal language is more accurately interpreted as asserting some logical implication . . . . To say that a right implies a duty is an elliptical way of saying that some statement about that right implies a statement asserting or implying the existence of that duty (1995, 156).

Wellman thinks that rights can be proactive because to say that someone has a right with a correlative duty is to say that the right implies the duty. This is an important insight.

Wellman's analysis of the rights of past individuals parallels his account of the rights of future individuals. He thinks that, just as there are proactive rights, rights that imply duties that exist after the right has ceased to exist, there are retroactive rights, rights that imply duties that exist before the right comes to exist. In the case of future individuals, the central problem concerns duties such as the duty to refrain from doing things that will injure future individuals. Examples of such duties include the duty not to do things that will result in children born with disabilities and the duty not to do things that will harm future generations by forcing them to deal with the pollution we produce. Just as Wellman holds that past individuals do not now have rights, he holds that future individuals do not now have rights. However, some of the rights that future individuals will have are retroactive and imply duties whose subjects are present individuals. This is not mysterious, on Wellman's view, once one recognizes that talk of "a right creating a duty" is best understood as a reference to a logical implication between the right and the duty.

There is a crucial insight in Wellman's view but without modification it will not do. The problem with Wellman's view is that his theory of relational obligation, which was discussed in Chapter 4, does not sit well with his theory of the rights of past and future individuals. On Wellman's view,

> a relative [i.e., a relational] duty is a duty to the party with the moral power of claiming performance of that duty (1999, 218).

He holds that the power to claim performance

> is exercised when the party to whom the duty is owed requests or demands performance of the duty and presents title to the duty-bearer (1999, 218).

Finally, presenting title occurs when

> one refers to or otherwise indicates the basis of one's moral claim in one's act of claiming (1999, 218).

Unfortunately for Wellman, it seems clear that past and future individuals cannot present title because one who does not exist cannot refer to or otherwise indicate the basis of his or her claim. Those who do not exist cannot do anything, so they cannot refer to or indicate the basis of a claim. The obligation to keep a deathbed promise is not, on Wellman's view, a relational obligation, and since Wellman holds that rights imply relational obligations, Wellman is committed to the view that there are no retroactive or proactive rights. His view is inconsistent.

There is an obvious move that Wellman might make. He might assert that a person does not have to present her own titles. Others can represent a person and present her titles. However, when defending his view that human infants cannot have rights, Wellman has rejected the view that one can represent an individual that does not have a will or agency.

> Right-holders can sometimes, at least in the case of normal adults, be represented by others who claim, exercise or waive their rights for them. Because infants have no will, their agency cannot be represented by other moral agents (1995, 116).

Note here that Wellman rejects the view that one can represent infants even though, while they are not now agents, most will become agents. If infants do not have agency, then obviously past and future individuals do not have agency either. To remain consistent with his views on the rights of infants, Wellman cannot assert that representatives can present the titles of past and future individuals. Therefore, he cannot follow this route to remove the inconsistency between his theory of relational obligation and his views on the rights of past and future individuals.

4. TIME AND RIGHTS

The puzzles concerning the rights of the past and future individuals are clearly puzzles that revolve around time and truth. We seek answers to questions such as, "When is 'Makeba has a right that James keep the promise he made to her on her deathbed' true?" The crucial words in this question are the first and last words— "when" and "true." Unfortunately, consensus in the literature on time and truth is hard to find. There are many different views, and this is not the place to attempt to resolve the difficult issues that arise when considering the nature of time and truth. Because of this lack of consensus, it is best to refer to "a standard view," rather than "the standard view." Let us focus on one of the standard and most intuitive theories on these subjects and then apply this theory to the justified-constraint conception of rights. Assume that time is linear and infinite into both the past and future. Let us ignore theories of relativistic time, discrete time, circular time, beginning time, and ending time. Assume a correspondence theory of truth. Having presented the justified-constraint view under these simplifying assumptions, it will become apparent that they are not necessary to the argument for the view. (One interested in tense logic could begin by seeing Prior (1967). This book is not an easy read. A less complete but more accessible text is Rescher and Urquhart (1971). An accessible presentation of a standard and simple tense logic can be found in Nolt (1997). For a discussion of various sorts of correspondence theories of truth, one might see David (1994).)

The most important point concerning time and truth is a simple one. The truth of statements is often time-relative.

> Truth . . . must . . . be . . . relativized to times. It is true now that I am sitting at my computer, but this will not be true a few hours hence. Thus the statement 'I am sitting at my computer' is true at one time and not at another . . . (Nolt, 1997, 369).

It is not clear that the truth of all statements is time-relative. Statements of mathematics and logic (e.g., two plus five equals seven) may not be time-relative. Fortunately, for the purposes of rights theory, we need not worry about whether or not the truths of mathematics and logic are time-relative. We need only be concerned with non-mathematical non-logical statements.

Take the sentence "George is at his computer." The truth of this sentence is time-relative. It is true at some times (now for instance) but not true at other times (3 hours ago). "George is at his computer" is ambiguous because no time is specified. If someone asserts "George is at his computer" do they mean that

"At 12:55 *p.m.* on August 7, 2003, George is at his computer,"

or that

"At 12:55 *a.m.* on August 7, 2003, George is at his computer?"

The first sentence is true but the second is false. But what of the sentence

"At 12:55 p.m. on August 7, 2003, George is at his computer?"

When is this sentence true? Is it true at all times? Is it timelessly true? Or perhaps the question "What is the truth value of 'At 12:55 p.m. on August 7, 2003, George is at his computer'?" is to be rejected as a question with a false presupposition. It might be like the question "When did George get the J.D.?" This question presupposes that I have a J.D., but I do not have one.

On a standard view, the answer to the question "What is the truth value of 'At 12:55 p.m. on August 7, 2003, George is at his computer'?" depends on whether determinism or indeterminism is true. (For the classic statement of this view, see Thomason (1970).)

If determinism is true and if I was at my computer at 12:55 p.m. on August 7, 2003, then "At 12:55 p.m. on August 7, 2003, George is at his computer" is true at all times. If determinism is true and if I was not at my computer at 12:55 p.m. on August 7, 2003, then "At 12:55 p.m. on August 7, 2003, George is at his computer" is false at all times. If determinism is true, this view is a natural one.

If indeterminism is true, then the truth value of "At 12:55 p.m. on August 7, 2003, George is at his computer" depends on when it became inevitable that I would be at my computer at 12:55 p.m. on August 7, 2003. If indeterminism is true, at those times *before* my being at my computer at 12:55 p.m. on August 7, 2003, becomes inevitable, the sentence "At 12:55 p.m. on August 7, 2003, George is at his computer" is neither true nor false. Indeterminism requires a three-valued logic. Moreover, if indeterminism is true, at those times before my *not* being at my computer at 12:55 p.m. on August 7, 2003, becomes inevitable, the sentence is also neither true nor false. This view is a natural one because, if indeterminism is true, before it is inevitable that I will be/not be at my computer at 12:55 p.m. on August 7, 2003, the sentence could be either true or false depending on what I do. If indeterminism is true, at the moment my being at my computer at 12:55 p.m. on August 7, 2003, becomes inevitable, the sentence "At 12:55 p.m. on August 7, 2003, George is at his computer" becomes true and remains true at every time thereafter. If indeterminism is true, at the moment my *not* being at my computer at 12:55 p.m. on August 7, 2003, becomes inevitable, the sentence "At 12:55 p.m. on August 7, 2003, George is at his computer" becomes false and remains false at every time thereafter. Rather than attempting to resolve the controversy between determinism and indeterminism, let us consider the rights of past and future individuals twice, once assuming that determinism is true and again assuming that indeterminism is true.

Some notation will be useful. We need to refer to the "earlier than" relation and the "same as" relation. Let us use "t" to refer to a time (what some call a "moment"). So, "t_x is earlier than t_y" means that a time, t_x, is earlier than a time, t_y. The earlier than relation is linearly ordered. For any two times, t_x and t_y, either

t_x is earlier than t_y, or t_y is earlier than t_x, or t_x is the same as t_y. It is also transitive. For any three times, t_x, t_y, and t_z, if t_x is earlier than t_y and t_y is earlier than t_z, then t_x is earlier than t_z.

To this point, and still ignoring impossibilities in order to simplify presentation, I have argued that

> X has an S right against Y that Y do A if and only if
> in the possible world identical to the actual world except that X has no features other than F and those logically and nomologically entailed by F, there is a sound instance of the following argument form:
> 1. X is F.
> 2. If X is F, then Y has an S obligation to do A.
> 3. Therefore, Y has an S obligation to do A.

It is now apparent that this analysis is inadequate because it is filled with time ambiguity. To remove the time ambiguity, one needs to insert a time reference before the assertion that someone has a right and before each claim in the key argument form.

> At t_r, X has an S right against Y that, at t_o, Y do A if and only if
> in the possible world identical to the actual world except that X has no features other than F and those logically and nomologically entailed by F, there is a sound instance of the following argument form:
> 1. At t_f, X is F.
> 2. At t_s, if, at t_f, X is F, then, at t_o, Y has an S obligation to do A.
> 3. Therefore, at t_o, Y has an S obligation to do A.

"t_r" refers to a time that X has the right. "t_f" refers to a time when X has the feature. "t_o" refers to a time at which Y has the obligation. "t_s" refers to a time at which the statement is a part of the relevant rule system.

We need to refer to t_s because a rule system can change. In the case of the legal rule system, what was the law at one time need not be the law at an earlier or later time. In the town square of the town in which I live, there is an old sign that has been preserved and encased in glass by the local historical society. The sign reads, "No horse and buggy parking on the square." Consider the statement: "It is illegal to park a horse and buggy on the town square." There was a time, before the city ordinance banning horse and buggy parking on the square was passed, when this statement was false. Later, after the ordinance was passed but before it was repealed, there was a time when this statement was true. Now, after the ordinance has been repealed, the statement is false again.

When is "At t_r, X has an S right against Y that Y do A" true? It is true at those times when the relevant instance of the key argument form is sound. All instances of the argument are valid at all times, so an instance of the form is sound when the two premises are true. Therefore,

At t_r, X has an S right against Y that Y do A

is true at those times when both

At t_f, X is F.

and

At t_s, if, at t_f, X is F, then, at t_o, Y has an S obligation to do A.

are true.

It must be the case that t_s is the same as t_o. Let us consider the case of legal obligations. One only has a legal obligation when the law is in effect at the time of one's obligation. Suppose that on January 1 of a year, a government passes a law saying that everyone must hold hands with someone else at noon on March 4 of that year. But, on March 1 of that year, the law that was passed on January 1 is repealed. In that case, one does not have a legal obligation to hold hands on March 4.

Because it must be the case that t_s is the same as t_o, there are only three possible time orderings of t_f, t_s, and t_o:

Case One, t_s is the same as t_o and t_o is the same as t_f.
Case Two, t_f is earlier than t_s and t_s is the same as t_o.
Case Three, t_s is the same as t_o and t_o is earlier than t_f.

We must consider when

At t_r, X has an S right against Y that Y do A

is true in each of these three cases.

The actual world is a relatively stable one. It will be useful to consider a mythical world in which things can and do change more often than they do in our world. Let us consider a mythical country, Corcyra, in which there are three races of moral agents. Some moral agents are humans, others are centaurs, and some are changelings who can be either humans or centaurs as they wish. The political forces in Corcyra are in turmoil because of racial prejudice between the races. The government is of a parliamentary type and unstable, with governments coming and going as political alliances shift. This causes the laws of Corcyra to change much more often and much more radically than they typically do in our world. Let consider three individuals living in Corcyra. Proteus is a changeling. Diane is a human. Nessus is an arms manufacturer.

4.1. Case One: The Right Not to Be Spit Upon

Let us suppose that, because of the political instability, the laws on spitting upon centaurs and humans are changed repeatedly. Sometimes spitting upon a centaur is illegal and sometimes it is not. When does Proteus have a Corcyra legal right not to

222

be spit upon by Diane? It depends on when Proteus is a centaur and when the law says that one has an obligation not to spit upon centaurs. Consider the following, fully time-disambiguated instance of the key argument form

1. At noon on January 1 of the year 1 (1/1/01),
   Proteus has the feature of being a centaur.
2. At noon on 1/1/01,
   if, at noon on 1/1/01,
   Proteus has the feature of being a centaur,
   then, at noon on 1/1/01,
   Diane has a Corcyra legal obligation not to spit upon Proteus.
3. Therefore, at noon on 1/1/01,
   Diane has a Corcyra legal obligation not to spit upon Proteus.

(Expressing dates in this numerical shorthand just used will improve the clarity of the arguments to come.) The sentence "At noon on 1/1/01, Proteus has the right not to be spit upon by Diane" is true at those times when this instance of the key argument form is sound. The argument, an instance of modus ponens, is valid at all times so it is sound at those times when both premises are true. Whether premise 1 is true or not depends on what shape Proteus has chosen to take at noon on 1/1/01. Whether premise 2 is true or not depends on the state of the law in Corcyra at noon on 1/1/01. If, at noon on 1/1/01, Proteus is not a centaur, then the argument is not sound and so (if there are no other relevant arguments) Proteus has no Corcyra right not to be spit upon. If, at noon on 1/1/01, the law of Corcyra did not state that it was forbidden to spit upon centaurs, then the argument is not sound and so (if there are no other relevant arguments) Proteus has no Corcyra right not to be spit upon.

If determinism is true, then the fully time-disambiguated statement "At noon on 1/1/01, Proteus has a right not to be spit upon by Diane" will never come to be true but, if it is true, will always be true at all times. If indeterminism is true, then this statement will become true at the moment it becomes inevitable that Proteus will be a centaur at noon on 1/1/01 *and* that the laws of Corcyra will, at noon on 1/1/01, hold that Diane has an obligation not to spit upon centaurs. Given that Proteus can change his shape at will, the point of inevitability might well be noon on 1/1/01.

There are some rights that past and future individuals cannot have. Past and future individuals cannot have the right to be treated in a certain way. They cannot have the right not to be killed, the right not to be struck or the right not to be spit upon. In each of these cases, the obligatory action must take place at some time when the right-holder exists. I cannot have an obligation to shake the hand of George Washington or the first person born in the year 3000. These rights require that t_s, t_o, and t_f be the same time. If past and future individuals have rights, they must have rights that do not require that t_s, t_o, and t_f be the same time. Past and future individuals cannot have rights whose contents require that they be alive to be treated in some way. If past and future individuals have rights, they can only have rights that others do or not do something that does not involve treatment of them. They might have a right that another person stick her feet in Squam Lake or the right that someone burn some money in their honor.

4.2. Case Two: The Right That Someone Retrospectively Burn $1,000 in One's Honor

The political situation in Corcyra deteriorates into a brutal civil war between humans and centaurs. After some time, the civil war ends. The humans feel remorse for a series of brutal tortures inflicted on the centaurs. Nessus profited handsomely during the civil war by selling instruments to be used for tortures and massacres. Corcyra passes a law requiring that, at noon on January 1 of the year 5 (1/1/05) (which is both t_s and t_o), Nessus must burn $1,000 for each being who was a centaur at noon on 1/1/04 (t_f). Proteus was a centaur at noon on 1/1/04. At noon on 1/1/05, Nessus burns $1,000 in Proteus' honor. Proteus has a Corcyra right that Nessus burn $1,000 in his honor at noon on 1/1/05. When did he gain this right? At the moment the following instance of the key argument form became sound:

1. At noon on 1/1/04,
   Proteus has the feature of being a centaur.
2. At noon on 1/1/05,
   if, at noon on 1/1/04,
   Proteus has the feature of being a centaur,
   then, at noon on 1/1/05,
   Nessus has a Corcyra legal obligation to burn $1,000 in Proteus' honor.
3. Therefore, at noon on 1/1/05,
   Nessus has a Corcyra legal obligation to burn $1,000 in Proteus' honor.

As before, this instance of the key argument form is sound when the premises are true. If determinism is true, then the fully time-disambiguated statements are true at all times and therefore it is true at all times that Proteus has a Corcyra legal right that, at noon on 1/1/05, Nessus burn $1,000 in Proteus' honor. On the assumption that determinism is true, this is a natural result. If indeterminism is true, then this statement will become true at the moment it becomes inevitable that this instance of the key argument form will be sound. It will remain true at every time thereafter. Suppose that Proteus changes shape often and so it does not become inevitable that Proteus will be a centaur at noon on 1/1/04 until noon on 1/1/04. At noon on 1/1/04 Proteus still does not have the right yet. He gains the right at the moment it becomes inevitable that the law requiring Nessus to burn $1,000 in his honor would not be repealed before noon on 1/1/05. If that became inevitable at noon on 7/1/04, then that is the moment that Proteus gained the right.

This case allows us to see an important point. An event can be inevitable or determined to occur without anyone knowing it. Therefore, it is possible for someone to have a right without anyone knowing it. This is not a problematic implication of the justified-constraint analysis. Indeed, it is a common situation. Recently, the state of Georgia passed a bill to reallocate the funds used to build highways (Pruitt, 1999). To simplify a bit, the bill required that state highway funds be spent equally, per capita, in every county. At the time the bill was passed, everyone assumed that Fulton County, the county containing the city of Atlanta, was getting more money to build highways than the county would get if the money were divided equally per capita among all counties. Everyone assumed that the effect of the bill would be to reduce the amount of money going to Fulton County and increase the amount of money going to other counties. Indeed, that was the point of the bill. Later it became apparent that Fulton County was in fact getting *less* money to build highways than the county would get if the money were divided equally per capita among all counties. Therefore, the effect of the bill was to give Fulton County a right to more money. This right came into existence when the bill was signed by the Governor. But the effect of the bill was not discovered until several months after it was signed. During the period from signing to discovery, Fulton County had a right that no one knew about.

To this point, we have assumed that Proteus was alive at noon on 1/1/05. How, if at all, does the situation change if Proteus dies on 8/1/04? The answer is that, as far as Proteus' rights are concerned, the situation has not changed at all. Proteus gained the right when it became inevitable that the law would not be repealed. Even after he has died, he still has this right because the instance of the key argument form remains sound. The sound instance of the key argument form makes no reference to whether Proteus is alive or not. As far as this right is concerned, whether Proteus is alive or not is irrelevant. There is nothing paradoxical about obligations to past individuals.

It may seem that I have pulled a rabbit out of a hat. Who is the subject of the right that a past individual has? The past individual who is F, Proteus in the case above, is the subject of the rights. Feinberg is right to hold that the antemortem individual is the subject of this right. The subject of this right is the antemortem individual because it is a feature of the antemortem individual that justifies the obligation. In general, the subject of a right is the individual that is F. How does this solve the problem of the subject? There are two key steps. First, one must adopt the justified-constraint theory of rights. One must hold that one *has* a right when another person has an obligation that is *justified* in a particular way. As Wellman saw, when discussing rights the term "has" is metaphorical in a misleading way. One usually has physical objects. To have a right is not to have some odd sort of physical object. To have a right is to be the source, the ground, the justification of another's obligation. Second, one must note that justification is *trans-temporal*, i.e., it works both forward and backward in time. That some sentence was true in the past can justify some future sentence. Features of those who are now past individuals can be the justification of current obligations. Proteus' feature in the past justifies Nessus' current obligation. That is all that is required for Proteus to be the subject of a right that Nessus burn $1,000 in his honor. Whether or not he continues to be alive is irrelevant to having this right. The correct theory of rights is the justified-constraint theory. Justification is trans-temporal. Together, these two views imply that the same analysis of rights applies to both present and past individuals. The problem of the subject is solved.

4.3. Case Three: The Right That Someone Prospectively Burn $1,000 in One's Honor

To consider this case, it will be helpful to have more knowledge of the future than we have in the actual world. Therefore, let us assume that in Corcyra they have access to the Oracle at Delphi. The Oracle will, if asked, infallibly inform someone if a fully disambiguated sentence is true, false or not yet true or false. It will also inform someone when the sentence became true or false. If one asks the Oracle, "What is the truth value of 'At t_f, Proteus has the feature of being a centaur'?" the Oracle will say one of five things:

1. "The sentence 'At t_f, Proteus has the feature of being a centaur' is true at all times."
2. "The sentence 'At t_f, Proteus has the feature of being a centaur' is false at all times."
3. "At t_x, the sentence 'At t_f, Proteus has the feature of being a centaur' became true."
4. "At t_x, the sentence 'At t_f, Proteus has the feature of being a centaur' became false."
5. "At the current time, the sentence 'At t_f, Proteus has the feature of being a centaur' is indeterminate."

The Oracle allows those in Corcyra to know, with a precision that we cannot, when their rights came into existence.

Assume that, as in Case Two, the political situation in Corcyra deteriorates into a brutal civil war between humans and centaurs. The civil war ends and the humans feel remorse for the brutal tortures inflicted on the centaurs. Nessus again profited handsomely by selling munitions and instruments to be used for tortures and massacres. But in this case, Corcyra passes a slightly different law. The law requires that, at noon on 1/1/05 (which is both t_s and t_o), Nessus must burn $1,000 in honor of everyone who will be a centaur at noon on 1/1/06 (t_f). At noon on 12/31/04, Nessus consults the Oracle and the Oracle says either:

"At noon on 12/15/04, the sentence 'At noon on 1/1/06, Proteus has the feature of being a centaur' became true."

or

"The sentence 'At noon on 1/1/06, Proteus has the feature of being a centaur' is true at all times."

The law is not repealed and, at noon on 1/1/05, Nessus burns $1,000 in honor of Proteus who, just as the Oracle said he would be, is a centaur at noon on 1/1/06.

The existence of the Oracle gives the parliament of Corcyra options that legislative bodies in our world do not have. Because we cannot know, with precision, who will be alive even one year from now, no responsible legislative body in this world would actually pass a law such as the one just imagined. But the case is an instructive one because it allows us to more clearly distinguish the question of when individuals have rights from the question of when we know that individuals have rights.

Proteus has a right that Nessus burn $1,000 in his honor. When did he get this right? He gained the right when the following instance of the key argument form became sound:

1. At noon on 1/1/06,
   Proteus has the feature of being a centaur.
2. At noon on 1/1/05,
   if, at noon on 1/1/06,
   Proteus has the feature of being a centaur,
   then, at noon on 1/1/05,
   Nessus has a Corcyra legal obligation to burn $1,000 in Proteus' honor.
3. Therefore, at noon on 1/1/05,
   Nessus has a Corcyra legal obligation to burn $1,000 in Proteus' honor.

If determinism is true, then the fully time-disambiguated statements are true at all times and therefore Proteus has, at all times, a Corcyra legal right that, at noon on 1/1/05, Nessus burn $1,000 in Proteus' honor. Again, on the assumption that determinism is true, this is a natural result. If indeterminism is true, then this statement will become true at the moment it becomes inevitable that this instance of the key argument form will be sound. It will remain true at every time thereafter. The Oracle tells us that the first premise became true at noon on 12/15/04. Suppose that, by chance, at this same moment, it became inevitable that the law requiring Nessus to burn the $1,000 would not be repealed. In that case, Proteus gain the right at noon on 12/15/04.

The following case may seem to be an objection to the justified-constraint theory. In the case as described to this point, the first premise either was always true or became true at a time which is earlier than the time at which the second premise became true. Suppose, on the other hand, that indeterminism is true and that the first premise does not become true until after the time indicated in the second premise. Suppose that, when asked, the Oracle said, "At noon on 7/1/05, the sentence 'At noon on 1/1/06, Proteus has the feature of being a centaur' became true." In this case, the justified-constraint theory implies that Proteus gains a right that Nessus burn $1,000 in his honor after he had burned it. This may seem odd. It is indeed odd but not problematically so. It is odd, unusual, to have the kind of knowledge about the future that the Oracle gives those in Corcyra. Given our current technology, we do not possess this kind of knowledge. If one genuinely imagines that we did have the kind of information that the Oracle provides, this implication seems natural, not odd. What does the justified-constraint theory imply about Proteus' case in a world that did not contain an infallible Oracle? It correctly implies that no one in that world would know when Proteus gained his right. Our initial intuitions about this case are suspect because we are imagining a case different from any anyone in this world has actually experienced.

Although we have no Oracle, we do have some knowledge of the future. Joseph is saving for his retirement. He puts aside several hundred dollars each month. Suppose that Sherry were to challenge the reasonableness of his savings plan. She asks, "Why do you save several hundred dollars each month? Why not spend that money now?" Sherry is asking for a prudential justification of Joseph's savings plan. He can justify his savings plan by referring to the fact that in all probability, the future will contain a time when he will not be receiving a salary but will wish to have money to spend. This banal example shows that prudential justification can be trans-temporal. Just as the existence of future states of affairs can prudentially justify current actions, the existence of past or future states of affairs can be the normative justification for an obligation. The existence of past or future states of affairs frequently justifies moral or legal obligations.

How, if at all, does the situation change if Proteus does not exist until 7/15/05, after Nessus has burned the $1,000? The answer is that, as far as Proteus' rights are concerned, the situation has not changed at all. This instance of the key argument form makes no reference to whether Proteus is alive before or after noon on 1/1/06. As far as this right is concerned, Proteus' existence at any time other than noon on 1/1/06 is irrelevant.

Who is the subject of the right that a future individual has? The future individual who has feature F in the relevant instance of the key argument form is the subject of the rights. The justified-constraint theory of rights solves the problem of the subject for future individuals just as it did in the case of past individuals. As before, there are two keys to solving the problem. One must first see that the proper analysis of rights is a justified-constraint analysis. Then one must note that justification is trans-temporal. The problem of the subject is solved. Once we have removed the time ambiguity, the justified-constraint analysis applies without any modification to the rights of past, present, and future individuals. This is an important advantage of the justified-constraint theory of rights.

5. PARFIT AND THE NON-IDENTITY PROBLEM

Parfit (1984) was the first to see a crucial problem that any complete theory of the rights of future individuals must consider: the non-identity problem. The non-identity problem arises because the choices we make not only change the lives of those who will live in the future, they also change who will have a life in the future.

Suppose that a nation is considering two possible long-term resource-utilization policies. The "green plan" results in the conservation of resources so that each generation has the same resources as the preceding one. The "brown plan" results in the use of resources at a non-sustainable rate so that the generations who live in the first 200 years will have more resources than the generations who would live in the first 200 years under the green plan but that the generations who would live after the first 200 years will have substantially fewer resources than the generations who would live after the first 200 years under the green plan. Furthermore, the choice between the green plan and brown plan is an identity-defining choice. In other words, there is no overlap between the group of people who will live if the green plan is chosen and the group of people who will live if the brown plan is chosen. If the green plan is chosen, all of those who would have come to exist if the brown plan had been chosen will never exist. If the brown plan is chosen, all of those who would have come to exist if the green plan had been chosen will never exist. Finally, suppose that all those who will live if the brown plan is chosen will have lives that are worth living. The resource reduction that would occur after 200 years if the brown plan is chosen, while substantial, is not so horrific as to make those who would live if the brown plan were chosen wish that they did not live. The brown plan is not a black plan. Most people think that the brown plan is morally worse than the green plan. The problem of non-identity is this: Why is the brown plan morally worse than the green plan?

The question is hard because one answer will not do. One cannot say that those who would live after 200 years if the brown plan is chosen would be better off if the green plan had been chosen. This claim is false because if the green plan had been chosen, then those who would live after 200 years if the brown plan had been chosen would not have existed at all. Since their lives are worth living, those who would live after 200 years if the brown plan is chosen are better off if the brown plan is chosen.

What, if anything, does the justified-constraint theory imply about the problem of non-identity? It has no implications because Parfit's point is not relevant to the issue at hand. The non-identity problem is a problem for any *substantive* theory of the moral obligations of present individuals to future individuals that holds that those obligations are based on a certain feature of future individuals—that they will be better off (however, one wishes to understand the concept of being better off) if present individuals do some actions rather than other actions. More broadly, the non-identity problem is a problem for any substantive theory of moral obligations that calls upon present individuals to compare some future individuals to other future individuals. The non-identity problem could be used by defenders of non-comparative substantive theory of moral obligation (perhaps some kinds of deontological theories) to argue against theories of moral obligation that are comparative. The justified-constraint theory of rights does not take sides in this debate. It is not committed to this substantive view or any substantive view about which features of individuals are the source of moral obligations. The non-identity

229

problem is no objection to the justified-constraint theory, and the theory does not solve the non-identity problem.

Parfit's example points to an interesting dissimilarity between the rights of future individuals as compared to the rights of past and present individuals. If indeterminism is true, the justified-constraint theory of relational obligation implies that there is one difference between the rights of future individuals and the rights of past and present individuals. In the case of future individuals, it may become inevitable that *someone* will have an F that justifies an obligation before it is inevitable that *some particular person* will have the F. In the case of past and present individuals, this is not possible because, even if indeterminism is true, the past and present are fixed. One cannot change the past or present. If indeterminism is true, then the case of it becoming inevitable that someone, but no particular person, will have a feature that justifies current obligations is the usual case when it comes to the rights of future generations. It is unlikely, on the assumption that indeterminism is true, that the birth of any particular person in the year 2300 is now inevitable. It may be inevitable that there will be humans in the year 2300. Even if determinism is true, the rights of future individuals are rights about which we currently know little.

6. IMPLICATIONS

Let us discuss three implications of the justified-constraint view of the rights of past and future individuals.

First, consider the right to compensation for injuries caused by events before one's conception. Let us suppose that, during the civil war, the humans used a chemical weapon against the centaurs. Some of the children born of centaurs exposed to the chemical are born without the use of their legs. (For lack of a better term, let us refer to young centaurs as "children.") Suppose that no one knows who will be effected. The Oracle cannot tell us because we do not know the names of future centaurs and, therefore, we cannot formulate non-ambiguous questions to ask the Oracle. But an infallible soothsayer reveals the exact number of centaurs who will be born without the use of their legs. A law is passed requiring Nessus to place $1,000 for each of these centaurs into an investment account at noon on 1/1/05. The $1,000, plus the interest this $1,000 will earn, will be paid to the centaurs born without the use of their legs. At noon on 1/1/05, some of the centaurs who will be born without the use of their legs have not yet been conceived. Chiron is a centaur conceived after noon on 1/1/05 and born without the use of her legs. Does Chiron have a right that Nessus put the money into the account and, if so, when does she get it? Following the same line of argument, Chiron has a right that Nessus put $1,000 in the account at the moment it becomes inevitable that she will be born and that she will be born without the use of her legs. If we assume that centaurs always have children if they conceive them and that centaurs can be individuated by their genes, this moment would be when Chiron was conceived. This case is perfectly parallel to Proteus'.

On the justified-constraint view of rights, it is possible to violate someone's rights when she has not yet been conceived.

Second, the justified-constraint view of rights implies that future individuals cannot have a right to exist. Feinberg noticed this issue.

> Suppose ... that all humans beings at a given time voluntarily form a compact never again to produce children, thus leading within a few decades to the end of our species. [...] Would this arrangement violate the rights of anyone? (1980, 182).

Feinberg's answer is,

> that the suicide of our species would be deplorable, lamentable and a deeply moving tragedy, but that it would violate no one's rights. (1980, 182)

The justified-constraint view of rights implies that Feinberg is correct. If there were no future individuals, then the first premise of the relevant instance of the key argument form would never be true and no rights would exist. If it is true that an individual will not exist, then no feature of that individual can justify the obligations of other individuals. There is no right to come into existence.

Third, the justified-constraint view implies that it is possible for a past person to have a right that a future person do something. It also implies that it is possible for a future person to have a right that a past person do something. Suppose that X has a feature, F, until t_x, when X dies. Furthermore, Y is born at t_y. Finally suppose that the F that X has until t_x, justifies an obligation that Y has at t_z and that t_x is earlier than t_y which is earlier than t_z. In that case, between t_x and t_y, a past individual has a right that a future individual do something. Such a situation would occur if a law specified that the first ancestor born after an individual dies must, upon reaching the age of 18, perform a ritual in honor of the deceased. One can imagine a country with religious beliefs that might lead them to enact such a law. The reverse of this case is also possible.

As with the analysis of rights conflict offered in Chapter 6, the theory of the rights of past and future individuals offered here cannot be used to argue that the justified-constraint theory of rights is superior to the justification versions of the interest theory, the choice theory, or the will theory. The theory above could be adopted by any holder of a justification theory of rights. The difference between the analysis offered above and the one that could be offered by a defender of the justification version of the interest theory is that such a defender would have particular substantive views about which versions of the key argument form are sound. She would argue that whether or not particular past and/or future individuals have rights will depend on the interests of these past and future individuals. A defender of a justification version of the choice theory would argue the question can be resolved by looking at the importance of the choices of these individuals.

On the other hand, the above analysis of the rights of past and future individuals shows that there is an important respect in which any justification theory of rights is markedly superior to any protection theory of rights. A defender of a protection theory of rights cannot make the first of the two key steps needed to solve the problem of the subject. She must follow Feinberg, Lomasky, and Kramer and attempt to show that rights protect a feature that does not currently exist. Those attempts are bound to fail.

The justified-constraint theory of the rights of past and future individuals does not rely on the assumptions about time and truth made above. Those assumptions greatly simplify the presentation of the theory, but the theory itself does not in any way rely on them. The theory is perfectly consistent with any theory of time and perfectly consistent with all theories of truth and justification that hold that justification is trans-temporal.

9. A Final Comparison

As Rawls notes, "[a]ll theories are presumably mistaken in places. The real question at any given time is which of the views already proposed is the best approximation overall" (1971, 52). The evaluation of philosophical theories is a comparative matter. Although it might be possible in principle to show that one's preferred theory is correct without reference to other theories, in practice theories are compared to each other and judgments are made as to the relative merits of each. The justified-constraint theory is not the final word on rights. If I have succeeded, it is an example of philosophical progress in that it is superior to other theories of rights. Therefore, this final chapter compares the justified-constraint theory of rights to the others discussed in this book: Martin's, Feinberg's, Hart's, Raz's, and Wellman's. Another aim of this chapter is to step back from the detailed arguments presented in previous chapters to get an overarching picture of the six theories of rights presented in this book. Since we will be looking at the forest, not individual trees, many of the details that are included in previous chapters will be omitted here. In particular, when I present the objections to the other five theories, I will not restate all the possible responses to these objections that were considered in previous chapters.

1. OBJECTIONS TO THE JUSTIFIED-CONSTRAINT THEORY

On the justified-constraint theory of rights,

At t_r, X has an S right against Y that, at t_o, Y do A if and only if
in the possible world identical to the actual world except that X has no features other than F and those logically and nomologically entailed by F, there is a sound instance of the following argument form:
1. At t_f, X is F.
2. At t_s, if, at t_f, X is F, then, at t_o, Y has an S obligation/impossibility to do A.
3. Therefore, at t_o, Y has an S obligation/impossibility to do A.

In addition to many objections quickly considered in the preceding chapters, there were four objections that merited detailed discussion. The first two of these objections were raised by defenders of an alternative theory. The second two could be seen as flaws with the justified-constraint view that are so serious that an alternative theory of rights must be sought.

The justified-constraint theory holds that a single claim or a single immunity is a right. The possession of other relations is not necessary to have a right. As noted in Chapter 2, Section 4, Wellman argues that this is incorrect. He holds that only a collection of Hohfeldian relations can be a right. In a broad sense, Wellman's arguments for his theory of rights as advantaged wills are arguments for the view that no single relation can be a right. But in a debate between the justified-constraint theory and the advantaged will theory we seek theory-independent arguments either for the view that no single relation can be a right or for the view that a single relation can be a right. This issue is not an ideal platform upon which to build a case for or against a theory of rights. The discussion concerns the classification of a situation that exists rarely if ever in actual rule systems. I cannot think of a single actual case of a person who has a claim or an immunity and no other relations. The debate is over the classification of an imaginary normative situation. All else being equal, a theory's implications about imaginary positions are not as good a basis for objections as a theory's classifications of actual positions.

Wellman has two theory-independent arguments for his view. First, he considers the case of a creditor who has a legal claim to repayment against her debtor. He correctly points out that the legal right to repayment of a debt cannot be plausibly analyzed as a single claim. But a defender of the justified-constraint theory can and should acknowledge that the legal claim to repayment found in typical legal systems is not a mere claim. It is a rights package that contains many relations. However, the issue at hand is not the correct analysis of the right to repayment but whether a mere claim is a right. Second, he argues that a liberty must be part of any genuine right. He claims that the ordinary talk of rights indicates that all rights contain a liberty. This is not so. Much of the ordinary talk of rights is about rights that contain a liberty. All active rights necessarily contain a liberty. But there are also passive rights. A theme of this book is that philosophers have tended to overlook passive rights. There are many rights in which the right-holder has a right that someone else do or not do some act. Indeed, we saw that all active rights can be analyzed as passive rights. The recurring example used to illustrate this point was the right generated by your promise to me that you will stick your feet into Squam Lake. There are many passive rights. The ordinary talk of rights does not support the view that a liberty must be part of any genuine right.

The second objection to the justified-constraint theory is Hart's disadvantageous immunities argument. This objection is potentially more serious than Wellman's objection because disadvantageous immunities are common in actual rule systems. Hart is correct that

> Even in the loosest usage, the expression 'a right' is not used to refer to the fact that a man is . . . immune from *advantageous* change; the fact that . . . my neighbor has no power to exempt me from my duty to pay my income-tax, do[es] not constitute any legal right . . . for me (1982, 191).

There are five responses to this objection. As we saw in Chapter 2, Section 4, the first four do not fully respond to the objection. They merely limit its importance. The best response to the disadvantageous immunities objection was presented in Chapter 5, Section 1. The justified-constraint theory does not imply that my immunity to Donna's removing my duty to pay my income taxes is one of my rights. The justification for my immunity is not based on a feature of me. Rather, it is based on the fact that the revenues of the U.S. government would drop if individuals generally possessed the power to relieve their neighbors of their duties to pay their income taxes. The U.S. government is the object of Donna's disability. I am not. The justified-constraint conception of rights implies that, as far as the concept of rights in concerned, it is possible for my immunity to be one of my rights. One could adopt substantially odd views that would imply that my immunity is one of my rights. But this disability is not, as a substantive matter, justified in this way. When combined with plausible substantive views about the justification of Donna's disability, the justified-constraint theory of rights implies that her disability is regarding but not with respect to me and therefore that my immunity is not one of my rights. It is the U.S. government that has a right that Donna not relieves me of my duty to pay my income taxes. This analysis of the situation is natural and its plausibility is confirmed once one notices that cases such as this are common. In Chapter 1, Section 3 we examined the case of Evelyn, Joshua and Steve. Evelyn has both a claim against Joshua that Joshua not drive Evelyn's car and an immunity against Steve that Steve not change Joshua's duty not to drive Evelyn's car into a liberty to drive her car. This case shows that, in second-order relations, the object of primary relation can be a different person from the subject of both the original and resulting relations. Steve is the object of Evelyn's immunity but Joshua is the subject of the original and resulting relations. The case of my immunity to Donna's removing my duty to pay my income taxes is another case that follows this pattern. Steve/Donna has a disability with respect to Evelyn/the U.S. government to remove Joshua's/my duty.

The third objection to the justified-constraint theory is potentially even more serious than the disadvantageous immunities objection. In Chapter 5, Section 1 we considered the case of Brian the pedophile. Vinita has a right that her father, Jeffery, not leave her alone with Brian. The justified-constraint theory of rights places no restrictions on the features of a person which can justify rights. It might seem that the justified-constraint theory is committed to the view that *Brian* has a right that Jeffery not leave Vinita alone with him. The justified-constraint theory does not have this preposterous implication. The theory merely asserts that the *concept* of rights places no restrictions on the features of a person which can justify rights. As far as the conception of rights defended here is concerned, one could write a set of laws that implied that pedophiles have a right to a government payment of $1,000 per month. The justified-constraint theory implies that it is conceptually possible that Brian has a right that Jeffery not leave Vinita alone with him. It does not imply that Brian actually has this right. The justified-constraint analysis only has this preposterous implication when combined with preposterous substantive views about what features actually justify obligations.

The case of the rights of journalists was used as the basis of the fourth objection to the justified-constraint theory. As noted in Chapter 5, Section 2, journalists have a right to protect their sources, but there seems to be no feature of journalists that justifies this right. A journalist's interest in protecting her sources seems to be a redundant feature because the real justificatory work is being done by the general public interest. So, the objection continues, the justified-constraint view implausibly implies that journalists do not have a right to protect their sources, but the general public has a right that journalists not reveal their sources.

This objection overlooks the distinction between simple and complex justification. One must not confuse the justification of a rule system with justification of a person's rights within a system. The question of who, if anyone, is the object of an obligation/impossibility is a question of the entailments of the system of rules, not of the justification of the system of rules itself. When we seek the justification of an obligation to determine whether or not it is relational we seek the feature that does the work in the system as it is. We are not seeking a justification for the inclusion of this feature in the rule system. The system of giving journalists the right to protect their sources is justified by the public interest. The rights of a particular journalist are justified by the rules of the system. At the individual level, the end of justification is the fact that an individual is a journalist. Any further requests for justification move to the practice level, to the level of questioning the rules of the system.

These four objections point to implications of the justified-constraint theory that initially seem problematic. The second, third, and fourth objections require that the justified-constraint theory be made more complex. In that way, the objections do have some force. On the other hand, the complexities introduced are plausible ones. They are not introduced merely to respond to these objections. They are reflections of the complexity of rights. Although it is true that, all else being equal, a simpler theory is to be preferred to a more complex one, all else is rarely equally. A simple theory of a complex phenomenon is usually incorrect. Rights are complex. The complexities of the justified-constraint theory (and all other plausible theories of rights) merely reflect that complexity.

2. PROBLEMS WITH OTHER THEORIES OF RIGHTS

Martin (1993, 25, 26, 31, 42, 51) holds that rights are "ways of acting or . . . of being treated" that are "determinate," "individuated," "socially recognized," and provide "normative direction" to the actions of others (Chapter 2, Section 5). Martin's theory is the most subtle and well-developed version of the view that social recognition is a necessary condition for the existence of rights. Martin tells us that a way of acting is socially recognized when it is "backed up" or has an "appropriate social ratification" (1993, 27, 36). Because he thinks that social recognition is a necessary condition for the existence of a right, his view implies that it is logically impossible for there to be rights that no one knows about. Furthermore, because one society may recognize a way of acting while another does not, Martin's view implies that all rights are relative to a society.

Chapter 2, Section 5 considers Martin's arguments for the view that social recognition is a necessary condition for the existence of rights as well as his arguments against the view that social recognition is not a necessary condition. Both sets of arguments are weak. Central documents in the history of rights (such as the U.S. Declaration of Independence) and banal documents that can be found in any newspaper indicate that social recognition is not a necessary condition for the existence of rights.

Feinberg (1980, 149) holds that "a right *is* a kind of claim" (Chapter 3, Section 4). He then provides an analysis of claiming. According to Feinberg, we must distinguish making claim to, claiming that, and having a claim. Making claim to is an activity we perform when we "petition or seek by virtue of some right, to demand as due" (1980, 149–150). For example, I can make claim to a seat in a theater on the basis of the ticket I purchased. Making claim to something is performative in the sense that making claim to something causes things to happen. It creates a duty for someone to give the claimant the thing to which claim was made. Claiming that, on the other hand, is not performative. To claim that something is the case is merely to assert that it is true. I can, for example, claim that I like baseball. One has a claim when one is in a position to make a claim to or to claim that. Many individuals might have a claim to something, might have a case meriting consideration. According to Feinberg, the only person who has a right to it is the person who has the best or strongest case. Thus, in the final analysis, Feinberg holds that rights are valid claims. To have a right is to have a claim recognized as valid by a set of rules or moral principles.

There are three flaws in Feinberg's analysis. First, his view cannot account for immunity rights. Feinberg's theory of rights is entirely focused on claims. No account of rights can be plausible unless it can account for the immunity rights found in such central documents as the U.S. Bill of Rights. Feinberg has overlooked the fact that two Hohfeldian relations imply constraints on others. Feinberg notes that duties, the correlative of claims, constrain others. "A duty, whatever else it be, is something *required* of one. That is to say ... that a duty ... is something that *obliges*" (1980, 136). Feinberg's "obliges" or "required of one," and the "constrains" found in the justified-constraint theory are referring to the same feature of duties. Feinberg fails to notice the similarity between duties and disabilities, and this leads him to formulate a theory that cannot account for immunity rights. He has overlooked the fact that in addition to actions that rule systems tell us we *may not* do, there are actions that rule systems tell us we *cannot* do.

The second problem with Feinberg's view is that it has no theory of the relational nature of rights. Feinberg is aware that some obligations are to others while others are not. He holds, for example, that "indebtedness is the clearest example of one person *owing* something to another; and owing, in turn, is perspicuous model for the interpretation of that treacherous little preposition 'to' as it occurs in the phrase 'obligation *to* someone' " (1980, 130). But Feinberg's discussion of making claim to, claiming that, and having a claim does not provide any clue as to why the obligations and immunities correlative to rights are relational. Feinberg cannot answer the question: "Why are the obligations correlative to rights obligations to the right-holder?"

The third problem with Feinberg's view is that it provides no link to central normative concepts. For example, there is no link between rights and obligations. Feinberg analyzes rights in terms of claims and then distinguishes three kinds of claims and claiming. This provides a link between rights and duties because one can analyze claims in terms of duties. But this does not tell us how rights relate to non-Hohfeldian moral concepts—such as those discussed in Chapter 3. How does claiming relate to obligation? How does claiming relate to what one may not or cannot do?

Raz holds a justification version of the interest theory of rights. He holds that X has a right if and only if other things being equal, an aspect of X's well-being (his interest) is a sufficient reason for holding some other person to be under an obligation (Chapter 4, Section 2). There are counterexamples to Raz's theory. First, it seems to imply that all rights must be in the interest of the right-holder. But there are many rights that are not in the interest of the right-holder. One might, for example, inherit some property that is literally more trouble than it is worth. Suppose that the property in question is bound up in complex legal proceedings that prevent its sale but require time and attention. Imagine that it is far from one's home and is generally of no use. Consider one's liberty right, under U.S. law, to cut off one's little toe. This right is of no benefit to most people. Most people have no desire to cut off their little toe. Useless rights are conceptually possible. It is not the case that "rights are to benefits" (1994, 32).

The second problem with Raz's view is that it incorrectly implies that rights must be justified by the interests of the right-holder. A judge has a right to impose sentence. But it is not the judge's interest in imposing sentence that justifies his right to do so. This right is justified by the interests of other individuals in having criminals punished.

The basic reason that all interest theories of rights are inadequate is that there are many rights that are not in the interest of the right-holder. As rule systems have grown and changed over the course of centuries they have not all grown in rational and coherent ways. They have laid rules on top of rules like so many layers of sediment at the bottom of an ocean. In this way, they have created odd rights. Many rule systems are amazingly complex. They create completely unanticipated rights. Many rule systems are unintentionally of poor design. Many of their rules do not serve the interests of those who are subject to them. Other rules systems are designed by people seeking their own gain and/or by people who seek to make those they dislike suffer. To account for all these features of rule system, interest theorists must layer qualification after qualification to their view. Rather than go down that road, one should simply admit that the interest theory distorts the nature of rights.

Hart holds a protection version of the choice theory. He believes that rights are protected choices (Chapter 4, Section 3). I have a right to look over the fence at my neighbor's yard because I have a choice (the liberty to look over the fence and the liberty not to look over the fence) that is protected by duties not to interfere with these liberties. Because he suggests that rights are protected choices, he thinks that every right contains a bilateral liberty—a liberty to do or not to do A. According to Hart, power rights are liberty rights in which what one has the liberty to do is to change or not to change an Hohfeldian relation. Claim rights, on Hart's view, are power rights of a special sort. On his view, one has a claim right when one has a claim and powers that give one control over the actions of others. In the paradigm case, according to Hart, one has (a) the power to extinguish the duty correlative to the claim, (b) the power to enforce the duty correlative to the claim by taking legal action, and (c) the power to extinguish the duty to compensate that arises from the failure to perform the duty correlative to the claim. Hart holds that the following three relations are necessary and sufficient for the existence of a right: (1) a liberty to do A, (2) a liberty not to do A, and (3) at least one claim that protects these liberties.

There are five problems with Hart's theory. First, Hart is unable to account for duty rights. He thinks that rights necessarily contain a bilateral liberty but duty rights contain only a unilateral liberty. A duty right occurs when a duty is protected by a claim. One example of a duty right is the right to vote found in some legal rule systems. In those countries where one has a duty right to vote, one's choices concerning voting are not protected. One has a duty to vote and it is this duty, not a choice, that is protected by claims.

A second problem with Hart's view is that it cannot account for disability rights. Recall the disability right that you had if you were a first-year faculty member. Here the right does not protect a choice but protects you from having to make choices you do not want to make. As a first-year faculty member you have a disability to give anyone tenure. This is true whether you want to give someone tenure or not. Disability rights do not protect choices for there is no choice to be protected.

Third, the Squam Lake example shows that Hart's claim that a liberty is a necessary condition for the existence of a right is false. I could have a right that you stick your feet in Squam Lake even if I had no liberties at all.

Fourth, Hart's view implies that those who violate the criminal law do not violate the legal rights of their victims. On his view, the criminal law does not grant a woman a right not to be raped because it is the state, not the woman, who has the power to file a charge of rape. This view is counterintuitive. Let us imagine a country whose legal rule system contains only criminal law. Ordinary individual citizens have no power to bring legal actions. On Hart's view, such a legal rule system grants no legal rights. Pretheoretically, it is much more plausible to hold that the legal rule system of this country does create legal rights. Any theory of rights that implies that the criminal law does not create rights has a serious flaw.

The fifth problem with Hart's view is that it implies that human infants cannot have rights. On Hart's view, they cannot have rights because they cannot make choices. There are three arguments against the view that infants do not have rights. First, the view that infants do not have rights conflicts with the settled law of all jurisdictions in the Anglo-Saxon world. "[I]t is manifest that [infants] have legal rights recognized and easily enforced by the courts" (Feinberg, 1980, 163). Second, the view implies that the moral reasons we have for not killing an infant are different from the moral reasons we have for not killing a typical adult. The choice theorist must assert that, although the reasons we have to refrain from killing an infant are just as strong as the reasons we have to refrain from killing a typical adult, the reasons are not the same. According to the choice theorist, we may cite the rights of an adult as a reason not to kill her but we cannot cite the rights of an infant as a reason not kill him. Third, the view that infants do not have rights is radically at odds with the ordinary language of rights. The over-whelming majority of competent speakers of English not only reject but recoil from the view that infants do not have rights.

Wellman holds that a right is a complex advantage to which the right-holder can appeal should there be a confrontation with one or more second parties. On his view, rights are advantages in that they favor the right-holder's will over the will of an opposing second party (Chapter 4, Section 4). Wellman believes that every right is a set of Hohfeldian relations that may be broken down into two parts—the core relation(s) and the associated elements. The core relation defines the essential content of the right. The core determines whether the right in question is a claim right, a liberty right, a power right, etc. The core also serves to individuate rights. The associated elements give the right-holder freedom or control over the core relation. Wellman conceives of the conferring of an advantage as something that necessarily involves a third-party. Every right has three parties–the right-holder, the person against whom the right holds, and a third-party to whom the right-holder can appeal to intervene if there is a conflict of wills between the right-holder and the person against whom the right holds.

Wellman's theory has at least three problems. First, the idea of the core of a right is not sufficiently clear. A person's right to look over the fence at a neighbor's lawn is composed of the liberty to look over the fence, the liberty not to look over the fence, and the claim against the neighbor's interfering with attempts to look over the fence. It seems that each of these relations is individually necessary to having the right to look over one's fence.

The second and third problems with Wellman's view are those it shares with Hart's view. Wellman's view, like Hart's, implies that those who violate the criminal law do not violate the legal rights of their victims. Wellman's view is also similar to Hart's in that it implies that infants do not have rights.

3. ADVANTAGES OF THE JUSTIFIED-CONSTRAINT THEORY

The problems with Martin's, Feinberg's, Raz's, Hart's, and Wellman's theories of rights are much more serious than the problems with the justified-constraint theory. In addition to having less serious problems than these five opposing theories, the justified-constraint view has a long list of advantages over them. Steiner provides the following useful list of features that at least some people have thought are features of rights.

> Here are some features which have been attributed to rights... I list these in loosely ascending order of contestability...
> 1. Rights are constituted by rules. [...]
> 2. Right signify a bilateral normative relation between those who hold them (their subjects) and those against whom are held (their objects).
> 3. These relations entail the presence or absence of constraints on the conduct... of objects (i.e., the individuals who are the objects of rights).
> 4. These constraints consist in objects' duties (obligations) or in their disabilities (lack of capacities to alter subjects' normative relations with objects).
> 5. Rights are exercisable.
> 6. The exercisability consists in subjects' capacity to control objects' constraints by either extinguishing them or securing compliance with them.
> 7. This capacity to control objects' constraints is a capacity to determine whether objects' actions should be prevented.
> 8. Rights prescribe interpersonal distributions of pure negative liberty.
> [...] Most accounts of what rights are accept features (1) to (4) on this list. Only some accept (5) and (6), and fewer still have included (7) and (8) as features of rights. I believe that all eight items are features of any right... (1994, 56–57).

One strength of the justified-constraint theory of rights is that it provides a plausible analysis of items (1) to (4) on Steiner's list, the items accepted by "most accounts of what rights are." As noted in Chapter 3, Section 4, the justified-constraint theory implies that a right is always the right of a particular rule system. One might have a right to drive under U.S. law without having a right to drive under French law. What Steiner calls the "bilateral normative relation" between the subject and the object of a right is referred to in this book as the relational nature of rights, and Chapter 5 provides a detailed analysis of this feature of rights. The justified-constraint theory implies that rights are normative constraints on others and so accounts for the third item on Steiner's list. Chapter 2, Section 1 noted that only claims and immunities impose constraints on others. Item (4) makes this same point by noting that duties and disabilities constrain the actions of their subjects (i.e., the objects of the correlative rights).

Steiner argues for (5) on the grounds that it is implied by the choice theory of rights. (5) is implied by the choice theory of rights, but we saw in Chapter 4,

Section 4 that the choice theory of rights is flawed. Steiner's arguments for (6), (7), and (8) all rely on claim (5).

Another advantage of the justified-constraint view is that it unifies all rights as either claim and immunity rights or packages of Hohfeldian relations that contain either a claim, an immunity, or both (Chapter 2, Sections 2 and 3). The theory explains why both claims and immunities are rights. Both claims and immunities are rights because they (and only they) entail normative constraints on the actions of another. Rights entail a normative constraint on the actions of others. Therefore, we find a claim or an immunity in every rights package.

The justified-constraint analysis also unifies Hohfeldian analysis with the analysis of rights in terms of the deontic and alethic normative concepts (Chapter 3). Rights theory has historically been somewhat cut off from the rest of social and political philosophy because it is traditionally done in Hohfeldian terms and most social and political philosophers do not know Hohfeld's work. The justified-constraint view shows that claims are relational obligations and immunities are relational impossibilities. The justified-constraint analysis provides a bridge across which one can walk to connect Hohfeldian analysis to the rest of social and political philosophy. In addition, the analysis is metaethically thin. It is compatible with almost all metaethical views. This is an advantage for a theory of rights because it explains why the large literature on metaethical issues does not refer to debates over rights.

As argued in Chapter 2, the justified-constraint theory of rights provides the best analysis of the notion of normative constraint. To the question, "What is a moral normative constraint?" the justified-constraint theory responds, "One is under a normative constraint when one may not or cannot do some action." The analysis of rights defend in this book is built on the notions of what one may not do and what one cannot do. These two notions allow us to pull together all rights under the rubric of obligations or impossibilities. Both obligations and impossibilities constrain, limit, the actions of the person who has the obligation/impossibility. These last two advantages of the justified-constraint theory of rights can be summed up as follows: the theory integrates rights into a broad web of moral concepts.

The justified-constraint theory of rights resolves or dissolves many puzzles of rights simply by individuating them correctly (Chapter 5, Section 5). On the justified-constraint view, only claims/obligations and immunities/impossibilities are rights. Almost all the things we refer to as *a* right are in fact packages of normative relations. Once one defines a right as a claim or an immunity, there is no need to seek and define some relations as the core of a right and relegate the other relations to the status of associated relations. There is no need to hold that a right somehow exists over time, implying one set of correlative obligations at one time and another set of correlative obligations at a later time.

The theory provides an enlightening response to the puzzle of the relational nature of rights (Chapter 5). On the justified-constraint view, an obligation correlative to a right is *to* the right-holder when it is a feature of the right-holder that justifies the obligation. Rights are normative constraints on others justified by a feature of the right-holder. This analysis accounts for the observation that if X has a right that Y do A, then Y's obligation to do A is *to* X. It also provides for a plausible and interesting understanding of the relationship between rights and consequentialism. It explains why consequentialists have found it difficult to account for rights.

The justified-constraint theory allows one to resolve the problems of rights conflict and the rights of past and future individuals. Because rights are obligations with a certain sort of justification and because justification is understood in terms of arguments, it becomes apparent that rights conflict occurs when there are plausible arguments both for the view that a person has a relational obligation/impossibility to do A and for the view that this person does not have a relational obligation/impossibility to do A (Chapter 6).

The analysis implies that any sort of individual or group can have rights (Chapter 7). This is a crucial advantage of the justified-constraint theory over Hart's and Wellman theories. Unlike their views, the justified-constraint view implies that human infants can have rights. Finally, the view that rights are obligations with a certain sort of justification and that justification is trans-temporal allows one to solve the problem of the subject, a problem that has bedeviled philosophers since Epicurus' time (Chapter 8). In sum, a comparison of major theories of rights shows that the justified-constraint theory "is the best approximation overall."

This book began with the following examples of statements of rights: "The Chinese are violating Tibetan rights," "Landlords have a right that their tenants pay their rent," "Students have a right to be graded fairly," "Dogs have a right not to suffer merely to bring pleasure to humans," "Abortion violates a fetus' right to life," "We violate the rights of future generations when we pollute the water." What is it that Tibetans, landlords, students, dogs, fetuses, and future generations all have in common? They all have relational obligations and/or relational impossibilities under some rule system or other.

The justifications of obligations/impossibilities that are rights rest essentially on the features of persons. In this sense, one who believes that there are rights believes that individuals are a source of obligations. This is deep and important point. To treat someone as a right-holder is to acknowledge that person as a source of obligations. This sort of acknowledgment is an important kind of respect. Thus, to respect a person's rights is, in a fundamental sense, to respect that person. It is to see that person as a source of constraints on one's own actions. The justified-constraint theory of rights thus explains why people feel violated when their rights are not respected. A person who violates another's rights "says" that the other person is not a source of obligations/impossibilities. He says that the other person is not important. This can be a profound hurt, a hurt over and above the direct harm that rights violations typically cause.

Conceptually, rights serve to indicate that a person is to be respected. Substantively, when people assert that some rights exist while others do not, they are revealing what features of persons they think are important. A defender of the choice theory thinks that choices are important, important enough to justify constraints on the actions of others. A defender of the interest theory thinks that interests are important enough to justify these constraints. Both conceptually and substantively, a person's views on rights tell us about that person's views on central moral matters. People's views on rights tell us whether or not they think that individual people are important and, if they believe that there are rights, why they think that individual people are important. Rights are not the whole of normative analysis. But the justified-constraint theory of rights reveals why some have died for them. The respect of others is an essential part of human flourishing. Without it, life may not be worth living.

References

Anderson, A.R., "Logic, Norms and Rules", *Ratio* 4 (1962), pp. 36–49.

Badhwar, N., "Friendship, Justice, and Supererogation", *American Philosophical Quarterly* 22 (1985), pp. 123–132.

Benditt, T.M., *Rights* (Totowa, NJ: Rowman and Littlefield 1982).

Bentham, J., "Anarchical Fallacies", in J. Waldron (ed.), *Nonsense Upon Stilts* (London: Methuen & Co 1987).

Corbin, A., "Legal Analysis and Terminology", *Yale Law Journal* 29 (1918), pp. 163–173.

Dancy, J., "On Moral Properties", *Mind* 90 (1981), pp. 367–385.

Darby, D., "Unnatural Rights", *Canadian Journal of Philosophy* 33 (2003), pp. 49–82.

Darby, D., "Rights Externalism", *Philosophy and Phenomenological Research* 68 (2004), pp. 620–634.

David, M., *Correspondence and Disquotation* (Oxford: Oxford University Press 1994).

DeGeorge, R., "The Environment, Rights and Future Generations", in E. Partridge (ed.), *Responsibilities to Future Generations* (Buffalo, NY: Promethus Books 1981), pp. 157–165.

Dworkin, R., *Taking Rights Seriously* (Cambridge, MA: Harvard University Press 1978).

Dworkin, R., "Rights as Trumps", in J. Waldron (ed.), *Theories of Rights* (London: Oxford University Press 1984), pp. 153–167.

Edmundson, W., *An Introduction to Rights* (Cambridge: Cambridge University Press 2004).

Epicurus, "Letter to Menoeceus", in E. O'Connor (trans.), *The Essential Epicurus* (Amherst, NY: Prometheus Books 1993), pp. 61–68.

Feinberg, J., *Social Philosophy* (Englewood Cliffs, NJ: Prentice-Hall 1973).

Feinberg, J., *Rights, Justice and the Bounds of Liberty* (Princeton: Princeton University Press 1980).

Feinberg, J., *Harm to Others* (Oxford: Oxford University Press 1984).

Feinberg, J., *Freedom and Fulfillment* (Princeton: Princeton University Press 1992).

Finkelstein, C.O. "Two Men and a Plank", *Legal Theory* 7 (2001), pp. 279–306.

Finnis, J., *Natural Law and Natural Rights* (Oxford: Clarendon Press 1980).

Fitch, F., "A Revision of Hohfeld's Theory of Legal Concepts", *Logique et Analyse* 10 (1967), pp. 269–276.

Frey, R.G., *Interests and Rights, The Case Against Animals* (Oxford: Clarendon Press 1980).

Georgia State University. *Undergraduate Catalog* (Atlanta: Georgia State University 2005).

Hart, H.L.A., "Are There Any Natural Rights", in D. Lyons (ed.), *Rights* (Belmont, CA: Wadsworth Publishing Company 1979), pp. 14–25.

Hart, H.L.A., *Essays on Bentham* (Oxford: Oxford University Press 1982).

Hart, H.L.A., *The Concept of Law* (2nd edn.) (Oxford: Clarendon Press 1994).

Hartney, M., "Some Confusions Concerning Group Rights", *The Canadian Journal of Law and Jurisprudence* 4 (1991), pp. 293–314.

Heyd, D., *Supererogation* (New York: Cambridge University Press 1982).

Hobbes, T., *Leviathan* (New York: Macmillan 1962).

Hohfeld, W.N., In D. Campbell and P. Thomas (eds.), *Fundamental Legal Conceptions as Applied in Judicial Reasoning* (Burlington, VT: Ashgate Publishing Company 2001).

REFERENCES

Hurd, H., *Moral Combat* (Cambridge: Cambridge University Press 1999).
Jones, P., "Group Rights and Group Oppression", *The Journal of Political Philosophy* 7 (1999), pp. 353–377.
Kanger, S., "New Foundations for Ethical Theory", in R. Hilpinen (ed.), *Deontic Logic* (Boston: Reidel 1981), pp. 36–58.
Katz, L., "Conflicting Rights and the Outbreak of the First World War", *Legal Theory* 7 (2001), pp. 341–367.
Kramer, M., "Getting Rights Right", in M. Kramer (ed.), *Rights, Wrongs, and Responsibilities* (New York: Palgrave 2001), pp. 28–95.
Kramer, M., Simmonds, N.E., and Steiner, H., *A Debate Over Rights* (Oxford: Oxford University Press 1998).
Lindahl, L., *Position and Change* (Dordrecht: D. Reidel Publishing 1977).
Lomasky, L., *Persons, Rights and the Moral Community* (Oxford: Oxford University Press 1987).
Lyons, D., "The Correlativity of Rights and Duties", *Nous* 4 (1970), pp. 45–55.
Lyons, D., *Rights, Welfare and Mill's Moral Theory* (Oxford: Oxford University Press 1994).
MacCormick, N., "Rights in Legislation", in P.M.S. Hacker and J. Raz (eds.), *Law, Morality and Society* (Oxford: Oxford University Press 1977), pp. 189–209.
MacCormick, N., *H.L.A. Hart* (Stanford, CA: Stanford University Press 1981).
MacCormick, N., *Legal Right and Social Democracy: Essays in Legal and Political Philosophy* (New York: Clarendon Press 1982).
Mackie, J.L., *Ethics* (New York: Penguin Books 1977).
Martin, R., *A System of Rights* (Oxford: Clarendon Press 1993).
Martin, R., "Human Rights: Constitutional and International", in M.N.S. Sellers and D. Reidy (eds.), *Universal Human Rights: Moral Order in a Divided World* (Totowa, NJ: Rowman and Littlefield 2005), pp. 37–57.
May, L., *The Morality of Groups* (Notre Dame: University of Notre Dame Press 1987).
Mellema, G., *Beyond the Call of Duty* (Albany: State University of New York Press 1991).
Mill, J.S., *Utilitarianism* (Indianapolis: Hackett Publishing Company 1979).
Montague, P., "Two Concepts of Rights", *Philosophy and Public Affairs* 9 (1980), pp. 372–384.
Montague, P., "When Rights Conflict", *Legal Theory* 7 (2001), pp. 257–277.
Morris, H., "Persons and Punishment", *Monist* 52 (1968), pp. 475–501.
Nolt, J., *Logics* (Belmont, CA: Wadsworth Publishing 1997).
Nozick, R., *Anarchy, State and Utopia* (New York: Basic Books 1974).
Parfit, D., *Reasons and Persons* (Oxford: Clarendon Press 1984).
Partridge, E., "Posthumous Interests and Posthumous Respect", *Ethics* 91 (1981), pp. 243–264.
Pietroski, P., "Prima Facie Obligations, Ceteris Paribus Laws in Moral Theory", *Ethics* 103 (1993), pp. 489–515.
Pitcher, G., "The Misfortunes of the Dead", *American Philosophical Quarterly* 21 (1984), pp. 183–188.
Porn, I., *The Logic of Power* (New York: Barnes and Noble 1970).
Primus, R., *The American Language of Rights* (Cambridge: Cambridge University Press 1999).
Prior, A., *Past, Present and Future* (Oxford: Oxford University Press 1967).
Pruitt, K., "Governor Says Road Allocations Need Fixing, Lawmakers Acknowledge Formula was a Mistake", *The Atlanta Journal and Constitution*, July 8 (1999).
Rainbolt, G., "Rights as Normative Constraints on Others", *Philosophy and Phenomenological Research* 53 (1993), pp. 93–112.

Rainbolt, G., "Perfect and Imperfect Obligations", *Philosophical Studies* 98 (2000), pp. 233–256.

Rainbolt, G., "What are Group Rights?" in L. May, L. Francis, and C. Sistare (eds.), *Groups and Group Rights* (Lawrence, KS: University Press of Kansas 2001), pp. 71–81.

Rawls, J., *A Theory of Justice* (Cambridge, MA: Harvard University Press 1971).

Rawls, J., *John Rawls: Collected Papers* (Cambridge, MA: Harvard University Press 1999).

Raz, J., "Promises and Obligations", in P.M.S. Hacker and J. Raz (eds.), *Law, Morality, and Society* (Oxford: Clarendon Press 1977), pp. 210–228.

Raz, J., *The Concept of a Legal System* (2nd edn.) (Oxford: Clarendon Press 1980).

Raz, J., "Legal Rights", *Oxford Journal of Legal Studies* 4 (1984), pp. 1–21.

Raz, J., *The Morality of Freedom* (New York: Oxford University Press 1986).

Raz, J., "Rights and Individual Well-being", *Ratio Juris* 5 (1992), pp. 127–142.

Raz, J., *Ethics in the Public Domain* (Oxford: Clarendon Press 1994).

Réaume, D., "Individuals, Groups and Rights to Public Goods", *University of Toronto Law Journal* 38 (1988), 1–27.

Réaume, D., "The Group Right to Linguistic Security: Whose Right, What Duties?" in J. Baker (ed.), *Group Rights* (Toronto: University of Toronto Press, 1994), pp. 118–141.

Regan, T., "The Case for Animal Rights", in J. Olen and V. Barry (eds.), *Applying Ethics* (Belmont, CA: Wadsworth Publishing Co 1992), pp. 356–363.

Rescher, N. and Urquhart, A., *Temporal Logic* (New York: Springer-Verlag 1971).

Robinson, R.E., Coval, S.C., and Smith, J.C., "The Logic of Rights", *University of Toronto Law Journal* 33 (1983), pp. 267–278.

Rohter, L., "Secretive Colombian Courts Survive Protests Over Rights", *New York Times*, June 20 (1999).

Ross, A., *Directives and Norms* (London: Routledge & Kegan Paul 1968).

Ross, W.D., *The Right and the Good* (Oxford: Clarendon Press 1930).

Rowan, J., *Conflicts of Rights* (Boulder, CO: Westview Press 1999).

Sayre-McCord, G., "Introduction: The Many Moral Realisms", in G. Sayre-McCord (ed.), *Essays on Moral Realism* (Ithaca: Cornell University Press 1988), pp. 1–26.

Scheffler, S., *The Rejection of Consequentialism* (revised edn.) (Oxford: Clarendon Press 1994).

Shafer-Landau, R., "Moral Rules", *Ethics* 107 (1997), pp. 588–591.

Steiner, H., *An Essay on Rights* (Oxford: Blackwell Publishers 1994).

Stoljar, S., *An Analysis of Rights* (London: The Macmillan Press 1984).

Sumner, L.W., *The Moral Foundation of Rights* (Oxford: Clarendon Press 1987).

Thomason, R., "Indeterminist Time and Truth-value Gaps", *Theoria* 36 (1970), pp. 264–281.

Thomson, J.J., *Rights, Restitution and Risk* (Cambridge, MA: Harvard University Press 1986).

Thomson, J.J., *The Realm of Rights* (Cambridge, MA: Harvard University Press 1990).

Tuck, R., *Natural Rights Theories* (Cambridge: Cambridge University Press 1979).

Waldron, J., "A Right to Do Wrong", *Ethics* 92 (1981), pp. 21–39.

Waldron, J., "Conflicts of Rights", in *Liberal Rights* (Cambridge: Cambridge University Press 1993a), pp. 203–224.

Waldron, J., "Can Communal Goods be Human Rights?" in *Liberal Rights* (New York: Cambridge University Press 1993b), pp. 339–369.

Wellman, C., *Welfare Rights* (Totowa, NJ: Rowman and Littlefield 1982).

Wellman, C., "The Growth of Children's Rights", *ARSP* 70 (1984), pp. 441–453.

247

REFERENCES

Wellman, C., *A Theory of Rights* (Totawa, NJ: Rowman and Allanheld 1985).
Wellman, C., *Real Rights* (Oxford: Oxford University Press 1995).
Wellman, C., *An Approach to Rights* (Dordrechet: Kluwer Academic Publishers 1997).
Wellman, C., "Relative Moral Duties", *American Philosophical Quarterly* 36 (1999), p. 218.
Wellman, C. (ed.), *Rights and Duties*, Vol. 6 (London: Routledge 2002).
Wellman, C.H., "On Conflicts between Rights", *Law and Philosophy* 14 (1995), pp. 271–295.

Index

249

Law and Philosophy Library

1. E. Bulygin, J.-L. Gardies and I. Niiniluoto (eds.): *Man, Law and Modern Forms of Life*. With an Introduction by M.D. Bayles. 1985   ISBN 90-277-1869-5

2. W. Sadurski: *Giving Desert Its Due*. Social Justice and Legal Theory. 1985
        ISBN 90-277-1941-1

3. N. MacCormick and O. Weinberger: *An Institutional Theory of Law*. New Approaches to Legal Positivism. 1986   ISBN 90-277-2079-7

4. A. Aarnio: *The Rational as Reasonable*. A Treatise on Legal Justification. 1987
        ISBN 90-277-2276-5

5. M.D. Bayles: *Principles of Law*. A Normative Analysis. 1987
        ISBN 90-277-2412-1; Pb: 90-277-2413-X

6. A. Soeteman: *Logic in Law*. Remarks on Logic and Rationality in Normative Reasoning, Especially in Law. 1989   ISBN 0-7923-0042-4

7. C.T. Sistare: *Responsibility and Criminal Liability*. 1989   ISBN 0-7923-0396-2

8. A. Peczenik: *On Law and Reason*. 1989   ISBN 0-7923-0444-6

9. W. Sadurski: *Moral Pluralism and Legal Neutrality*. 1990   ISBN 0-7923-0565-5

10. M.D. Bayles: *Procedural Justice*. Allocating to Individuals. 1990   ISBN 0-7923-0567-1

11. P. Nerhot (ed.): *Law, Interpretation and Reality*. Essays in Epistemology, Hermeneutics and Jurisprudence. 1990   ISBN 0-7923-0593-0

12. A.W. Norrie: *Law, Ideology and Punishment*. Retrieval and Critique of the Liberal Ideal of Criminal Justice. 1991   ISBN 0-7923-1013-6

13. P. Nerhot (ed.): *Legal Knowledge and Analogy*. Fragments of Legal Epistemology, Hermeneutics and Linguistics. 1991   ISBN 0-7923-1065-9

14. O. Weinberger: *Law, Institution and Legal Politics*. Fundamental Problems of Legal Theory and Social Philosophy. 1991   ISBN 0-7923-1143-4

15. J. Wróblewski: *The Judicial Application of Law*. Edited by Z. Bańkowski and N. MacCormick. 1992   ISBN 0-7923-1569-3

16. T. Wilhelmsson: *Critical Studies in Private Law*. A Treatise on Need-Rational Principles in Modern Law. 1992   ISBN 0-7923-1659-2

17. M.D. Bayles: *Hart's Legal Philosophy*. An Examination. 1992   ISBN 0-7923-1981-8

18. D.W.P. Ruiter: *Institutional Legal Facts*. Legal Powers and their Effects. 1993
        ISBN 0-7923-2441-2

19. J. Schonsheck: *On Criminalization*. An Essay in the Philosophy of the Criminal Law. 1994
        ISBN 0-7923-2663-6

20. R.P. Malloy and J. Evensky (eds.): *Adam Smith and the Philosophy of Law and Economics*. 1994   ISBN 0-7923-2796-9

21. Z. Bańkowski, I. White and U. Hahn (eds.): *Informatics and the Foundations of Legal Reasoning*. 1995   ISBN 0-7923-3455-8

22. E. Lagerspetz: *The Opposite Mirrors*. An Essay on the Conventionalist Theory of Institutions. 1995   ISBN 0-7923-3325-X

Law and Philosophy Library

23. M. van Hees: *Rights and Decisions*. Formal Models of Law and Liberalism. 1995
ISBN 0-7923-3754-9

24. B. Anderson: *"Discovery" in Legal Decision-Making*. 1996 ISBN 0-7923-3981-9

25. S. Urbina: *Reason, Democracy, Society*. A Study on the Basis of Legal Thinking. 1996
ISBN 0-7923-4262-3

26. E. Attwooll: *The Tapestry of the Law*. Scotland, Legal Culture and Legal Theory. 1997
ISBN 0-7923-4310-7

27. J.C. Hage: *Reasoning with Rules*. An Essay on Legal Reasoning and Its Underlying Logic.
1997   ISBN 0-7923-4325-5

28. R.A. Hillman: *The Richness of Contract Law*. An Analysis and Critique of Contemporary
Theories of Contract Law. 1997   ISBN 0-7923-4336-0; 0-7923-5063-4 (Pb)

29. C. Wellman: *An Approach to Rights*. Studies in the Philosophy of Law and Morals. 1997
ISBN 0-7923-4467-7

30. B. van Roermund: *Law, Narrative and Reality*. An Essay in Intercepting Politics. 1997
ISBN 0-7923-4621-1

31. I. Ward: *Kantianism, Postmodernism and Critical Legal Thought*. 1997
ISBN 0-7923-4745-5

32. H. Prakken: *Logical Tools for Modelling Legal Argument*. A Study of Defeasible Reasoning
in Law. 1997   ISBN 0-7923-4776-5

33. T. May: *Autonomy, Authority and Moral Responsibility*. 1998   ISBN 0-7923-4851-6

34. M. Atienza and J.R. Manero: *A Theory of Legal Sentences*. 1998   ISBN 0-7923-4856-7

35. E.A. Christodoulidis: *Law and Reflexive Politics*. 1998   ISBN 0-7923-4954-7

36. L.M.M. Royakkers: *Extending Deontic Logic for the Formalisation of Legal Rules*. 1998
ISBN 0-7923-4982-2

37. J.J. Moreso: *Legal Indeterminacy and Constitutional Interpretation*. 1998
ISBN 0-7923-5156-8

38. W. Sadurski: *Freedom of Speech and Its Limits*. 1999   ISBN 0-7923-5523-7

39. J. Wolenski (ed.): *Kazimierz Opalek Selected Papers in Legal Philosophy*. 1999
ISBN 0-7923-5732-9

40. H.P. Visser 't Hooft: *Justice to Future Generations and the Environment*. 1999
ISBN 0-7923-5756-6

41. L.J. Wintgens (ed.): *The Law in Philosophical Perspectives*. My Philosophy of Law. 1999
ISBN 0-7923-5796-5

42. A.R. Lodder: *DiaLaw*. On Legal Justification and Dialogical Models of Argumentation. 1999
ISBN 0-7923-5830-9

43. C. Redondo: *Reasons for Action and the Law*. 1999   ISBN 0-7923-5912-7

44. M. Friedman, L. May, K. Parsons and J. Stiff (eds.): *Rights and Reason*. Essays in Honor of
Carl Wellman. 2000   ISBN 0-7923-6198-9

45. G.C. Christie: *The Notion of an Ideal Audience in Legal Argument*. 2000   ISBN 0-7923-6283-7

Law and Philosophy Library

Law and Philosophy Library